TRUE TALES
of the
EASTERN SHORE

By Kirk Mariner

Miona Publications
New Church, Virginia
23415

For information write:
    Miona Publications
    194 Mill Neck Road
    Williamsburg, Virginia 23185
or E-mail mionapub@yahoo.com

ISBN 0-9648393-8-5

Table of Contents

INTRODUCTION

1   **DEFINITELY NOT MARYLAND:**   1
    Explaining the "Va" in "DelMarVa"
    The Battle of the Pocomoke • The Maryland-Virginia Boundary:
    Who Cheated Whom? • The Almost State of Delmarva

2   **INDIANS AND EUROPEANS**   11
    The First Eastern Shoremen • A "Strange Mortalitie"
    • What Do You Call a "Laughing King"? • The Indian Makes His Mark
    • Our Indian Placenames: A Moveable Feast • Indiantown

3   **A CAST OF CHARACTERS (Part I)**   26
    Francis Makemie, Presbyterian Founder • Blackbeard the Pirate
    • Warner Mifflin, Abolitionist, Pacifist • "Black Harry" Hosier, Preacher
    Extraordinaire • Stephen Gunter, The Reverend Blacksmith
    • Jean G. Potts, Pugnacious Painter

4   **THE LATE UNPLEASANTNESS:**   52
    Stories of the Civil War
    Ten Miles to New Church • The Union Telegraph • John Yates Beall,
    Rebel Raider of the Chesapeake • The Rebel Raid That Never Was
    • Richard B. Winder, War Criminal?

5   **A CAST OF CHARACTERS (Part II)**   75
    George D. Watson, Evangelist • William B. Judefind, Hymnwriter • Robert
    P. Woodward, Eccentric Adventurer • Carry Nation, Enemy of Demon
    Rum • Billy Sunday, Revival Preacher • Frances Benjamin Johnston,
    Photographer • Aliens in Accomack: The Visitors Who Never Arrived

6   **PRESIDENTIAL VISITATIONS**   98
    The President Who Loved the Eastern Shore • A Tale of Two Presidents
    • Presidential Spy • Piscatorial Presidents • An Elephant Stampede

7   **MURDER, MAYHEM, AND A GHOST OR TWO**   113
    Epitaph in Bulbegger • Shootout in Eastville • The Ghost of Marino
    • Love and Death in Deep Hole • Who Shot the Shooter? • Murder by Mail

8   **ALMOST FORGOTTEN:**   129
    Little Places That Are No More
    Wagram • Atlantic Female College • Mr. Boykin's School • Belinda • Little
    Hell • Luna Park • The Pleasure Pier • Alive and Well and Living in Maryland

9   **AS THE WORLD WATCHES:**   152
    Brief Moments in the Limelight
    The Wreck of the *Despatch* • The "Battle of the Chesapeake"
    • The *Graf Zeppelin* Makes Its American Debut • An Elephant for Tangier

    NOTES   171
    BIBLIOGRAPHY   178
    INDEX   184

In memoriam
L. FLOYD NOCK III
1932-1997

Architect
Historian
Gentleman
Friend

Introduction

When are you going to put all that stuff in a book?

I've heard that question for almost two decades, since 1985 when the *Eastern Shore News* first opened its pages to my proposal for a column of local history.

When I began writing "Chronicles," I promised the *News* only occasional, not regular, submissions, and it wasn't long before the column turned out to be far more occasional than I had envisioned. Even so, it all adds up over time, enough for even some of it to fill a book. Now here, at last, is the book that I've been promising others, and myself, for a long time.

Behind these "tales" stands the rewarding experience of getting to know many people from the Eastern Shore, and some from elsewhere, whose knowledge and memories were crucial to what is printed here. Many people helped not with the writing but with the re-writing, by contacting me to correct and/or improve the original column. I have welcomed their input also. Since this collection has been almost twenty years in the making, a number of those who helped with it are no longer living, and I am proud to be the one who "chronicled" what they knew and remembered.

Among the many who contributed to this effort, a few deserve special thanks here at the front.

Jean Mihalyka is always a congenial and helpful colleague, and I especially enjoyed the opportunity to partner with her in writing the sketch on Stephen Gunter. (We still think that the scholarly journals should have accepted it for publication, but since they didn't, here it is.)

B. Miles Barnes is, in a word, indispensable to any and all who would research the history of Virginia's Eastern Shore. Once again he has helped in more ways than either of us can remember.

Thanks to Bill Sterling, editor of the *News*, always encouraging and always willing (thus far) to print whatever I submit without alterations.

And with special appreciation I dedicate this book to the memory of Floyd Nock, who is so sorely missed not only as cohort in local history but also as friend. Was ever there anyone who had as many stories about the Eastern Shore of Virginia as he did? A number of these "tales" bear the stamp of his counsel and directions, and at least one of them came almost entirely from his immense store of knowledge and local lore. I thankfully dedicate all of what follows to his memory.

Kirk Mariner
Williamsburg, Virginia
March 5, 2003

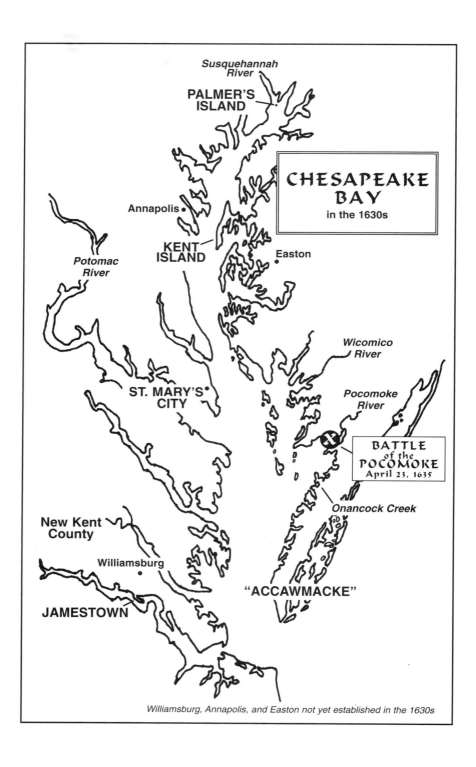

Susquehannah River

PALMER'S ISLAND

Annapolis •

KENT ISLAND

Easton •

Potomac River

CHESAPEAKE BAY
in the 1630s

Wicomico River

ST. MARY'S CITY •

Pocomoke River

BATTLE
of the
POCOMOKE
April 23, 1635

Onancock Creek

New Kent County

Williamsburg •

"ACCAWMACKE"

JAMESTOWN

Williamsburg, Annapolis, and Easton not yet established in the 1630s

1

Definitely Not Maryland
Explaining the "Va" in "DelMarVa"

The Battle of the Pocomoke

On a map, the Eastern Shore of Virginia looks like it ought to be a part of Maryland. In fact many maps show it as such, or leave it off altogether.

Why is this little section of the Delmarva Peninsula a part of Virginia? The answer is a simple one, having nothing to do with geography and everything to do with history: this part of the Eastern Shore was Virginia before there was such a thing as Maryland.

And therein hangs a tale of what is said to be the first naval battle in what is now the United States.

In June 1632, King Charles I granted to Cecil, Baron of Baltimore, the right to establish a new province in America on the northern shores of Chesapeake Bay. Two years later, in 1634, two small ships named the *Ark* and the *Dove* sailed into the bay bringing nearly two hundred settlers. In that year they established St. Mary's City on the northern banks of the Potomac River, the first of the settlements of the new province called Maryland.[1]

But the upper Chesapeake Bay was an area to which Virginia also had a claim. By then, Virginia had been settled for a quarter century, and Virginians lived on both sides of the Bay. In fact, Kent Island, settled by Virginians in 1631 under the leadership of the influential William Claiborne (1600-1677), lay fully 45 miles further north than the new Maryland capital. Already thriving on the fur trade with the Indians, Kent Island had a walled fort, an Anglican church and priest, and a population of over 100 who were represented in the Virginia House of Burgesses in Jamestown. In the minds of its settlers, this was clearly Virginia territory, specifically a part of the Eastern Shore of Virginia. Nor was it the furthest reach of Virginia up the Chesapeake, for Claiborne had another smaller outpost on Palmer's Island at the mouth of the Susquehanna River, at the very head of the bay.[2]

1

The Marylanders were at first conciliatory to the Virginians in their midst. Lord Baltimore had given instructions that Claiborne was to be permitted to keep his lands and his business interests if the Virginian would simply acknowledge that he was now a part of Maryland. This Claiborne was not about to do, and it was only a matter of time until each side had goaded the other into action.

William Claiborne

In the spring of 1635, Claiborne dispatched his ship the *Long Tayle* to trade with the Indians on the Western Shore, almost within shouting distance of St. Mary's City. The *Long Tayle* was a pinnace, Claiborne's favorite, and the first ship to be built on the Eastern Shore. The Maryland authorities promptly seized the ship, its cargo, and its men.[3] The fight was on.

Claiborne was infuriated that the *Long Tayle* had been seized, particularly since it had been sent to trade for corn which was sorely needed by the Kent Islanders. When he learned that the Marylanders had dispatched a ship to trade with the Indians on the Eastern Shore, at a site on the Pocomoke River where his own people had been trading, he retaliated by sending a second ship, the *Cockatrice*, to seize the Maryland vessel.[4]

On April 23, 1635, Lt. Radcliffe Warren and his small band of Virginians armed with "gonnes and pistolls, swords and other weapons" sailed the *Cockatrice* into Pocomoke Sound and encountered the Maryland ship, the *St. Helen*, near the creek "that Trencheth out of the North side of the river" at Jenkin's Point (now William's Point), the last spit of land before the Sound turns northward and narrows into the Pocomoke River. The Virginians bore down on the *St. Helen*, bent on boarding and seizing her, but just as they drew near a second Maryland vessel sailed unexpectedly into view, the much larger and well-armed *St. Margaret*.

Though clearly outnumbered, Lt. Warren veered towards the larger vessel and ignored the shouts of Captain Thomas Cornwallis, the Maryland commander, that they were approaching "at their own peril." With the *Cockatrice* barreling on, Warren ordered his men to prepare to board, and Cornwallis ordered his men to open fire. A "thunderous volley of musket and pistol fire" shattered the Pocomoke quiet, and when the roar and the smoke had died down three Virginians, among them Lt. Warren, lay dead, three more wounded.

Battle of the Pocomoke
by Artist Jacob Riegel, Jr.

One Marylander, shot "in his breste on the left side," was the only Marylander casualty.[5]

In 1636 Claiborne sailed to England to argue his case, leaving Kent Island under the command of George Evelin, who promptly acknowledged Maryland's claim to the settlement without seeking the approval of the islanders. In February 1638 an expedition from St. Mary's landed at sunrise, gained entrance to the fort, and seized the entire island. The islanders submitted to the Maryland government, which tried a number of their leaders and hanged one of them, Captain Thomas Smith, for piracy.[6]

The site of this brief but bloody battle was most likely just west of Jolley's Neck in upper Accomack County, near William's Point. The best view of the general vicinity of the battle from the Virginia side is from Flag Pond Landing at the eastern end of Sanford. Here the vista is wide across Pocomoke Sound to the mouth of Pocomoke River, and somewhere in this vicinity, straddling what is today the boundary between the two states, the encounter took place.

Two unlikely "monuments" to this all-but-forgotten battle stand today, far from this spot. One is a rural county of Virginia between Williamsburg and Richmond, the place William Claiborne settled, safely deep in Virginia, after losing Kent Island. He named his new home in honor of his Eastern Shore island: New Kent.[7]

The other stands 75 miles north of the Eastern Shore of Virginia, where large roadsigns greet the travelers who cross Kent Island today hurrying to and from the beach via the Chesapeake Bay Bridge. "First English Settlement Within Maryland," reads the sign. "Within," not "in" Maryland—for when Maryland first came into being this was already a part of Virginia's Eastern Shore.

The Maryland-Virginia Boundary:
Who Cheated Whom?

"Maryland Welcomes You, Please Drive Gently."

The sign marking the border between Virginia and Maryland looms over the highway just above the village of New Church, Virginia. But if Maryland had had her way, the sign might well have been located several miles to the south, below the village of Nelsonia. Or if Virginia had had her way, the sign would stand well north of Princess Anne in Somerset County, Maryland. And leaving aside what could have been, the boundary should have crossed Route 13 not above New Church, but below it.

With the creation of the new colony of Maryland came official documents specifying where its boundary with Virginia would cross the Eastern Shore. The line was to begin at a place called Watkins' Point, on the Chesapeake, and from there to head East across the peninsula to the ocean. Watkins' Point was the name Captain John Smith gave to the southwestern corner of Somerset County, near today's Crisfield, Maryland. Though his map of the Chesapeake, published in London in 1612, was then the best available, it was not sufficiently detailed to specify exactly where, in that general region, Watkins' Point was located.[8]

For twenty years after the founding of Maryland neither colony worried much about the boundary across the Eastern Shore. On the Virginia portion of the peninsula there were no English settlements further north than what is today Eastville. Not even the extravagant claim of the Maryland governor that the boundary lay as far south as Onancock Creek caused much consternation, for no Marylanders lived anywhere near that far south.[9]

Then in 1660, by which time settlement on the Eastern Shore of Virginia reached as far north as Deep Creek, the Virginia legislature passed a series of stringent anti-Quaker laws, hoping to rid the colony of that "radical" sect. As a result, a number of Virginians moved north, settling the region west of Pocomoke River in today's Somerset County. The Maryland governor quickly appointed three commissioners to grant lands in Somerset to any who would take an oath of fidelity to Lord Baltimore, and thus become Marylanders.[10]

Ironically one of the three Maryland commissioners appointed for this purpose was Edmund Scarburgh, a militant Virginian. By 1662 Maryland, aware of his militancy for the older colony, had dropped him as a commissioner, and he himself was gearing up to lay claim to Somerset for Virginia. In 1663 Scarburgh influenced the Virginia legislature to pass an "Act Concerning the Bounds of This Colony on the Eastern Shore" which claimed that Watkins' Point was not located on the Pocomoke River at all, but much further north. On Smith's map the Pocomoke is labeled the "Wighco River," by which, reasoned Scarburgh, Smith had obviously intended the Wicomico River, not the Pocomoke. By this reckoning the former Virginians who had settled in

Somerset were therefore still in Virginia.

To enforce this claim, Scarburgh and a force of 40 armed horsemen set out on October 11, 1663, crossed into Somerset County, and rousted the Marylanders from their beds, forcing them at gunpoint to claim allegiance to Virginia.[11]

Virginia quickly disavowed Scarburgh's actions, but the exact location of the boundary had now become a matter no longer to be ignored. The two colonies agreed at last to draw a boundary acceptable to both, and in May 1668 Scarburgh of Virginia and Phillip Calvert of Maryland met at Watkins' Point to do so. They determined that a line drawn due east from that point would cross the Pocomoke River at "the land of Robert Holston's," and there they marked "Certain Trees which are so Continued by an East Line Running over Swansecute [Swan's Gut] Creek" to the ocean. In fact, the only part of the boundary they actually marked was between Pocomoke River and the ocean. They did not mark the line west of the Pocomoke, in today's Somerset County, because it passed through an area where there were as yet no settlements.

In one regard their work was a success: The Calvert-Scarburgh line of 1668 was quickly recognized by the locals who lived on either side of it, and with minor variations is still the line that separates Accomack County, Virginia, from Worcester County, Maryland.

But Calvert and Scarburgh failed to settle the issue completely.

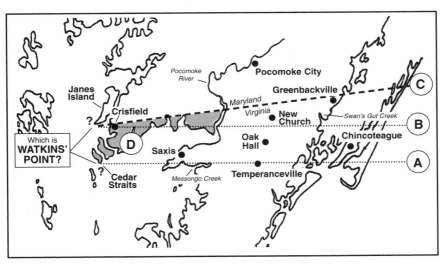

The Scarburgh-Calvert Boundary of 1668
Had the boundary run due East of Cedar Straits (A), Chincoteague, Temperanceville, and Saxis would have been included in Maryland, or due East of Janes Island (B), New Church and Greenbackville would have been Maryland. Because it ran NNE from Janes Island (C), Virginia gained territory east of the Pocomoke River that should probably have been Maryland's. Yet should not the territory west of the river and south of the line (D) have been Virginia's?

More than a century later both states still considered the Eastern Shore boundary to be "doubtful."[12] And not for almost two centuries would the maps show the boundary correctly.

At issue was the exact location of Watkins' Point. Today's Watkins' Point is the southwesternmost point of land in Somerset County, at Cedar Straits just above Fox Island, about four miles south of Crisfield. Had Calvert and Scarburgh run a line east from that point to the ocean, much of northern Accomack County—everything north of Temperanceville, including Saxis, Chincoteague, and all points in between—would have been in Maryland.

But take a map of the Eastern Shore, and with a ruler extend the present boundary west from Pocomoke River to Chesapeake Bay. Your line will hit the bay not at Watkins' Point but three miles north of it, just below Janes Island on the Little Annemessex River, and it might have hit Janes Island itself had not the southern tip of that island eroded significantly over the past two centuries. The southernmost point of Janes Island was once a much higher and more visible "promontory" than it is today. To Calvert and Scarburgh, this was Watkins' Point, and it was from this point, now under water, that they ran their line to the ocean.[13]

In 1670, only two years after the boundary was established, a new map of the Chesapeake published by Augustine Herrmann of Maryland became the first to show it. But Herrmann assumed that Watkins' Point was where it is today, not at Janes Island but at Cedar Straits, and he drew the boundary as a straight line heading east to the ocean from that point. As a result, his map showed the boundary crossing the Eastern Shore mainland near Messongo Creek, making it appear as if Saxis Island and Chincoteague Island were actually in Maryland.[14]

In 1691, Daniel Jenifer of Accomack produced a map of the Eastern Shore of Virginia. It too showed the boundary heading due east from Watkins' Point, but located Watkins' Point at Janes Island.[15] But it was Herrmann's map, not Jenifer's, that became definitive for the Chesapeake region, and for almost two centuries mapmakers reproduced the Maryland version of the boundary. As late as the middle 1800s mapmakers were showing the line to be east-west from Cedar Straits. Even some Virginia maps were vague about the boundary.[16]

By the mid-1800s the two states were again in dispute over the "doubtful" boundary, and an agreement was reached to re-survey the line. On November 29, 1858, topographic engineer Nathaniel Michler arrived in Horntown with a crew of six to begin the work. Michler found "many traces of the work of Calvert and Scarburgh," including a number of the trees that they had marked almost two centuries earlier. He discovered that the Calvert-Scarburgh line ran not from west to east, but west-southwest to east-northeast, giving to Virginia approximately 23 square miles of territory, including New Church, Horntown, and Greenbackville, that should have been in Maryland.[17]

The Calvert-Scarburgh line was surveyed again in 1883, when it was discovered that at its eastern end it was 80 feet too far north, and at its western end 275 feet too far south. Virginia thus gained a small strip of Assateague Island, Maryland three times as much on the Pocomoke River.[18]

Today just east of where Route 13 crosses the boundary, at the edge of a cemetery on Marva Road, there stands a marker from that 1883 survey. And today everyone agrees that the boundary runs through the straight line etched across the top of the stone.

But it might have gone otherwise. So which state got the better end of the deal?

Did Edmund Scarburgh deceive Calvert by running the line not east, but east-

The boundary stone (1883)

northeast? Scarburgh was a surveyor who should have known what he was doing, so it may have been he who thus gained New Church, Horntown, and Greenbackville for Virginia.

Did Scarburgh gain even more for Virginia by persuading Calvert to run the line from Janes Island, instead of from Cedar Straits? If so, Virginia has him to thank for Chincoteague, Temperanceville, Saxis, and points in between.

But Maryland, too, scored her gains. If the boundary runs from Janes Island, then everything south of that line should have been Virginia territory, west of the Pocomoke River as well as east of it. That means that a significant section of what is today Somerset County was, perhaps, to have been Virginia's. That territory, which includes the town of Crisfield, is part of Maryland today, not by virtue of the 1668 boundary agreement but by uncontested "possession" of it. For though unsettled at the time, it was later assumed to be Maryland (based probably, on Herrmann's map) and settled by Marylanders without Virginia's ever laying claim to it.[19]

So it might have been Crisfield, Virginia.

Or Chincoteague, Maryland.

Who cheated whom?

The Almost State of Delmarva

What a splendid state this Delmarva Peninsula would make. A rich country, close to city markets, but far enough away to avoid its contamination, and its political influence. A unified people with common interests, ideals and aspirations. What a great "free state" we could have—a state with more than one-half million people, with no dominating large cities—fourteen rich, prosperous counties in the best section of the United States.

So wrote the editor of the Federalsburg (Md.) *Times* in 1931, after columnist H. L. Mencken had once again blasted the Eastern Shore in the Baltimore papers.[20]

Did he know that a century before him the state of Delmarva had almost come into being?

The Eastern Shore of Maryland's sense of separation from the rest of the state dates back to colonial times, when it enjoyed its own land offices, treasurers, surveyors, and judges quite apart from those of the Western Shore. There were times during the Revolution when the British held control of the Bay, and the Eastern Shore, effectively cut off from the rest of Maryland, functioned as a separate unit. When in the 1770s a new state constitution was written, it specified that six of Maryland's fifteen state senators must come from the Eastern Shore, required the General Court to sit alternately on either side of the Bay, and provided that "nothing...which relates to the Eastern Shore particularly shall at any time hereafter be altered, unless...at least two-thirds of the members of each branch of the General Assembly shall concur."

There was, for a while, even an unofficial "capital" of the Eastern Shore of Maryland. In the 1770s the General Assembly decreed that a new town be laid out on the Choptank River in Talbot County, as the place where the court "shall be forever held" when it met on the Eastern Shore. The town was to be named Dover—not a great choice, given the proximity of that other capital city Dover, Delaware—but Dover, Maryland, never really came into being. Instead, when a new courthouse was built in nearby Easton, the legislature named that town as the site of the court and of the other government offices for the Eastern Shore. The courthouse that stands today in Easton is larger than most, at the time of its completion in 1794 second only to the State House in Annapolis itself, and it was built large in expectation that the state legislature, also, might choose to sit alternatively at Annapolis and Easton, the "Little Capital."

By the 1830s the rest of Maryland was clearly outdistancing the rural Eastern Shore. Baltimore, blossoming into a metropolis, was demanding its share of representation, and canals and railroads were being constructed to further commerce and industry. Though taxed for them, the rural Shore counties saw few of these new "internal improvements," and began to feel overlooked and restless, a mood which did not go unnoticed across the line in Delaware.

On February 4, 1833, the state legislature in Dover—Delaware, not Maryland—passed a resolution that "the people of the Eastern Shore of Maryland and of this State should be united under one government." No sooner had the idea been conveyed to the Maryland legislature in Annapolis than the newspapers took up the issue. "Delaware grows [too] ambitious," insisted the *Baltimore American and Daily Advertiser*. But "the people of the Peninsula...form one people, [and] nature intended their territory to constitute one state," countered the *Delaware State Journal* of Wilmington. The new state would be named Delaware ("Delmarva" was not yet a term in general use during the 1830s). The new capital would be, most likely, Easton.[21]

The Talbot County Courthouse, Easton, Maryland
Larger than most—designed to serve as capitol of the Eastern Shore?

What about Virginia's two Eastern Shore counties? "If natural boundaries had been originally considered," wrote the Wilmington editor, "the whole Peninsula, including the counties in Maryland and the two counties of Accomac and Northampton, which by some queer accident belong to Virginia, would have been included in one government." But Virginians were said to be "cold to the proposal, scornfully unwilling to sell their birthright for what seemed to them an unsavory mess of pottage."[22]

On March 20, 1833, the Maryland House voted 40 to 24 to call a "general convention" to ascertain the wishes of the citizens of the Eastern Shore of Maryland about uniting with Delaware. The following day the measure went to the Maryland Senate, which promptly referred the matter to a special committee of three senators, all of whom were from the Eastern Shore: Thomas Emory of Queen Anne's County, William Hughlett of Talbot, and Littleton P. Dennis of

Somerset, who lived at "Beverly," on the Pocomoke River just across the line from Virginia. It took the committee all of one day to report back to the Senate that they were "of the opinion that [the proposal] ought to be assented to." The Senate voted on March 21, 1833, but despite the committee's report the measure was defeated 5 to 4.

Thus the proposal to consider uniting the Eastern Shore of Maryland with Delaware lost "by the exceedingly slim margin of one vote." Had the vote gone the other way, it seems likely that the Shore counties would have voted to leave Maryland for Delaware. In fact, defeat of the measure did little to allay interest in the idea, or to quell the restlessness of the Eastern Shore counties. A similar proposal was submitted and defeated in 1834. Eight years later, in the legislature of 1842, Delegate Levi Cathell of Worcester proposed that "the Eastern Shore...attach themselves to the State of Delaware." Again a select committee was appointed, again it urged adoption, but again the measure was defeated, 45-18, with all of the delegates from the Eastern Shore voting for it. "It was abundantly evident," writes one modern historian, "that there still existed on the Eastern Shore a considerable sentiment for secession from Maryland and merger with Delaware."

There was yet one more attempt. When a new state constitution was being written in 1850-1851, Thomas Holliday Hicks of Dorchester tried in vain to include a provision that would allow the Eastern Shore counties to separate from Maryland and unite with Delaware if a majority of Shore voters so decided. By now, however, improved transportation and communication, especially the steamboats that linked the Eastern Shore to the rest of the state, had taken the fire out of the separatist mood of the Shore. Not only did the new constitution not include Hicks' motion, it also eliminated the separate treasurer for the Eastern Shore. After 1851, all state offices were consolidated in Annapolis and Baltimore, and Easton's days as the "Little Capital" were over.[23]

It is, however, an idea that has never fully died out. In 1931 when Mencken raised the dander of the Eastern Shore's editors, in 1949 when the proposed Chesapeake Bay Bridge seemed to threaten the Shore's way of life, in 1964 when the Shore's representation in Annapolis was about to be reduced by redistricting, a few people again dreamed of the Delmarva Peninsula as a unified state. And in 1992, when the issue was the toll on the Chesapeake Bay Bridge-Tunnel, some Virginians wondered whether union with the rest of the peninsula might not be preferable.[24]

It seems safe to predict that it will never happen—at least until one remembers what almost happened in 1833....

2

Indians and Europeans

The First Eastern Shoremen

When English settlement of Virginia began, the Indians on the Eastern Shore of Virginia numbered about 2,000 people,[1] two "tribes"—or three, depending upon how they are classified—who lived in small settlements scattered evenly across the peninsula.

The Eastern Shore Indians lived in villages that were always located conveniently close to water, and today, almost four centuries later, it sometimes seems as if there must have been an Indian village at virtually every spot along the coastline of the peninsula. Perhaps there was, at one time or another, for the first Eastern Shoremen lived a "transhumant" existence, migrating among several locations as game and fields demanded. After a couple of years of planting one field, they would move to another, taking with them the wooden framework of their "houses" and the mats they used to cover those frames. A day's work—work performed largely by the women—could find the "village" relocated at a different site. Thus almost any location that was easily accessible to water, high enough to be safe from tide, and inland enough to give protection from storm could, and probably did, serve as a "village."[2]

The southern portion of the Shore, from Cape Charles north to approximately Hungars Creek, was occupied by the Accomacks, who were the first Indians encountered by the English. The Accomacks were related culturally to the Indians across the Bay near Jamestown, spoke the same language as Powhatan, and were at least nominally a part of Powhatan's "empire," though they had never actually been invaded or subjugated by that great chief, who lacked the means to wage war across the broad expanse of the Chesapeake.[3]

The chief "village" of the Accomacks, from which their name is taken, was located on the banks of King's Creek in the region of Cheriton and Cape Charles. Here lived the most famous Indian of the Eastern Shore of Virginia, their chief, or "werowance," whom the English called the "Laughing King."[4]

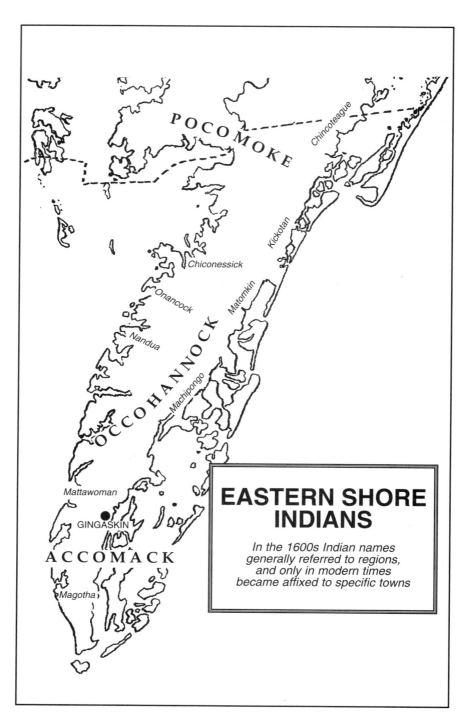

POCOMOKE

Chincoteague

Kickotan

Chiconessick

Onancock

Matomkin

Nandua

OCCOHANNOCK

Machipongo

Mattawoman

GINGASKIN

ACCOMACK

Magotha

EASTERN SHORE INDIANS

In the 1600s Indian names generally referred to regions, and only in modern times became affixed to specific towns

Within the territory of the Accomacks were at least two smaller outlying companies. Further down the peninsula lived the Magothas, near the present village of that name,[5] further up the peninsula lived the Mattawomans, or Matoones, on Mattawoman Creek north of Eastville. The Mattawomans were the first Indians on the Shore to be displaced by English settlement. Forced out of their home in Old Town Neck, they settled by 1641 in a new location which they called Gingaskin, on the Seaside east of Eastville. After moving to this location they were no longer known as the Mattawomans but as the Gingaskins, for the Indians took their names from the locations in which they lived.[6]

North of the Accomacks lived the Occohannocks, who were of the same culture and language; in fact, in 1621 their werowance Kiptopeake was the brother of the "Laughing King."[7] Some scholars, noting the similarity between the two tribes, list the Occohannocks as a sub-tribe of the Accomacks.[8] However, as far back as 1608 the English always listed the two as separate tribes, and most scholars continue that differentiation.

The Occohannocks take their name from their chief village, which was located on the south bank of Occohannock Creek about three miles west of Exmore.[9] The Indians of a number of other villages, from northern Northampton to upper Accomack, were also considered Occohannocks.

On the Seaside the Occohannocks included the Machipongos, who lived at various times in what is now the town of Wachapreague, at "Brownsville" near Nassawadox, and at "Woodlands" across the creek from Brownsville.[10] North of them lived the Matomkins, who had at least two villages in the region stretching from Finney Creek to Parker Creek, Locustville to Pastoria. Above them were the Kickotans, who lived on Hog Neck south of Modest Town.[11]

The Bayside Occohannocks included the Nanduas, also known as the Nassawadox Indians, who lived in Hacks Neck,[12] the Onancocks, who occupied both sides of Onancock Creek but whose chief village was probably at "Oatlands" near Poplar Cove on the north bank, and the Chesconessex Indians, who lived between Deep Creek and Hunting Creek.[13]

At the northern end of the Shore the English encountered an altogether different tribe of Indians, smaller in stature, more warlike, with a language and culture related not to the Powhatans across the Bay but to the Nanticokes and other tribes further up the Delmarva Peninsula.[14] These were the Pocomokes, who lived in several waterside locations principally in Maryland. Among them were the Chincoteagues, who lived not on Chincoteague Island but on the mainland opposite it, south of Horntown on Mosquito Creek.[15] Also in Virginia, perhaps, was the principal Pocomoke village, known as Wighcocomoco. In 1608, when the English first explored the region, it was located on the southern bank of the Pocomoke River, perhaps at or near Pitts Wharf west of New Church. At a later time the

Pocomokes moved to the northern side of the river.[16]

The Indians of the Eastern Shore did not long survive the arrival of the white man. Less than a century after English settlement began, the native Americans who had numbered in the thousands on the Virginia portion of the Delmarva Peninsula were reduced to a "mere remnant," gathered into eight small villages of just a handful of people apiece.[17] Though war and violence played its part in the eradication of the original inhabitants, it was for the most part disease that carried them away.[18]

A "Strange Mortalitie"

The decimation of the Eastern Shore's Indians began even before Englishmen settled upon these shores. The native inhabitants of America lacked the immunization to certain diseases that Europeans, after centuries of exposure to plague and epidemic, had built up naturally. As a consequence, contact with Europeans, many of whom arrived in America in a less than healthy state after a perilous voyage, was followed by a rapid decline in population as entire Indian communities and cultures perished in the face of unchecked epidemic. In central Mexico the native population, approximately 25 million people when the Spanish landed, shrank to less than two million within the space of a century, and in other places a century's decline was as much as 90% of the population. In what is now the United States "the raging epidemics of Europe's most tragic centuries repeated themselves" once contact was made, with the result that the settlement of America by Europeans was more like "a resettlement, a reoccupation of a land made waste by the diseases and demoralization introduced by the newcomers."[19]

The transmission of deadly diseases to a people without the genetic make-up to fight them did not depend upon the establishment of permanent settlements. Eastern Shore history suggests that even brief, fleeting contact with Europeans was sufficient to unleash among the Indians the sicknesses that proved so deadly to them.[20]

Capt. John Smith

Though permanent English settlement of the Eastern Shore of Virginia began in 1620,[21] the history of the Shore is usually measured from 1608, when Captain John Smith of the new Jamestown colony visited the Bayside in his exploration of Chesapeake Bay. Smith visited only two Indian villages, Accomack and Occohannock, but judging from a tale that the werowance of the Accomacks told Smith, it is not unlikely that the Indian population was already on the decline on the Eastern Shore even before the English arrived.

The Indian king described a "strange mortalitie" that had lately visited his tribe. Following the death of two children, *the extreame passions of their parents, or some dreaming visions, phantasie, or affection moved [the parents] again to visit their dead carkases, whose benummed bodies reflected to the eyes of the beholders such pleasant delightfull countenances [as to suggest that] they had regained their vital spirits. This as a miracle drew many to behold [the dead], all which (being a great part of his people) not long after died, and not any one escaped.*[22]

Modern scholars have been unable, from Smith's description, to identify the sickness that killed the children, but it does seem clear that shortly before Smith's arrival a "great part" of the Accomacks had died from contact with corpses ridden with disease.[23] The likelihood is that this "strange mortalitie" was the result of previous European contact with the Eastern Shore, and it is known that there were at least two recorded visits to the peninsula before John Smith, and perhaps others as well.

English vessels were visiting the Chesapeake Bay as early as 1546, but the first European settlement on the bay was made by the Spanish in 1570 in the region of today's Williamsburg. This settlement was very quickly massacred by the Indians, but the Spanish presence in the Chesapeake region—the Bahia de Madre de Dios, as they called it, the "Bay of the Mother of God"—continued for a number of years. And it is known that at least one Spanish ship put in, or almost so, at the Eastern Shore of Virginia.

In 1588 the Spanish captain Vicente Gonzales explored the Chesapeake as far as the Susquehanna River, and at the conclusion of his exploration touched upon the Eastern Shore of Virginia, one of the first Europeans to do so. Gonzales landed at what he called "some islands which are within view of the mouth of the bay," most likely the tiny islets at the mouth of Cherrystone Creek known today as Wescoat Point and Sandy Island. An 1852 map of the Chesapeake indicates that they were in that year a single, much larger Sandy Island, and it is not unlikely that three centuries before that the island was even larger.[24]

It was at this point that Gonzales...*steered for land, but because the water had little depth, they could not reach it. Many Indians, both men and women, came to the beach. When some came to the bank, after wading in water up to their knees, the Spaniards seized one of them and sailed away.*[25] There are frequent references to such attempts by European explorers to kidnap native American children; a child of seven or eight, already fluent in the native tongue, could be taught the white man's language and then used as a valuable interpreter on subsequent explorations. This incident at Cherrystone Creek was but a minimal contact between the two races, hardly enough, it would seem, to communicate European diseases to the native Americans, yet it is known that the Indian who was kidnapped at this time died soon afterwards.[26]

The most likely source of the contagion that decimated the Accomacks before Captain John Smith's arrival was a landing by Bartholemew Gilbert, nephew of Sir Walter Raleigh, who touched upon the southern tip of the Eastern Shore on July 29, 1603. Gilbert himself went ashore in a small boat with six others, found arrows and bows on the shore as if Indians who had been watching had withdrawn, and was only a short distance from the beach when he was set upon by an Indian ambush. He and one of his men were killed, and it was only with great difficulty that the other four of the party returned to the safety of the ship.[27] At least one historian believes that the "strange mortalitie" described to John Smith five years later was "probably the result of small pox picked up during the earlier visit of white explorers," and names Gilbert's landing as "perhaps the proximate cause of the epidemic."[28]

Did the natives of the Eastern Shore greet Gilbert with hostility because they remembered earlier European incursions that were accompanied by the kidnapping of their people, or by sickness?[29] Were the Accomack Indians who greeted Captain John Smith in 1608 the remnant of a much larger tribe recently reduced in numbers by the introduction of the white man's diseases? The irony is that after 1608 the English found the Indians of the Eastern Shore of Virginia to be far more peaceable, friendly, and "civil" than those of the Western Shore.[30] Their peaceful welcoming of the white man might well have worked to preserve the Indians of this isolated peninsula, had not biology already written the script for their destruction.

What Do You Call a "Laughing King"?

Without a doubt the most famous Indian of the Eastern Shore of Virginia was the "Laughing King" of the Accomacks. This peaceful werowance, unlike his contemporaries on the Western Shore, welcomed the English settlers, gave them land on which to live, counted them among his friends, and kept his people from going to war against them.

We know him as Debedeavon, but that was almost certainly not his name. A careful examination of the original documents of that period suggests that Debedeavon and the "Laughing King" were two entirely different persons.

It may have been the "Laughing King" himself whom Captain John Smith met in 1608 and called the "comeliest, [most] proper, and civil Salvage [sic.] we encountered." Yet not until 1621 is there specific mention of the "Laughing King" by that name.[31] After that the old records speak of him frequently, always by that name and always in the region of lower Northampton County. The last mention of him pertains to the 1630s, and his name drops from the record after that because, presumably, he died about that time. And not once in any of the original documents is this "Laughing King" identified as "Debedeavon."[32]

Debedeavon, on the other hand, does not enter the pages of history until 1648, well after the "Laughing King" has dropped from the record. For a number of years after that he appears in the old documents, always by the name Debedeavon (spelled in a variety of ways: Deabedanba, Depatiavon, Tabatiabum, Tapatiaton), and always in the region of Accomack County, not Northampton. It is he who is sometimes referred to as "King of Nandua," or "King of Great Nuswattocks," which was an early name for Nandua Creek. And not once in any of the original documents is this Debedeavon called the "Laughing King."[33]

Two different names, two different periods, two different areas, never once joined in the same place or identified as the same person—the conclusion seems inescapable: in giving the name of Debedeavon to the "Laughing King" we have confused two separate Indian chiefs, and merged them into one personality.

It is only since the twentieth century that we have done so, and the mistaken identity seems to have begun with Thomas Teackle Upshur (1844-1910), a prominent student of the Shore's history and arguably its first historian. In 1900, Upshur gave an address on

Monument to Debedeavon, Eastville, Virginia
Rightly remembered, but wrongly identified, for Debedeavon was not the "Laughing King"

Eastern Shore history in Accomac, which he published the following year in a scholarly journal. This article is the earliest known source linking the identities of the "Laughing King" and Debedeavon.[34] Since Upshur, most historians who have written about the Eastern Shore's Indians have relied on his identification, and "Debedeavon" as the name of the "Laughing King" has long since become a commonplace of Eastern Shore history.[35]

No matter what his name, there is no mistaking the legacy of the "Laughing King." Throughout the time that his name appears in the records, relations between the Indians and the Englishmen of the Eastern Shore were remarkably peaceful. When the Western Shore Indians conspired to massacre the English, the "Laughing King" of the Accomacks refused to participate.[36] When a 1631 law ordered that no Englishman should "speak or parlie with any Indian either in the woods or in any plantation if he can possibly avoide it," an exemption was granted to Eastern Shore residents, perhaps because Indians and whites there were already on friendly terms.[37] The "Laughing King" granted large tracts of land to Thomas Savage (still known as Savage Neck) and to George Yeardley (Oldtown Neck), apparently welcoming English settlement among his people. And once a year he visited in the home of Colonel Obedience Robins at Cherrystone, who was his trusted friend.[38]

Thomas Savage, first settler of the Eastern Shore, Interpreter
Thomas Savage, traded to the Indians as a boy, learned their language and was valued as an interpreter by the English. Here he is seen (the small figure in the center of the group) interpreting at a "parley" between Indians and Englishmen, as depicted by Theodore de Bry of Amsterdam (who imagines an American scene he never saw) in 1631.

By the 1640s the Eastern Shore was entering a new era of less peaceful relations between the two races.[39] Conflict was inevitable as whites came in increasing numbers, moving always further up and into the peninsula. But another factor in the increased tensions, border incidents, and outright warfare that characterized the mid-1600s may well have been that, by then, the old "Laughing King" was dead, no longer able to set the tone for race relations. A new generation of Indians, among whom was the chief named Debedeavon, faced a period of increased tension and growing hostility.

If not "Debedeavon," what was the name of the "Laughing King"? It is tempting, on the one hand, to suggest that his name was nothing other than "Laughing King"—that is, that "Laughing King" is an Anglicization of whatever Indian word or words made up his name or title. Since the documents make no mention of his being jolly, it is tempting to suggest that the English called him "Laughing King" not because he was jovial but because what the Indians called him and what he called himself sounded, to English ears, like the two English words "Laughing King."

There is, on the other hand, a record of 1635 which preserves the name he used when he granted Savage Neck to young Thomas Savage. According to Savage's widow Hanna, her husband received his gift of land from the "King of the Eastern shoare ...calling himself Esmy Schichans."[40]

Today on the courthouse green in Eastville the small monument to the "Laughing King" names him Debedeavon. He is rightly remembered, but long since, in the Eastern Shore's memory, wrongly identified.

The Indian Makes His Mark

For centuries, in fact until relatively recent times, it was not uncommon for someone signing a deed or an official document to be unable to write his name. In those instances, the literate scribe who was writing out the document would fill in the name of the illiterate person who was to sign, leaving a blank space for him to make his own "mark," which was most often a simple "X." In the old county record books in Eastville and Accomac are innumerable documents that end with a scribbled "X" beneath a notation like "John Smith, his mark."

In the 1650s and 1660s white settlers of the Shore began to purchase land from the Indians, and as a result there are in the old records documents which some of the Eastern Shore's own native Americans signed with their "mark."

The most remarkable of the Indian signatures is found in Eastville, where on October 10, 1650, Okiawampe, king of the Occohannocks, and his "great man" Norris signed a deed granting lands on Occohannock Creek to Edmund Scarburgh. Their signatures were no

Signatures of Indians Okiawampe (L) and Norris (R)
The clerk has written each man's name in English letters, next to which the Indians have added their "signatures." Northampton County Court Records, October 10, 1650.

simple "X," but little picture-like figures of men, as if each were drawing a quick, stylized image of himself.[41] Such signatures are rare among the Algonquin Indians, and unique on the Eastern Shore of Virginia.[42]

Among the Indians whose signatures appear in the records of Accomack County is Ekeeks, the "king" of the Onancocks. In 1663 he sold the land on which South Chesconnessex now stands to John Wise, who paid him six Dutch blankets (so insists the Wise family tradition). The deed on record makes no mention of the blankets, but right in the Clerk's Office can be found today the little squiggle that Ekeeks himself made right under the words "Ekeeks his mark" and the date, July 3, 1663.[43]

And so we have the "signatures" of such long forgotten men as Matom, chief of the Metompkins,[44] Matahoquid of Onancock,[45] Nowthothrawen, "king" of the Chesconessex Indians, and his "great man" Awosseconsul,[46] and Kokewiss and Watchesagon, "great men" of the Occohannocks.[47]

No single Indian signed the records more frequently that Debedeavon—or Tapatiapon, Tabatiabum, Tapatiaton, or Tepiatavon, for the county clerks seemed unable to agree on how to transliterate his name into English. His signature appears at least half a dozen times, and is remarkably consistent, like a capital "W" with an extra loop. It usually appears above that of Kokewiss and Watchesagon, for like other local Indian "kings" Debedeavon would frequently bring his "great men" along to witness the transaction with the English.[48]

The various Indian signatures are usually non-figural marks whose meaning or significance is unknown to us. Kokewiss' looks like elaborations upon the letter "Z," Matom's something like a half-moon, Nowthothrawen's like two overlapped circles, one of them flattened into an ellipse. Watchesagon seems to have been inconsistent in how he made his mark—did he, like many of us, have more than one way to sign his name?

The sad story behind these signatures is that they witness contracts between Englishmen and Indians who did not really understand each other. Englishmen thought they were purchasing land as Europeans had done for years—John Wise, for example, had already purchased his Chesconessex lands from another Englishman even before he sealed his ownership by purchasing it also from Ekeeks.[49] Indians, however, had no concept of the private ownership of land. Among them, land was understood to be common ground, and the chiefs who "sold" it to the English were, in their own minds, granting them the right to use it, not to hold it in perpetuity.[50] Yet the English claimed the land, and occupied it, and within a short time the Indians found themselves dispossessed of

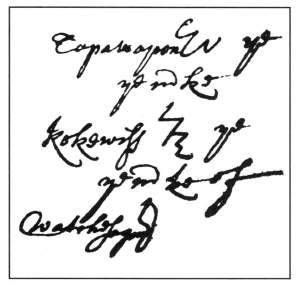

Three Indian Signatures
Tapatiapon (Debedeavon), king of the Occohannocks (top); Kokewiss (center); Watchesagon (bottom). Each man's "mark" is to the right of his name in English. Accomack County Court Records, November 9, 1663.

it. By the end of the 1660s, after the local "kings" had done with selling their lands, the tribes were left on ever smaller enclaves of territory.[51] After little more than a century of English settlement, the entire Eastern Shore of Virginia, with the exception of one Indian reservation near Eastville, was in English hands.

Today, ironically, the very signatures of the men who hastened its demise are among the most prized of the visible evidences of this now vanished culture.

Our Indian Placenames: A Movable Feast

Accomack, Chincoteague, Onancock, Machipongo—today the Eastern Shore revels in the Indian placenames that dot the map. But these Indian names do not necessarily refer to the same places now as they did when the Indians used them.

As the English filled the land, what had been the names of the Indian tribes who inhabited the peninsula became at first the names of regions and sections of the Shore, and only later the names of specific English towns and villages. Those towns that bear Indian names today may or may not be on or even near the site of the old Indian villages, with the result that modern readers of the early history of the Shore should not assume that an Indian placename then meant the same thing as it does now.

Accomack is the most obvious case in point. The Indians of this name lived nowhere near the modern town of Accomac, or even in Accomack County, but on King's Creek in lower Northampton County in the region of Cheriton and Cape Charles. Because they were the closest tribe when the English arrived, "Accomack" became the term the English used to refer to the entire Eastern Shore (in the 1600s Virginia was sometimes known as "Ye Colony of Virginia and Ye Kingdome of Accawmacke"). In time the Indian name Accomack was applied to the upper county of the peninsula, not to the lower one where the Accomacks had lived. For many years after that Drummondtown, the county seat, was known as Accomack Court House. It was only in 1893 that Drummondtown officially took the name "Accomac"—without the final "k," to the on-going confusion of virtually everyone who does not live on the Shore. The result is that the ancient Indian name is preserved today, but at a location fully forty miles distant from where the Indians of that name lived.[52]

Pocomoke is a similar case. In the old parlance, Pocomoke was that section of the Bayside bordering on the Pocomoke Sound and Pocomoke River. So when the Methodists established a church in this region in 1855, just east of what is Sanford, it was only natural to name it Pocomoke Church. Newtown, up the Pocomoke River and across the state boundary in Maryland, did not change its name to Pocomoke City until 1878.[53] Since then, the Indian name has been associated with a specific town in Maryland, though a portion of Virginia has an older claim to it.

Nassawadox, similarly, was in the 1600s the section bordering on the creek of that name, and Nassawadox Meetinghouse, built by the Quakers in the 1600s, stood not in today's Nassawadox but in Franktown. Machipongo was associated not with central Northampton County but with the Seaside of lower Accomack and upper Northampton, near the vicinity of the Machipongo River. Assawoman was not simply today's village but an entire region which included the creek, the island, and the bay of the same name— and this particular Indian name is also found as far north as Delaware.[54]

No Indian name took longer to settle down than Messongo. Messongo Creek, on the Bayside in upper Accomack, has borne its name since the earliest days of English settlement, and by the mid-1700s Messongo (sometimes "Messongoes" or "Messongers" in the old records) referred to the general region on both sides of the creek. When a small community formed south of the creek, near the point where it is bridged by the Bayside Road at today's "Skin Point," its post office was given the name Messongo in 1837.

Since that time Messongo has jumped on the map, not once but twice. In 1893 the original post office closed (the old village was by then declining), and when a new Messongo post office opened in 1900 it was four miles west at an entirely different point on the north side of the creek, at Hammock's Landing between Sanford and Saxis. This, officially, was Messongo until 1904, when this post office also ceased to function. Then in 1909 a third Messongo post office opened in yet another location, a mile north of the creek, a mile south of Grotons, about three miles from the original site. Though this post office no longer functions, the small village that clusters around it is the latest location of "Messongo."[55]

Though modern Chincoteague clings tenaciously to the tradition that the Indians inhabited the island of that name, in fact the early records prove that the Chincoteague Indians lived on the mainland opposite the island. In early English usage, "Chincoteague" referred not so much to today's island as to an entire region of the upper Accomack Seaside. Corbin Hall, the elegant plantation north of Horntown, was "Chincoteague Farm." Chincoteague Baptist Church is to this day located not on the island but a mile north of New Church, where it was founded in 1786 when this neighborhood was known as "Chincoteague." The post office at Atlantic on the mainland was known as Chincoteague as late as 1872 (the island's post office, in that same year, was named "Gingotig"). Though in our own time "Chincoteague" means a specific community on a specific island, one cannot make that assumption in reading the local records throughout most of the Shore's long history.[56]

Indiantown

There is one other Indian placename on the Shore. Not without reason is the region east of Eastville on the Seaside known as Indiantown Neck. Here for almost two hundred years was located Gingaskin, largest and last of the Indian settlements on the Eastern Shore of Virginia, and its only official Indian reservation.

The displacement of the Indians from their lands began within twenty years of the coming of white settlers to the Eastern Shore of Virginia. The influential William Stone was probably the first to move them aside. When he settled in Wilsonia Neck west of Machipongo in 1635, the small Mattawoman tribe that had lived there was relocated across the creek to Oldtown Neck. Then in 1640 when Argoll Yeardley, son of the former governor, laid claim to Oldtown Neck, the Mattawomans were moved again, to the thinly populated Seaside east of today's Eastville.

The Indians knew, as the white men did not, that the place to which they had been relocated was known as Gingaskin, and as was their custom they called themselves, thereafter, by the name of the place. By the end of the 1600s, virtually all of the remaining Indians of the southern part of the peninsula, including what was left of the Mattawomans and the Accomacks, were living at Gingaskin and were

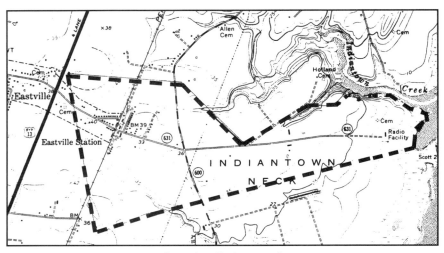

Gingaskin, "Indiantown"

The Eastern Shore's only Indian reservation stretched from the water almost to Route 13. Its boundaries are superimposed on this modern map of the area.

known as Gingaskins. By 1705 there were only nine Indian settlements left on the Shore, and Gingaskin, the only one in Northampton County, was almost as populous as all the others combined, though it contained only about 40 or 50 families.

The Indian reservation, created in 1640, was to have contained 1,500 acres, but when surveyed in 1641 it turned out to be only 640 acres. Philip Taylor, the neighbor to the south, claimed 200 acres of even that much, and the authorities had to order him not to "disturb or molest the Indians," nor to clear or work their ground without which "they in noe wise can subsist." Taylor was only the first of many Eastern Shoremen to covet this Indian land, and the Gingaskins had often to do battle in court to retain possession of it.[57]

With their "fondness for fishing, fowling, and hunting," and their "disinclination to Agriculture," the Gingaskins seemed, by white standards of that time, to be wasting valuable land, and white planters continued to look begrudgingly and longingly at the square mile of Indian land that lay virtually at the front door of the Northampton County seat. What made the Indian town even more a problem to many of that day was the fact that as the years passed the tribe mingled and intermarried with free blacks. By the 1780s local whites were insisting that the reservation contained "not more than three or four genuine Indians at most," and had become a haven for "an idle set of free negroes who had of late years connected [married] themselves with the Indians."

White pressure to obtain the Indian lands began in earnest in the late 1700s. In 1769, when Gingaskin's population was about 30 and its lands were still largely uncultivated, the Vestry of Hungars Parish, who had the responsibility for the poor and indigent of the county, petitioned the Legislature to rent out the reservation lands, and to use the proceeds to care for the needy among the tribe. Accordingly 200 unused acres were leased, and the profits turned over to the Vestry. In 1773 and again in 1792 white Trustees were appointed to oversee the reservation. Among them was one who disliked the Indians, and believed that "Indolence and aversion from every kind of profitable labour" were the "true characteristics of the Gingaskin Indians." In 1784 and again in 1787 the whites petitioned the Legislature to dismember the reservation, prompting the tribe to address their own petition to the Legislature in 1786.

Finally in 1812 eleven Gingaskins proposed that the land be divided and sold to individuals of the tribe, their argument being that they were trying to support themselves by farming while most of the reservation lands were being leased to whites. With this argument the Indians, perhaps unwittingly, played into the hands of the whites, who had always assumed that once the individual members of the tribe held title to specific plots of land each one could be quickly and cheaply bought out—the Indians being, it was assumed, "illiterate, naive, and irresponsible."[58]

In 1812 an "Act Authorizing A Division of the Land of the Gingaskin Tribe of Indians" was passed, and the following year surveyors carved up the reservation into lots of 25.5 acres, each of which was deeded to one of the 27 Gingaskins "who appear to us to be all of the said tribe who are adults."[59]

But the swift transfer of lands to white buyers did not occur. Gingaskin retained its identity for another twenty years, only to disappear in the wave of anti-Negro reaction that swept the Eastern Shore following an insurrection of slaves led by Nat Turner in Southampton County in 1831. In this period of heightened racial tension, most of the remaining Gingaskins were persuaded to sell their lands to local whites. Thereafter some of the tribe moved off the Shore, and those who remained merged completely into the black population of Northampton. Today a number of African American families in Northampton County can lay good claim to be descendants of the Gingaskins, and those descended from Edmund Press (1816-1889?), who was identified by the Smithsonian as Gingaskin in 1889, can document the claim.[60]

Once in the hands of the whites, Gingaskin very quickly became just another part of the country landscape. In 1884 the railroad cut through the western portion of the reservation, and here arose Eastville Station. Today the eastern end of the Town of Eastville sits on what was once the Indian town of Gingaskin. East of Seaside Road in "Indiantown Neck" arose two large farms named, as if in honor of the Indians, "Powhatan" and "Pocahontas."[61]

But there is a sad irony in the choice of those two names. Although both are Indian, neither is Gingaskin or even Eastern Shore in origin. And by the time they were chosen Indian culture was, tragically, all but erased from the Eastern Shore of Virginia.

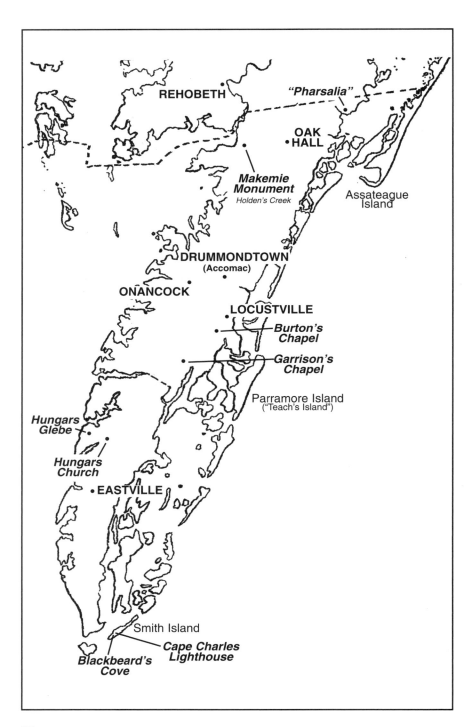

REHOBETH

"Pharsalia"

OAK
•HALL

*Makemie
Monument*
Holden's Creek

Assateague
Island

DRUMMONDTOWN
(Accomac)

ONANCOCK

LOCUSTVILLE

*Burton's
Chapel*

*Garrison's
Chapel*

Parramore Island
("Teach's Island")

Hungars
Glebe

Hungars
Church

•EASTVILLE

Smith Island

*Cape Charles
Lighthouse*

*Blackbeard's
Cove*

26

3

A Cast of Characters
Part I

Francis Makemie,
Presbyterian Pioneer

An elderly woman died near Jenkin's Bridge in 1788, and a part of her will read:

"I Give the two Pictures of Father and Mother to Samuel Wilson."[1]

If these two antique pictures were still in existence today they would be not merely valuable but priceless. For the woman who owned them was Anne Makemie Holden, and the "Father" and "Mother" that they depicted were none other than Francis Makemie (1635?-1708), the "Father of American Presbyterianism," and his wife Naomi Anderson Makemie.

In 1680 the Presbyterians of Scotland received an appeal from William Stevens, who lived in what is now Worcester County, Maryland, for a Presbyterian minister to come to the Eastern Shore. The call inspired young Irish-born Francis Makemie to enter the ministry. He was ordained in 1682, booked passage to America in 1683, and after several years in which he pursued various business interests settled in Accomack County in 1687.

Makemie chose Onancock as his home, married Naomi Anderson of that town, and with the backing of her affluent father became a successful tradesman and landowner. Business was his main pursuit (it

27

took him to Barbados in the West Indies for six years) and ministry a sideline until in 1699 he registered as a minister—the second "dissenter" to do so in Virginia—and began holding services at his two residences, in Onancock, and on Holden's Creek in upper Accomack County. He built no church, but became the pastor of Rehobeth in Maryland, the church just across the line that had called for a minister back in 1680.

In 1706 Makemie was instrumental in organizing the first presbytery in America, and he served as its moderator at its first meeting in Philadelphia. Shortly thereafter he undertook a preaching tour to the North, promoting the new denomination, when in 1707 he was catapulted into prominence by being arrested in New York for preaching without a license. His trial was highly publicized, and his acquittal seen to this day as a landmark decision in the evolution of religious liberty in America. Bad health soon forced him to return home, and there in 1708 he died at his home on Holden's Creek.[2]

Where and when in this busy life the portraits of Makemie and his wife were painted is not known, perhaps in Philadelphia or New York after he had become financially secure. Almost nothing is known about the paintings. In his daughter's will they sound like a matched set, and the reminiscences of those who saw them suggest that they were in color, so they may have been oil paintings. Makemie died in 1708, so if his portrait were painted from life it was undoubtedly almost a century old by the time of his daughter's death in 1788.[3]

Samuel Wilson, who inherited the pictures, lived in Somerset County, owned land in Accomack County, and was a friend and fellow Presbyterian of Mrs. Holden.[4] From his family the portraits passed into the hands of Stephen Bloomer Balch, a Presbyterian minister who served in Snow Hill.[5] In retirement Balch moved to Georgetown, the oldest section of Washington, D.C., and there in his home the two portraits hung among an extensive collection of books and papers until one night in 1831 Balch's house caught fire, and he and his wife barely managed to escape with their lives. Among the treasures that went up in flames was the only known true likeness of Francis Makemie.[6]

Two artists later drew from their imagination to produce "likenesses" of Makemie. The first was Henry Alexander Ogden (1856-1936), a Philadelphia-born artist and illustrator who specialized in the drawing of military uniforms. Ogden painted Makemie's most celebrated moment: his appearance before Lord Cornbury in New York during the celebrated trial of 1707. The painting, a watercolor, hangs today in the Presbyterian Historical Society in Philadelphia. It has been frequently reproduced, and in 1982 the Irish government reproduced it fully a million times when it became the basis for Makemie's portrait on a postage stamp.[7]

Alexander Stirling Calder (1870-1945) a sculptor from a family of sculptors (he followed his father into the field, and his son Alexander Calder became world famous for his "mobile" sculptures), produced

Francis Makemie's Trial before Lord Cornbury
This painting by Henry Alexander Ogden became the basis for...

another likeness of Makemie for the facade of the Witherspoon Building in Philadelphia, erected in 1896. Like Ogden's painting, Calder's statue is now at the Presbyterian Historical Society.[8] It too has been reproduced, much less often but much more familiarly for the peninsula, for it is the basis for the two Makemie Monuments on the Eastern Shore of Virginia.

Ireland's 1982 Stamp
marking the 300th anniversary of Makemie's ordination

In 1908 a statue to Makemie was dedicated on the site of Makemie's home near Sanford in upper Accomack County.[9] The statue bears no signature, and in all the materials printed about Makemie and his Eastern Shore monument no mention is made of the artist who produced it. It seems likely that the Presbyterians simply hired a stonecutter to copy the Calder statue, and that the Accomack County version is not the work of a master sculptor but of a tradesman, perhaps a carver of tombstones. Sarah B. Smith, the Onancock-born sculptor who restored the statue in 1984, points out its uneven workmanship: a head carved with more skill than the rest of the statue, differing sleeve styles, a disparity in the size of the two hands (somewhat but not fully

A Cast of Characters (I)   29

eliminated by Smith's restoration). Though the design is Calder's, the work is that of an unknown, and lesser, artist.[10]

In 1984 this statue, having suffered from neglect and vandalism at its original site on Holden's Creek, was moved to Accomac and

Francis Makemie Statue
Accomac, Virginia

restored, and since that year has stood behind Makemie Presbyterian Church in that town. The pedestal on which it remained at Holden's Creek, and in 2001 it received a new statue, cast in bronze from the older stone version.

There is one curious similarity in the two modern depictions of Makemie. In both Ogden's painting and Calder's statue the pose that Makemie strikes is virtually the same. In each, he holds a Bible in his right hand and, as if left-handed, with his left reaches upward to point or to bless. In each work also, more to be expected, he wears the "Geneva robe," black with white tabs at the neck.

Are these similarities by coincidence, or design? Neither artist, certainly, could have consulted the lost portrait that showed Makemie as he really looked, for Ogden was born 25 years and Calder 39 years after it went up in flames. But either or both of them could have consulted with those who had seen it. One person who remembered the lost portrait was the daughter of Stephen Balch, and the Eastern Shore author Littleton P. Bowen interviewed her before he published his book *The Days of Makemie* in 1885. Half a century after the loss of the portrait she could still remember the face in it: "the intellectual forehead crowned with brown locks, the fair complexion, the expressive blue eyes [and] mien of a true Irish gentleman" in a Geneva gown.[11] Did she remember also a pose—left hand raised, right hand holding a Bible—in which an earlier artist had painted Makemie as he really looked?

Today Francis Makemie raises his hand—the left one—over the old monument grounds and over a safer location in Accomac behind the church that bears his name. It has been centuries since anyone could say with certainty what this renowned resident of the Shore looked like, but the man if not the face is far from forgotten on the Eastern Shore of Virginia.

Blackbeard the Pirate

The Eastern Shore abounds with legends about the pirate Blackbeard. Said by some to have been a native of Accomack County, or of Franktown, he frequented many of the Barrier Islands, including Assateague, Revels, Hog, and Parramore. Rogue Island still bears a name dating from his pirate days. "There is little doubt" that his main headquarters was Parramore Island, at least until his "Eastern Shore haunts became too hot for his safety." One of his fourteen wives, presumably number 11, lived and died on Assateague, an island to which

Blackbeard often repaired when pursued. And somewhere on Assateague, perhaps, lies his buried treasure, for as one recent writer asserts, "There is an excellent chance that he chose Assateague Island as the final resting place for at least a portion of his ill-gotten gain."[12]

Or so the story goes. In fact, little or none of it is true. And most likely the Eastern Shore's legends about Blackbeard were born of nothing more exciting than a mapmaker's error.

Edward Teach (16??-1718)—alias "Blackbeard," alias Edward Tash, Tatch,

Edward Teach, alias "Blackbeard"

Tack, Tache, or Thatch, depending upon which of his contemporaries was doing the writing and the spelling—was probably born in Bristol, England. According to another tradition his name was Edward Drummond, a family name still found on the Eastern Shore, as was the name Teach up through the late 1800s.[13] Teach is thought to have been active as a privateer for the British during the War of the Spanish Succession (1703-1713), and after the war to have ended up in Jamaica.[14] By 1716 he had become a pirate in the company of Captain Benjamin Hornigold, who placed him in command of a sloop they had captured in combat. Hornigold and Teach plundered merchant shipping up and down the East Coast in 1717, then sailed back to the West Indies where, in December 1717, they captured a Dutch ship which Teach refitted, renamed *Queen Anne's Revenge*, armed with "forty gunes," and used to set out on his own career as an independent pirate captain.[15]

Blackbeard was, to be sure, a frightening figure. Tall, strong, possessed of a booming voice, a ferocious temper, and a sadistic personality, he sported a beard that grew from just below his eyes down to his belly. Often he would twist parts of it into "small tails" tied with tiny ribbons, and sling some of them up about his ears. Before battle, after donning a sling-holster which carried three pistols ready for firing, he would hang loosely twisted hemp cords from the brim of his hat and light them; these slow-burning "matches," wreathing his face in fire and smoke, gave him the appearance of a "Fury from Hell." He could and did best any of his men in endurance contests, doublecross his followers at whim, and cripple one of them with a gunshot to the knees just to remind them who was in charge.[16]

Such was the man who, by 1718, had gathered a small flotilla of four ships, armed with over sixty guns and manned by almost 700 men.[17] After plundering in the West Indies, off the coast of Central America, and in the Bahamas, Teach headed north up the East Coast. In May 1718 he blockaded the harbor of Charleston, South Carolina, and without firing a shot brought to its knees one of the largest and most important cities of English America. The following month he chose the Outer Banks of North Carolina as headquarters, then made a big display of accepting an offer of clemency from the king and giving up piracy. Yet by the end of the month he had sailed off to Philadelphia and Bermuda, pirating again. After making an agreement to share booty with Governor Charles Eden of North Carolina, who was either too frightened to resist, or corrupt, or both, Teach made such a terror of the waters of North Carolina and Virginia that

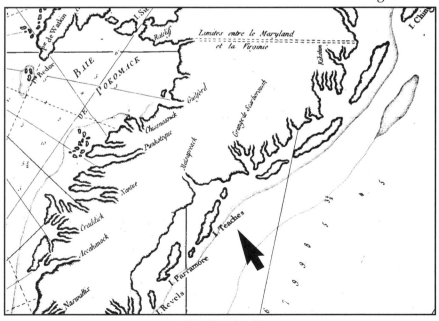

"Teach's Island"
from an 18th century French map showing the Barrier Islands of the Eastern Shore

Virginia Governor Alexander Spotswood dispatched a naval force to get rid of him. Ignoring colonial boundaries, the Virginia force sailed into North Carolina in November 1718, cornered Teach near Ocracoke, and under the leadership of Lt. Robert Maynard killed him in a furious battle. Many of Blackbeard's crew were returned to Williamsburg as prisoners, tried, and hanged. Blackbeard's head, severed from his body, returned to Virginia hanging from the bowsprit of Maynard's ship.[18]

For all the terror that it inspired, this pirate career lasted only about two years, and there is no record that the *Queen Anne*'s Revenge ever plied the waters of the Eastern Shore of Virginia.

So whence came the Eastern Shore legends? In 1635 when what is today known as Parramore Island began to appear on maps of the region, it was labeled Fets Island, or Fetches Island. Early deeds to the island refer to it as Feaks, or Feches, or some other variation of that name, for spellings varied widely in those days. For half a century it remained Fetches Island on most maps, but in 1676 an anonymous map published in London labeled it Tetches Island, and it became the first of many more to do so. By 1700 Fetches Island had become Tetches Island on most maps, and no fewer than eleven known maps published between 1676 and 1776 refer to it as Tetches, Teches, or finally Teaches Island. In 1750 the island was purchased by Thomas Parramore, and shortly thereafter it began appearing on maps as Parramore Island. But for the better part of a century the change of one letter, probably accidental, had made it Teach's Island. Local stories associating it with Edward Teach were rarely wanting in the Eastern Shore's imagination, and the legend grew and expanded.[19]

Despite the dubious legends, there is one place on the Eastern Shore of Virginia that can claim a legitimate historical connection with Blackbeard. In late summer or early fall of 1717, Hornigold and Teach

Blackbeard's Cove on Smith Island,
the only part of the Eastern Shore known to have seen Blackbeard

reached the Virginia Capes in their plundering expedition up the East Coast, and found it necessary to beach their ships to clean their fouled hulls. For this task they selected an "isolated backwater on the Eastern Shore of Virginia" which scholars believe to be Smith Island, just off Cape Charles. Here they hauled their ships ashore, emptied them, and "careened" them: leaning them first to one side then to the other, they burned the grass, shells, seaweed, and ooze off the bottoms with lighted torches. This safely done, they were again at sea by the end of September, seizing vessels just off the coast of Cape Charles and, by October, as far north as Delaware Bay.[20]

All of this was before Blackbeard's name had become a terror up and down the coast. Since it was before he seized the *Queen Anne's Revenge*, we do not even know the name of the sloop that he careened at Smith Island.

It was not an exciting moment in the Blackbeard story, hardly the stuff of which legend is made. But to this day the cove at the southern end of Smith Island is known as Blackbeard's Cove, or Blackbeard's Creek. And despite what other sections of the Shore may claim, this is one place that probably really did see the man they called the "Fury from Hell."

Warner Mifflin,
Abolitionist and Pacifist

Warner Mifflin was a boy of fourteen, at play among the blacks on the family plantation, when one of them made a remark that changed his life.

"Being in the field with my father's slaves, a young man among them questioned me whether I thought it could be right that they should be toiling in order to raise me, [so] that I might be sent to school, and that by and by their children must do the same for mine."

That question, wrote Warner Mifflin many years later when he was a famous enemy of slavery, was "never to be erased from my mind," and made him resolve "never to be a slaveholder."[21]

That encounter took place in 1759, in what is now Captain's Cove near Greenbackville. There Warner Mifflin was born in 1745, there he spent most of his childhood, and there he began to glimpse the evils of slavery and to resolve to fight them. It is because of this one very remarkable man that the Eastern Shore of Virginia can lay claim to a niche in two movements that were otherwise not much a part of its heritage, Quakerism, and the anti-slavery movement, as well as to a small chapter in the War for American Independence, which otherwise little touched the Shore.

Warner Mifflin (1745-1798) was the oldest son of Daniel and Mary Mifflin, who lived at "Pharsalia," the big house at the mouth of Swan's Gut Creek overlooking Chincoteague Bay in upper Accomack.

The Signature of Warner Mifflin
Despite his importance and renown, there are no known likenesses of Mifflin.

The Mifflins were Quakers, possibly the wealthiest and certainly among the last members of the Society of Friends to live on the Eastern Shore of Virginia. In 1660, even before Warner's great-great-grandfather first set foot in America, Virginia had passed laws designed to rid itself of these people who seemed, to the colonial authorities, a radical and troublesome sect. Virginia's anti-Quaker laws worked: most of the Quakers of Accomack and Northampton promptly moved north into Maryland. They left behind just two small congregations, or "meetings," in Guilford and Franktown, both of which then dwindled until they were virtually defunct by the time Warner was a boy. But he may have been present at the last known act of public worship among Quakers on the Eastern Shore of Virginia, which was a wedding held at Pharsalia in 1753.[22] Since as an adult Warner moved to Delaware and the rest of the clan left Virginia soon after his father's death some years later, the Quaker heritage, and with it the strongest anti-slavery sentiment and pacifist leanings of any Christian denomination in America, was lost to the Eastern Shore of Virginia. But not before Accomack County produced this one very noteworthy crusader.

By 1767, when he married Elizabeth Johns of Cecil County, Maryland, and set up house near the present town of Camden, Delaware, Warner Mifflin was not much of a practicing Quaker. Though Quakers generally shied away from participation in government, Mifflin accepted appointments as local magistrate in 1770, justice of the peace in 1771, and court justice in 1774. Though Quakers generally abstained from liquor, Mifflin "kept the bottle and the bowl on the table from morning till night." And despite his youthful vow, Mifflin soon became a slaveholder. Some of his slaves were really Elizabeth's, some of them gifts to him from his parents, and some of them people who had come up from Pharsalia on errands and elected to stay under his easy rule. Still he "rested quiet in the use of them," convinced that they were necessary "to support me in that mode of life," until "I became almost persuaded [that] I could not do without them."

A sudden turn-about occurred in Mifflin's life in or around 1774. He had spent several days in a dark mood of "debating, resolving, and re-resolving" about his life and its meaning when suddenly he found himself caught outdoors in a violent thunderstorm. It was a terrifying experience in which he feared for his life. When it was over, he came to the realization that "if taken hence in [this sinful] condition," he risked nothing less than an "eternal separation from heavenly enjoyment."

Almost immediately Mifflin changed his ways. He became serious about attendance at meetings at Duck Creek, the nearest Quaker meetinghouse, and rose quickly in the ranks to become a pillar of that congregation (elder in 1775, clerk in 1776). He resigned his government posts, and banished liquor from the Mifflin plantation. He adopted the plain and simple dress of the Quakers: gray suit without buttons or trim, hair without wig or powder, shoes fastened not with fancy buckles but with plain shoelaces, and flat-brimmed hat, which in Quaker fashion he would tip to no lady or remove for no man of whatever rank. He became pacifist in his attitudes toward war, so much so that his neighbors, convinced that he was anti-American in the gathering storm of revolution, shunned and threatened him.

Most important, Mifflin's sudden change re-awakened within him a concern for the condition of the enslaved blacks. Shortly after his thunderstorm experience, no doubt recalling the vow he had made as a boy in Accomack County, he freed the five slaves that belonged to him through Elizabeth. Not satisfied with that, he communicated with his father in Virginia to tell him either to reclaim the Pharsalia slaves or risk having them set free. Daniel told his son to do with them as he pleased, and in 1775 Warner manumitted another sixteen blacks—all that remained in his possession.

Freeing one's slaves, he soon discovered, was not as easy as it seemed, not in the agitated months before a war in a slaveholding state. "On setting my blacks free," he wrote, "I thought it best to put them from me, in order to manifest that they were free." But no sooner were the former slaves dispersed from the plantation than the word spread that "Mifflin had set free a parcel of lazy worthless negroes, that he could make nothing by them, and therefore had set them at liberty." To counter this accusation, Mifflin provided some of the blacks with land and stock in return for a payment from the produce of the land for a given period, only to discover that "the tune was turned and it was reported that Mifflin was making more money by his negroes than ever, and keeping them in more abject slavery under the pretence of being free."[23]

Mifflin was hardly the first to free his slaves. For twenty years or more the Quakers of the Eastern Shore of Maryland and Delaware had been exercised about the plight of the slaves. Now from Pennsylvania was radiating a stronger abolitionist mood among the Society of Friends, and the writings of Anthony Benezet and the frequent missionary journeys of the saintly John Woolman, two influential Quakers, seemed to be bearing fruit. In 1768 the Quakers of the Maryland Shore began to disown those of their number of who continued to hold slaves, until in 1788 they expelled altogether those who would not free them.[24]

Though Warner Mifflin did not initiate this movement, he influenced it by setting a new and higher standard for emancipating slaves. Slaves, argued Mifflin, need not only to be liberated but also recompensed for the time they had labored in bondage. "I found an engagement to make restitution to those I had held in a state of bondage," he wrote. According to one report he paid each slave 270 pounds per year of his labor as an adult, from age 21, which in the case of one slave named Jim came to 2,295 pounds, though Jim was not yet 30 years old.[25] That figure amounts to a fortune, and it is likely that the report exaggerates the amount Jim received from his former master. But that Mifflin made restitution to his slaves in some way is certain. Some received land on which to build, and all who chose to stay on the plantation were thereafter paid a fair wage for their work. As for those still of minor age when freed, Mifflin took upon himself the duty "to raise and educate them till they arrive to lawful age." Thus he reserved for himself "that prerogative over the males until they arrive to twenty-one years of age, and the females till they arrive to eighteen years of age."[26]

Only once after 1775 did Mifflin own another slave, and that was early in 1777 when he sought out and repurchased a slave from Kent County, Maryland, who had been owned by his father and sold. Mifflin purchased him and immediately set him free, citing the "uneasiness in my mind to remain till I purchased him to manumit and set him at liberty, which I have done."

These were impressive acts, even among Quakers who were not hesitant to follow the dictates of conscience that might require them to run counter to the practices of society. Though many had freed their slaves, few had been careful to see that those liberated were reimbursed for their labor, or set up in freedom. And few there were who, like Mifflin, had been concerned enough to seek out slaves they had formerly owned but sold to others in order to buy them back and set them free.

For the rest of his life, Warner Mifflin was a tireless and effective advocate for the slave. His example helped to swing more and more Quakers into the anti-slavery camp. One who followed him was his own father, Daniel Mifflin of Accomack County. The elder Mifflin owned almost a hundred slaves at Pharsalia. In April 1775, shortly after Warner set his slaves free, Daniel manumitted the 91 slaves who lived in the Virginia portion of his lands, and in January 1776 freed an additional seven who lived across the line in Maryland. Like his son, Daniel assumed responsibility for caring for the children of his former slaves.[27] And when in 1778 a committee of Quakers came down to Pharsalia to see the condition of those recently liberated (Warner was on the committee), they visited them in their homes and were able to report that the condition of the blacks had improved markedly with their manumission.

Within a few years Mifflin began to travel beyond the peninsula, and with these travels his fame and influence increased. When he expressed some "drawings in his mind" to attend other Quaker meetings, his congregation officially certified him to do so, and over the next several years he visited almost every "Yearly Meeting" of the Friends in the country: Pennsylvania (1780 and 1797), Long Island (1780), Rhode Island (1780), Virginia (1782 and 1787), North Carolina (1787), and New York (1795). With each visit he became more and more famous, and more and more influential among the Quakers.[28]

His attempts to persuade non-Quakers on the subject of slavery began in 1782 when he appeared before the legislature of Virginia to plead for the slaves. This particular assembly, in his opinion "a set of liberal-spirited members," passed a law that rescinded an earlier law forbidding slaveholders from freeing their slaves. When it became legal to do so again, many slaveholders freed thousands of slaves across Virginia in the next several years, and Warner joyfully claimed credit for these manumissions.[29]

He lobbied frequently after that, often in the company of other Quakers, before the U.S. Congress and the legislatures of Delaware, Maryland, and Pennsylvania.[30] In 1792 he gained a national renown, or notoriety, by presenting to Congress his own petition for freeing the slaves. William Smith, Federalist congressman from South Carolina, was incensed by Mifflin's proposal, which he labeled the "rant and rhapsody of a meddling fanatic." Even to read it would, he warned the House of Representatives, prove "highly dangerous." The house, following Smith, refused to accept Mifflin's petition.[31]

Stung by the label of "fanatic," Mifflin published a 16-page pamphlet entitled *A Serious Expostulation with the Members of the House of Representatives*, and in 1796 followed that with a longer and autobiographical *Defence of Warner Mifflin Against the Aspersions Cast on Him on Account of His Endeavors to Promote Righteousness, Mercy, and Peace Among Mankind*. In 1797 he was back again, heading yet another Quaker delegation to Congress with yet another "Address on Slavery."[32]

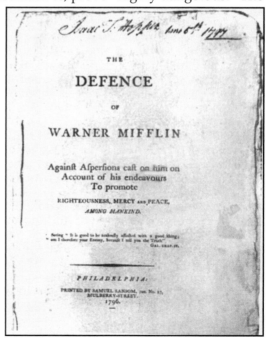

For all his efforts on behalf of the slaves, Mifflin was noted in his own time chiefly for his one effort to stay the course of war during the American Revolution.

In 1777, when the Yearly Meeting of the Society of Friends for Pennsylvania and New Jersey convened in Philadelphia, American and British armies were ranged about the city, and the slaughter of war was a cruel reality for the whole region. The Quakers, largely pacifist and opposed to war in all forms, took it upon themselves to try to arrange a truce between General Washington and General Howe, his British adversary. And to venture across the battlefield and enter the lines of each army they chose Warner Mifflin.

Going first to the British lines, Mifflin—so the story goes—was clapped into handcuffs and held under guard for more than two weeks. General Howe then received him, questioned him, and debated with him at length about the evils of war and the virtues of the Quaker stance on pacifism. In some versions the conversation between the two men is quite detailed, with Howe frequently red-faced and angry while Mifflin remains cool and logical. But in the end Howe informed him that he could not possibly meet with Washington without specific instructions from London to do so.

After leaving the British camp, the story continues, Mifflin crossed the enemy lines into Washington's camp, to do which "he had to walk in blood, and among the dead bodies of those who had fallen in battle," which he accomplished "with great freedom and intrepidity." Washington received him kindly, but Congress refused to allow the general to meet in truce with Howe. Though the attempt to arrange a truce was unsuccessful, Mifflin faced all the "dangers and difficulties of [this] undertaking" with eagerness and joy, the hero throughout.

Or so the story goes, as told by his admirers. The real story as told by the Quaker records is somewhat less spectacular. Mifflin was one of a committee of six who "proceeded to General Howe's headquarters near Germantown, and had a seasonable opportunity of a conference with him." Afterwards the committee "proceeded on our way to General Washington's camp, at which we arrived the next day without meeting any interruption." After a wait, Washington received them and they were "kindly entertained." At Washington's insistence they were not allowed to return directly home, but required to remain well behind the lines so that they would be unable to inform the enemy of American positions. A single officer held them under guard, while they were "hospitably entertained," then released in groups after three and four days.

It is a measure of Mifflin's stature and influence in the early anti-slavery movement that the stories of his life, like this one, became increasingly embellished, more and more legendary, and less and less grounded in actual fact as they were repeated by his admirers. Hector St. John de Crevecoeur, a Frenchman of noble birth who migrated to America as a youth, included a glowing account of Mifflin in his book *Letters from an American Farmer*, published in Paris in 1787. In this book Mifflin, who was then still living, had already been transformed into something of a saint. According to de Crevecoeur, the slave that Mifflin had sought out to re-purchase and emancipate had been sold not to Kent County, Maryland, but to far-off Jamaica, so that in order to bring him back to freedom he had to set sail for the West Indies. There is no record that Mifflin ever left the United States.

With the same intensity with which a pro-slavery congressman called him a "meddling fanatic," other admirers labeled Mifflin an "angel of peace" and spoke of his "undaunted firmness and zeal . . . on behalf of suffering humanity." J. P. Brissot de Warville, another Frenchman who met Mifflin in 1788, wrote of him, "What humanity! and what charity!"[33]

Though he was probably not the saint the stories made him out to be, Mifflin was undoubtedly moved by strongly humanitarian motives that issued straight from his Quaker religion. At various times he went to battle against war, alcohol, greed, and of course slavery, all the while concerned for the individual victim. The story of his second meeting with George Washington gives a glimpse into the sense of compassion of this improbable hero. When Mifflin visited Washington in New York some years after the Revolution, Washington recalled their earlier meeting on the battlefield and asked Mifflin to explain again "on what principles [he] had opposed the Revolution."

"Upon the same principles," replied Mifflin, "that I should be opposed to a change in this government. All that ever was gained by revolutions are not adequate compensation to the poor mangled soldier for his loss of life or limb."

Warner Mifflin was left a widower by the death of his wife Elizabeth in 1786, married Ann Emlen of Philadelphia in 1788, and was by his two wives the father of twelve children, seven of whom survived infancy. In 1798, when he was 53 years old, he attended the Yearly Meeting of the Friends in

Mifflin's tomb in Camden, Delaware

Philadelphia at a time when an epidemic of yellow fever was sweeping the city. He died on October 16, 1798, shortly after his return home to Delaware, probably of yellow fever contracted in the city. He was buried in the Quaker burial ground near his home. Not surprisingly, there are some versions of his life that insist that he caught yellow fever not by going to the church meeting but by actively ministering to those who were victims of the epidemic.[34]

Though the Virginia Eastern Shore where he was born does not remember him today, his admirers elsewhere, aware of his virtues and the genuineness of his Christianity, magnified him not only in life but also in death.

"Black Harry" Hosier, Preacher Extraordinaire

"I have now had the pleasure of hearing Harry preach several times," wrote Thomas Coke when he left Accomack County in 1784. "I really believe that he is one of the best preachers in the world, there is such an amazing power [that] attends his preaching.[35]

Thomas Coke (1747-1814) was a preacher himself, Oxford-educated, sophisticated, and recently arrived from England. Harry Hosier, the man whose preaching so impressed him, was black, born into slavery, completely uneducated, and unable to read or write.

Harry Hosier (1750?-1806)—"Black Harry," as his contemporaries called him—was gifted with extraordinary skills at public speaking, and in a day when few blacks were able to advance themselves in any way was called by some "the greatest orator in America."[36] "He was so illiterate he could not read a word," recalled one friend, but "he would repeat the hymn as if reading it, and quote his text with great accuracy. His voice was musical, and his tongue as the pen of a ready writer."[37] To the crowds who heard him he was both a curiosity and an inspiration, and usually far more popular than the more learned clergymen with whom he traveled.[38]

Little is known of the early life of Harry Hosier. He was born in North Carolina, a slave who somehow obtained or was granted his freedom.[39] Perhaps as early as 1780 he became the traveling companion of Francis Asbury, the itinerant preacher who covered the East Coast on horseback, nourishing the struggling Methodist movement. It was not long before it became obvious that the black man who attended Asbury as groom and assistant had preaching skills in his own right. By 1781 he was preaching to blacks who had come to hear Asbury, and shortly thereafter to whites who stayed to experience the novelty of a black man preaching.[40]

In late 1784, Thomas Coke arrived from England with instructions from John Wesley to organize the scattered Methodist societies in America into a separate and independent church. Asbury met Coke at

Barratt's Chapel near Frederica, Delaware, where the two men made plans for the organization. At the conclusion of their meeting Asbury gave Coke a horse, sent him southward down the Delmarva Peninsula to preach to the societies, and loaned him Harry Hosier as guide and assistant.[41]

Thomas Coke and Harry Hosier passed into Accomack County on September 24, 1784, and went first to the home of William Downing in Oak Hall, where Coke preached at noon. By evening the two had covered almost thirty miles to the home of Thomas Burton near Chancetown, where they lodged and Coke preached again.[42]

"Black Harry" Hosier

Methodism was then very new to the Eastern Shore of Virginia, and since there were not yet any Methodist chapels the congregations gathered in private homes for worship and preaching. In their four days in Accomack County, Coke and Hosier visited those homes where the principal societies were gathering: Downing's in Oak Hall, Burton's near Chancetown, William Paramore's south of Locustville, and Jonathan Garrison's in Mappsburg. In addition Coke preached in the courthouse at Drummondtown. Within a few years there would be a Methodist chapel standing in each of these communities, and Downings, Oak Grove, Locustville, Garrisons, and Drummondtown churches, respectively, all continue today from these early societies.[43]

Exactly when and where Harry Hosier spoke on this tour is not explicitly stated by Coke. "I sometimes give notice immediately after preaching," he noted, "that in a little time Harry will preach to the blacks; but the whites always stay to hear him. Sometimes I publish him to preach at candle light [dusk], as the Negroes can better attend at that time."[44] It seems likely, therefore, that Hosier preached in each of the places that he and Coke visited in Accomack. If he preached in even one of them, he was the first black preacher on the Eastern Shore of Virginia.

Leaving Accomack, Coke and Hosier preached their way northward towards Baltimore, where the organizing Conference was scheduled for Christmas. (Hosier's advice saved Coke from almost certain drowning as they ferried across the Choptank at Cambridge.)[45] At Baltimore the Methodist Episcopal Church was organized, and

Asbury and Coke assumed the title of Bishop (much to the displeasure of John Wesley). Only two black preachers were present at this famous "Christmas Conference": Harry Hosier, and Richard Allen of Philadelphia. The two became friends, and Allen attempted to teach Hosier to read and write. Hosier found that it constricted his freedom of expression in preaching, and gave up the effort.

For more than twenty years Harry Hosier continued to ride with the Methodist Bishops and preachers, a faithful guide and assistant as well as a popular preacher. In Wilmington, Delaware, latecomers hoping to hear Bishop Asbury were unable to get into the chapel because of the crowds, but could hear the sermon from outside. "If all Methodist preachers could preach like the bishop," one of them was heard to say, "we should like to be constant hearers." But the preacher they were hearing was Harry Hosier, not Francis Asbury. "If such be the servant," they replied when told of the preacher's identity, "what must the master be?"[46] In 1786 Hosier accompanied Asbury to New York City, and the first mention of Methodism in any New York newspaper is the report of Hosier's sermon on that tour. In 1789 Hosier joined Freeborn Garrettson for a tour of New England. On this trip he traveled as far north as Nova Scotia, and on one occasion preached to a crowd of more than 1,000 people.[47] Twice again, in 1804 and 1805, he touched again on the Delmarva peninsula though not, apparently, as far south as the Eastern Shore of Virginia.[48]

Towards the end of his life Harry Hosier had a brief bout with alcohol, but at his death in May 1806 he was again in good standing with the church. He was buried in Kensington, Pennsylvania. His funeral sermon was preached by William Colbert, who had been the preacher on the Accomack Circuit in 1795.[49]

American Methodism did not long continue the attitudes and practices of racial equality that characterized its early years. The potential rift between black and white was visible even during Hosier's day, and ten years after his death his friend Richard Allen withdrew from the denomination to establish the new, completely black African Methodist Episcopal Church (A.M.E.).[50] Back on the Eastern Shore, also, an integrated denomination slipped gradually towards racial segregation. Although by 1816 Methodist congregations on the Eastern Shore were still racially integrated, the preachers had largely ceased to preach against slavery or for the rights of the Negro, and white Methodists were increasingly unlikely to allow a black man to preach to them, or even to worship next to them. Within a few years the local churches were building galleries across the back of the chapels to separate blacks from whites at worship. One of the first to do so was Burton's Chapel, the very congregation that Hosier had visited and where he probably preached in 1784.[51]

By his early death Black Harry Hosier was spared the sight of this growing division. His own life is a startling success story from an earlier period when black and white Christians worked together as brothers.

Stephen Gunter,
The Reverend Blacksmith*

His body rests beneath a marble slab at the altar end of Hungars Episcopal Church in Northampton County, a place of honor in one of the most hallowed spots on the Eastern Shore.

He is the only rector buried in the venerable churchyard. Yet he was really a blacksmith, and a Methodist.[52]

Stephen Selby Gunter (1792-1835) was born in Accomack County and moved to Bridgetown in Northampton while still a young man. In 1814 he married Tamar Pearson, a local woman then eighteen years old. One of his earliest appearances in the records of the county was in 1816, when he purchased from the estate of a deceased neighbor an anvil, a vise, two hammers, and a box of "trumpery." If not already by then, Stephen Gunter was certainly after that engaged in the blacksmith's trade.[53]

By 1817 Gunter had become a Methodist, probably a member of nearby Johnson's Chapel. The local Methodist records reveal his quick climb towards the ministry in that denomination: class leader (1817), exhorter (1818), local preacher (1819), and ordained Deacon (1823). In 1822 he served as well as one of the managers of a Methodist camp meeting near Belle Haven.[54]

Soon after Stephen Gunter became a Deacon, Simon Wilmer, rector of Hungars Episcopal Church in Bridgetown, resigned his pastorate, and a few months later the Vestry of Hungars Parish invited Gunter, a Methodist, to succeed him. If it seems an odd choice today, it must have seemed even more so then, when differences between Methodists and Episcopalians were more pronounced and animosities closer to the surface. Gunter was obviously of a lower social stratum than most of his new congregation. His wife Tamar was illiterate;[55] he himself was not formally educated and probably had little or no direct experience of Episcopalianism. The good folk of Hungars, consciously among the "better part" of Eastern Shore society, were used to a learned and "proper" clergy, and had probably never dreamed of inviting a blacksmith to fill their pulpit.

It was, however, a marriage of convenience. Each party offered the other the solution to a problem of long standing.

The Vestry's problem concerned the Glebe, the farm in Church Neck which was both the house of residence and the chief means of support for the rector. By a complex and tightly-worded will of 1653, Stephen Charlton, one of the original vestrymen of the parish, had bequeathed the house and land "to be imployed wholly unto the use of an orthodoxe Divyne...for his Laboure in preachinge the word of the Lord unto the inhabitants of this Parish." There was one catch to this otherwise generous gift: "If by default of & vacancye of such a

---

*Jean M. Mihalyka is the co-author of this sketch.

Ministory in this parrish by the space of six months," the property was to revert to Charlton's heirs.

It was not until 1704, when Charlton's daughter died, that the parish took possession of the property, but by 1824 the Glebe had been home and support for every rector for over a century, and the parish had always been careful to make certain that it never stood vacant for more than six months. Though Hungars Parish had withered and almost died after the Revolution, the church building itself virtually a ruin until 1819, the Glebe had survived. Though Virginia had passed a law in 1802 permitting the state to seize all such glebe lands throughout the state, Hungars still retained possession of its Glebe, which unlike most others had not been purchased from public funds when Church and State were one.[56]

Stephen Gunter's problem concerned his entry into the ministry of the Methodist Episcopal Church. The Methodist clergy of that day were "circuit riders" who traveled constant rounds in a far-flung "itinerancy," and most of them were necessarily unmarried. It was difficult if not impossible to maintain family ties while serving in the itinerancy, or to support wife and family on the circuit rider's meager income. Gunter was not only married, he also had a growing family—two boys and two girls by 1823 (the oldest boy named John Wesley after the founder of Methodism), and a ward, his sister Ann. Ann left the household by marrying in April 1824, but was back home in two months, already a widow.[57] A family of six constituted no small encumbrance for a Methodist circuit rider, and no small drain on his income.

It seems likely that Gunter began work at Hungars early in 1824, so as to meet the six-months provision of the Charlton bequest, ministering in an informal capacity while negotiating with the Vestry. By mid-year both parties were ready to make the arrangement official. On July 3, 1824, Gunter withdrew from the Methodist "connection," and eleven days later was ordained Deacon a second time, by Bishop Richard Channing Moore of the Episcopal Diocese of Virginia. On August 18, well past the six-months deadline, he was officially invited to assume the pastorate at Hungars. Moderating the meeting that called him to the post was the prominent Abel Parker Upshur (1790-1844), who later became Secretary of State of the United States, and John Addison, a rich property owner from a well-established Northampton family.[58]

For a parson with a family, Hungars must have seemed a prize. In 1824 Methodist circuit riders were paid $100 a year, with no provision for housing. Gunter's salary at Hungars was $200, and he also had the Glebe in which to live and with which, if he proved able, to earn even more income. In further support, the vestry wrote to Bishop Moore in his behalf explaining the unusual "necessity of permitting Mr. Gunter to continue his present pursuits [of blacksmithing] for two years," and requesting a waiver of church laws that forbade a clergyman to have extra employment.[59]

The Gunters occupied the Glebe in late 1824, and though the widowed Ann was married (for good) a second time that December, still the family grew. Seven children were born to the Gunters while at the Glebe, for a total of eleven children, all of whom survived infancy. Indicative of their new Episcopalian status were the names of the younger boys: Stephen Charlton, born about 1829, named for the vestryman who donated the Glebe; Hobart, born about 1833, probably named for Bishop John Henry Hobart; and Richard Channing Moore, born 1834, named for the Episcopal Bishop of Virginia.[60]

With so many mouths to feed, life at the Glebe was not always easy. An old family tradition insists that the rector was forced to eat chicken so often that he grew to detest it, and finally ordered his wife to serve it to him no more. But Tamar, already adept at serving chicken, thereupon became adept at finding excuses for doing so. "We have to eat chicken tonight," she announced at one evening meal, "because one got its head caught in the fence, and I had to kill it so it wouldn't suffer." Yet Gunter made good use of the Glebe and, in time, built up a substantial farm.[61]

Hungars Glebe

There are two versions of how Gunter fared professionally in his adopted church, each of which probably contains some truth. The Methodist version insists that he quickly became an embarrassment to his flock. Gunter was a "natural orator" by Methodist standards, which meant that he preached a "plain and pointed" sermon. Though at first all came out eagerly to hear him, his Methodist-style preaching soon alienated the well-to-do and attendance dwindled. It is said that on some occasions he even read the service to completely empty pews.

According to the Methodist stories, the leaders of the parish soon regretted hiring Gunter and tried to dismiss him, only to find him possessed of a thick skin and a ready wit and firmly entrenched in his job. When one of the local gentry came to remonstrate with him, he ended by telling Gunter, "I know you from your birth—why you were born in a log cabin!" To which Gunter is said to have coolly replied, "I think it's very likely that I have been more fortunate under such circumstances than you, Colonel, would have been. If you had been born in a log cabin, there you would have remained."[62]

The other version of Gunter's professional career lies embedded in the records of the Episcopal church in Northampton County, and suggests that even if his parishioners had at first to adapt to him, he was for the most part accepted by them. For eleven years, the longest pastorate at Hungars for decades, he married, buried, baptized, and preached to the upper crust of the county. He was ordained an Elder by Bishop Moore in 1826, and thereafter it was he who met the Bishop when he came to the Eastern Shore for his episcopal rounds, riding with him up and down the peninsula to his appointments. It was Gunter who read the prayers at the service of consecration for a new church in Eastville when Bishop Moore preached. One yearly report from early in his pastorate speaks of how his parish was "growing attentive," and how under his leadership there was a "growing attachment to the service of the church."

It was, however, his fate to labor in what were lean years for the Episcopalians on the Eastern Shore of Virginia. While Methodism prospered and grew, Episcopalianism did little more than hold its own in Accomack and Northampton. When he assumed the pastorate, Hungars Parish had 29 communicants; eleven years later it had only 33—though Gunter had helped organize a missionary society, a tract society, a temperance and a Bible society, and had preached not only at Hungars but also regularly at a number of other places.[63]

It was in Eastville that the Episcopalians made their biggest gains during Gunter's ministry, and from Eastville that the greatest dissatisfaction with him radiated. A tiny band of Episcopalians had been worshiping in the county seat off and on since 1813, and under Gunter's predecessor had laid plans to build a church. Christ Church was erected in Eastville in 1829, the fourth year of Gunter's pastorate, at the then considerable cost of $2,960. Almost as soon as it was erected, a rivalry between it and Hungars developed, in which Gunter was somehow the issue. In 1834 a "goodly number" of Episcopalians engaged William H. Mitchell to serve as "missionary" and assistant to Gunter, but shortly after his arrival Gunter severed connections with the Eastville church.

Was the new church, and the hiring of the missionary, an attempt by some of the more sophisticated to circumvent the ministry of the former Methodist blacksmith? If so, the issue was defused by Gunter's death at the age of 43 on October 11, 1835. Within a few months the Vestry, refusing to acknowledge Mitchell's claim, invited William G. Jackson to the pulpit.[64]

That Gunter had earned the respect of most of his parish is indicated by his burial at an honored spot near the church altar in an expensive coffin costing $45 beneath a stone with a long and admiring inscription. His widow was offered the opportunity to continue living in the Glebe, and when she declined was granted $300 out of the rents of the Glebe for 1836. When in 1840 the church assigned and "rented out" its pews, the widow Gunter was presented with Pew #1.

That Stephen Gunter had made the right decision economically to enter the Episcopal ministry is indicated by his estate in 1835. His debts were many, but were well out-weighed by assets that included seven slaves, numerous cattle and other farm animals, ten horses (one named Shakespeare), a carriage, farming equipment, and—in the house—such refinements as silver teaspoons, bookcases and books, maps, mirrors, pictures, and china. While many a Methodist circuit rider left behind only the contents of his saddlebag, Gunter's assets totaled $9,012.65.[65]

Within weeks of Gunter's death the state began to press its claim to Hungars Glebe, based on the 1802 law permitting state seizure of such lands. Though Gunter's successors continued to live in the house, years of litigation followed, until it seemed as if "every lawyer of reputation in Virginia" had some part in it as it moved up the ladder to the State Supreme Court. During this struggle the Hungars rector John Cheevers died unexpectedly in 1857, and his successor Chauncy Colton held out for a higher salary before being installed in 1858. The Glebe stood vacant for more than six months, and in 1859 the parish gave up the struggle. Since there were no Charlton heirs, the state made good its claim to the property, and Hungars Glebe was divided into several parcels and sold.[66]

Today the rector of Hungars Parish lives in Eastville. The Glebe, for many years a ruin, is now beautifully restored. Gunter's descendants live scattered up and down the Eastern Shore, and one great-great-granddaughter owns the Bible from which he preached, each page of which contains not only the Biblical text but also exposition and commentary for the preacher's use.

Stephen Gunter himself lies at the back of Hungars Church beneath a stone that reads: *Sacred to the memory of the Rev. Stephen S. Gunter who was born in Accomack County, E.S. of Va. on the 20th of J... 1792. He was chosen Rector of Hungars Parish 1823 where he continued until October 1, 1835 when he was called at the age of 43 years to the rest which remaineth for the people of God. Let me die the death of the righteous and let my last end be like his.*

This stone was erected by his parishioners as a tribute of their affectionate remembrance.

Jean G. Potts,
Pugnacious Painter

Step inside St. James Episcopal Church in Accomac to see why the name of Jean G. Potts is still remembered on the Eastern Shore of Virginia.

The interior walls of this church are unlike any other on the Shore, adorned with classical columns and pilastres, ceiling medallions and exquisite moldings, fine panels and graceful arches.

It is all very lovely—but it is not for real. All of these arches and columns and panels are paintings, the sleight-of-hand of a skillful artist who has painted an illusion on a flat plaster surface. This type of painting is called *trompe d'oeil*, "fool the eye." And the *trompe d'oeil* that Jean G. Potts painted in St. James in the late 1850s or early 1860s is among the finest in the country.[67]

What the Eastern Shore does not remember is that the creator of such beauty was not a popular man when he lived in these parts. When Potts the painter laid down his paintbrushes he seldom won friends by either his views or his manner of expressing them. His contemporaries on the Shore knew him as pugnacious, opinionated, eccentric, vocal, and not an easy man to have as a neighbor.

Little is known about Jean G. Potts apart from his work on the

Columns and arches behind the altar at St. James Church,
illusionistic painting on a flat surface by Jean Potts

Eastern Shore. He was from Pennsylvania, and at various times painted in Norfolk and Delaware. By 1860 he was living in Drummondtown (Accomac) with his wife Nancy and his young son Andrew Jackson Potts. A second son, Thomas Jefferson Potts, was born in Accomack County the following year, and a daughter Nanette was born in Northampton in 1865.[68] The Potts family lived, most likely, across the street from the courthouse in Drummondtown, in Saunders Hotel where Henry A. Wise was born in 1806. Potts advertised himself in the local paper in 1860: "Interior Decorator, Grainer and Fresco Painter. Executes in all styles every ornamental painting in Fresco, Encaustic and Oil Colors — Architectural and scenographical — as Churches, halls, parlors, etc. Designs furnished, and the best of references given. Orders sent to Saunders Hotel, Drummondtown, or Wm. A. Byrd's store, Oak Hall, will meet with prompt attention."[69] It is known that Potts painted in a number of houses and buildings on the Eastern Shore, but only his work in St. James survives.[70]

When the Civil War began, Potts was a northerner repelled by slavery and secession surrounded by southern sympathizers, and he was very vocal about his differences with his neighbors. In those tense days the county seat was often buzzing with speeches, impromptu gatherings, even occasional mobs, and among those who could not keep quiet at such times was the Pennsylvania painter. On one such occasion he was threatened with tar-and-feathering for "trying to influence the masses for the Union." He escaped only because, in his own words, he himself "kept good sense in crowds of fools," and because his chief adversary was "too much a coward to try the experiment."

The Eastern Shore was already firmly back in the Union fold living under an army of occupation, but still divided into pro-northern and pro-southern camps, when in 1862 Potts took pen in hand and published an eleven-page pamphlet entitled *Address to the People of the Counties of Accomac and Northampton in General, and Particularly to the Mechanics, Tenants, and Laborers*. How many, if any, people on the Eastern Shore read Potts' *Address* is not known. Any southern sympathizers among his readers were undoubtedly unhappy with what he had to say.

"I shall be brief but perhaps a little too blunt for the coxcombs and rebels in our midst," began the painter. "There is a certain clique, an overbearing small-potato aristocracy who have governed you most despotically, by fair and unfair means...." These would-be aristocrats of the Shore always tried, insisted Potts, to "hand down those privileges [of public office] in their families to the fifteenth generation.... A certain clique have monopolized all offices and trust...[and always exercised] great care when Cousin John's term of office was out to get Cousin Sam in; and when Cousin Sam's term was out to get John in again...."

Lest his readers remain uncertain of whom he spoke Potts went on to mention names. Benjamin T. Gunter, later a State Senator, he labeled a "petty usurper" and the "little Accomac Cataline." John J. Wise, a prominent Drummondtown physician who was later a leader of the Readjuster movement, was the "ex-aesculapean, now arch-rebel and quasi-tactician" whose means to an end were often "brutal." One group of southern sympathizers he called a "swarm of hornets," another a "set of disappointed office-seekers and demagogues" and "petty tyrants." Secession was a "heresy," the assembly that voted for it a "bogus convention," and the Shore's support of it due to "deceptive addresses . . . which took many of the illiterate and dependent men unawares," and to "threats of tarring and feathering."[71]

It took either courage or folly for Potts to use such language, for who on the Eastern Shore except the "small-potato aristocracy" could afford to engage a skilled painter to decorate their homes or businesses? It was probably because of his politics that Potts wrangled a local political appointment, and perhaps because of the effects of his politics on his livelihood that he needed it. In 1865 he received an appointment as keeper of the Cape Charles Lighthouse, and moved his family to Smith Island at the tip of the Eastern Shore. There, apparently, he ceased to paint and there, certainly, he found it difficult to get along with his neighbors, and they with him.

In July 1867 Potts wrote from Smith Island to the Union military commander of the Eastern Shore to "lay before you my request for an investigation of the facts of malice and felony against me and my family." The problem was his neighbor David Hitchens, whom Potts accused of "theft and trespass on [government] Property, and with defiance to my authority from the Treasury Department concerning the care of Stock on the Island." Hitchens, he said, was the owner of a "vicious, sheep-killing dog which is trained by his wife and children to attack the members of my family on the public road, [and which] has lacerated the hand of my oldest son and attacked my children repeatedly." Furthermore, complained Potts, when these matters had been brought before the local law he had received no redress, "as a Union man," and he now petitioned for the removal of the local Northampton magistrate Edward P. Fitchett.[72]

What help, if any, the painter got from the military commander is not known. In fact, virtually nothing more is known about Potts after this correspondence from Cape Charles in 1867. Most likely he moved away from the Shore not long afterwards. His children remained and married among the locals. Andrew Potts, having survived dogbite on Smith Island, grew up and married twice, each time a Chincoteague woman, in 1876 and 1895. His brother Thomas married in Wachapreague in 1893, the same year in which his sister Nanette married a man from Chincoteague.[73] The whereabouts of the painter by this time, even when and where he died, is not known today.

More than likely many of the people on the Eastern Shore of Virginia in his own day were happy to see him go. The Eastern Shore of our own day is enriched by his paintings, if not by his polemics.

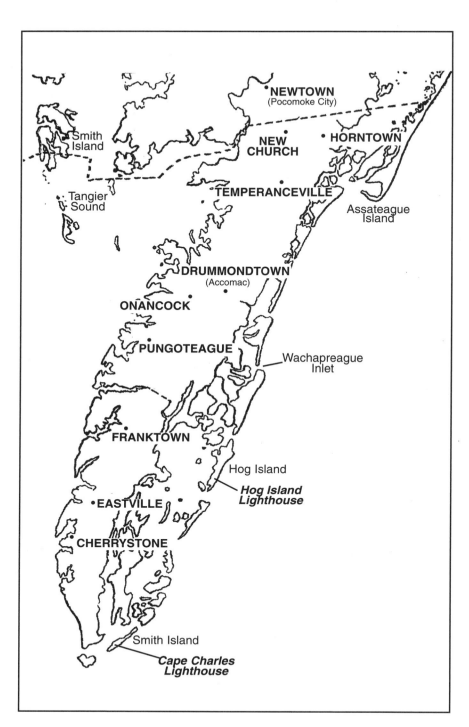

NEWTOWN
(Pocomoke City)

NEW
CHURCH

HORNTOWN

Smith
Island

Tangier
Sound

TEMPERANCEVILLE

Assateague
Island

DRUMMONDTOWN
(Accomac)

ONANCOCK

PUNGOTEAGUE

Wachapreague
Inlet

FRANKTOWN

Hog Island

Hog Island
Lighthouse

EASTVILLE

CHERRYSTONE

Smith Island

Cape Charles
Lighthouse

52

4

The Late Unpleasantness
Stories of the Civil War

Ten Miles to New Church

The Eastern Shore of Virginia does not loom large in the history of the Civil War. A few months after the conflict began the Union army marched down from Maryland and easily took control of the peninsula. The two Virginia counties saw no major battles, produced no great military leaders, and passed through the war safely in the Union, largely ignored by the rest of the nation.

Among those who deserve thanks for the happy fact that no battle was ever fought on the Shore are the Union officials who shaped the "invasion" in 1861, and, in his own way, John A. Brittingham (1823-1898) of New Church.

A battle seemed imminent in November 1861, when Union troops began to gather under General Henry H. Lockwood just across the river from Newtown (Pocomoke City), Maryland. Their objective: to march down the Eastern Shore of Virginia, disperse any pro-southern local troops, and secure the peninsula's allegiance to the Union. The Virginians that came up the Shore to meet them were few in number—between 1,500 and 2,000—and they were poorly equipped. Under the command of Colonel Charles Smith of Northampton, the Virginians built a breastwork across what is now Route 13 about a mile below New Church, and settled down in hopes of repelling the impending invasion.[1]

In addition to the main camp below New Church, an advance force of cavalry was sent ahead above the town to the Maryland line. There in early November they established pickets at the bridge over Pitts Creek just north of the boundary, and made camp in the front yard of the nearest farm, the home of John Brittingham. His big farmhouse, which dated from the early 1800s, stood until a few years ago just west of Route 13, back in the field in sight of the state line.

For more than two weeks the Brittinghams endured a small army of Confederate troops camped in the front yard, and officers sleeping on the floor downstairs at night. Though they were as sympathetic to the South as the next family, it was a situation filled with stress and danger. Like most people on the Virginia Shore, they assumed that the assembling troops were coming as conquerors intent on setting the slaves free. Even worse for Brittingham was the thought of what might happen to his family should they find themselves in the middle of a battle. It was in hopes of being able to evacuate his family to safety that he had made arrangements with

John A. Brittingham

Samuel C. Jones, his brother-in-law in Newtown, to inform him the moment the Yankees crossed the river.

On Friday, November 15, 1861, the Yankees made their first move, a surprise tactic that Smith and his southern troops had not anticipated. Under the white flag of truce Lockwood sent into Virginia a man named Dickinson to distribute copies of a proclamation. The proclamation was signed by General John A. Dix, commander of the Union forces in Maryland, and its contents were meant to reassure Virginians: the Union troops were coming not to invade but only to assert the control of the United States government. There would be no battle unless the "rebels" initiated it. Virginia laws, institutions, customs, and homes would not be violated. Slaves would not be set free, or allowed to come into the Union army camp. The Union troops, who constituted a "force too strong to be successfully opposed [would come] as friends, and with the earnest hope that they may not, by your own acts, be forced to become your enemies." Dix and Lockwood hoped that with such assurances the people of the Eastern Shore of Virginia would not take up arms against the United States, and that the peninsula could be returned from secession to the Union without bloodshed.[2]

That same night, well after dark, came Sam Jones to the farm with the long-awaited word of Yankee movements. He knocked on the front door, and though he and Brittingham whispered as they conferred, his message was overheard by some of the officers "asleep" in the parlor. The Union troops were crossing the river and preparing to march, and there were almost 5,000 of them—more than twice as many as the southerners gathered to meet them! The word of the size of the Union forces spread quickly among the officers, and by daybreak the cavalry had broken camp and headed south, taking the news with them to the main camp.

On Saturday, November 16, 1861, the first of the Union troops passed into Virginia, a small advance party under Captain John H. Knight. They crossed the creek, now unguarded, and came to the farm where Brittingham and his family, fearing retaliation, had attempted without success to erase the signs that southern troops had camped in their front yard. Knight, not fooled by their hasty efforts, questioned Brittingham, insisted that he escort his troops to New Church, and set out down the peninsula behind the farmer and his spirited horse.

They had no sooner started down the road towards New Church than they were stopped by fallen trees which the Virginians had deliberately laid across the road to slow their advance. "We then took a road through the woods," Knight later reported to his superiors. "Galloping along" through the countryside behind Brittingham they again "struck the main road...and came to New Church"—but not before they had covered ten miles.[3]

Did the Union officer realize that he had been duped by Brittingham? The road was then not Route 13 as we know it but Davis Road, which heads eastward from Brittingham's farm and then turns a sharp right angle south towards New Church. It was slightly more

Fallen Trees Stop the Advance of the Union Army
William McIlwaine, who served with Duryée's Zouaves from New York, painted many watercolors during his service with the Union Army in Virginia, including this event which occurred just north of New Church on November 16, 1861.

than two miles down this road from the boundary to New Church. But Brittingham, the immediate danger to his family now past, managed to add an extra eight miles to their route by leading the Yankees aside to Horntown and back, via Signpost Road and Horntown Road, delaying their advance down the Shore as long as possible in order to give the local troops extra time to get away to safety.

When he pulled into New Church, Brittingham handed his horse to a local boy, instructed him to conduct the soldiers down the road towards Drummondtown (Accomac), and winked, hoping the boy also would lead them astray. The boy rode off with the Union cavalry behind him, and Brittingham thought for sure he had sacrificed his best and favorite horse to the southern cause. He had not, for within a few days the horse was returned to him.

By then Knight's troops had enjoyed a "triumphant and uninterrupted march" down the county. The southern troops had simply disappeared. Many of them, trusting the proclamation, gave up soldiering and returned to their homes. Some, seeing the approach of the Union troops, "took to the woods, and others threw away their arms." Many of the officers and some of the enlisted men managed to cross the Chesapeake and join Confederate forces on the mainland. Less than a week after Lockwood's troops entered the Shore, the Federal War Department reported that about 1,800 "secessionists" had laid down their arms and that the Eastern Shore of Virginia was, without a shot fired, firmly in the hands of the United States.[4]

The Union "invasion" of the Shore is a study in restraint and even-handedness, and owes much of its success to men like Dix and Lockwood who were willing not to provoke a battle where one was not necessary. Among those on the Shore who recognized that indebtedness was Ellen Brittingham Nock (1868-1966), youngest child in the Brittingham household, who to her dying day defended Lockwood as a gentleman and a friend of the Eastern Shore of Virginia.

Her father, also, by finding an extra eight miles with which to distance the opposing forces, had played his own small part in seeing that bloodshed was avoided.

The Union Telegraph

Unlike the Eastern Shore, Hampton Roads was an important theatre in the Civil War. When Virginia seceded from the Union in April 1861, two strategic military installations in that vicinity remained in northern hands. The Norfolk Navy Yard (actually located in Portsmouth) was then as now the principal naval base of the East Coast. And at Old Point in Hampton stood Fort Monroe, "mighty and moated," the largest stone fort on the North American continent. Here, only a hundred miles from the Confederate capital in Richmond, was a vital northern stronghold, the base from which, eventually, Union forces would inch their way westward to

Richmond.

In the early months of the war, communication between Washington and Hampton Roads was slow because dispatches had to be sent by boat up the Chesapeake to Annapolis or Baltimore, then overland by telegraph to the capital.[5] The North urgently needed a direct connection by telegraph, and once the Eastern Shore was in Union hands that link became a possibility. In fact, among some military planners the need for a telegraphic link was a "leading motive" for the occupation of the Virginia Shore.[6]

Plans for the telegraph line were submitted within the month after the Union army entered the Eastern Shore of Virginia on November 16, 1861. Construction of the line overland from Wilmington, Delaware, began on January 15, 1862, and proceeded rapidly, for the Union's Signal Corps could string wire "about as fast as a man ordinarily walks." The workers passed through Drummondtown on February 4, 1862, reached Eastville a few days later,[7] and by February 13 stood at Cherrystone, 158 miles from the beginning. Almost immediately Union commanders began using the line, sending their dispatches by steamer to Cherrystone instead of to Maryland. What before had taken overnight could now be transmitted in less than two hours.

At Cherrystone the most daunting part of the task still lay ahead, for from that point the line was to pass 20 miles under the waters of Chesapeake Bay to Back Creek in Hampton.[8] The technology of submarine cables was then in its infancy. A cable laid beneath the Atlantic Ocean in 1858 had briefly enabled messages to be exchanged between Great Britain and the United States, but it went dead within a few weeks, and not until after the war was a permanent transatlantic connection achieved.[9] The only cable available on short notice for the Union was a light one which Signal Corps leaders feared might last only for a few months. It cost $300 per mile, was shipped from New York to Virginia in February,[10] and was laid across the bottom of the Chesapeake in three weeks. The telegraphic link was completed on Sunday afternoon, March 9, 1862.[11]

Meanwhile events in Hampton Roads had moved swiftly, and the connection was more urgent than ever. The Union had abandoned Norfolk and Portsmouth, after setting fire to the Navy Yard to make it useless to the rebels. The Confederates managed to salvage one ship from the drydocks, a sailing vessel named *Merrimack* which was burned to the deck, and in rebuilding her they plated everything above the water line with iron. On Saturday, March 8, the new *Merrimack,* now an entirely different kind of warship, steamed out of the Elizabeth River, crossed Hampton Roads, and tore into the wooden ships of the Union fleet anchored near Newport News, easily sinking the *Congress* and the *Minnesota.*[12] The last dispatch to go out from Fort Monroe to Washington by the "evening boat" was Gen. John E. Wool's description of the devastating losses to the Union fleet caused by the *Merrimack.*

The news of the *Merrimack* reached Washington on the morning of Sunday, March 9, creating despair among government officials and near panic among the citizens. At a meeting with Lincoln and his Cabinet, the Secretary of War paced the room "like a caged lion," while the usually calm President was "so excited...he could not deliberate." It was, as Gideon Welles, Secretary of the Navy, later remembered, the "worst moment of the war." Nothing like the *Merrimack* had ever been seen in all the history of warfare—was there a single Union vessel which could withstand the ironclad? What was to keep the *Merrimack* from sailing up the Potomac and bombarding Washington itself?[13]

The Battle of the *Monitor* (L) and the *Merrimack* (R)
...the news of which went to Washington, D.C. via the new telegraph from Cherrystone up the Eastern Shore

Yet Washington's information, dependent as it was upon dispatches by boat, was a day old, and back in Hampton Roads events had already taken a turn for the better for the Union. On Saturday, the very day of the *Merrimack's* appearance, even while General Wool was composing the report that caused such terror in Washington, the Union's own new warship was entering Chesapeake Bay. The *Monitor* was, like the *Merrimack*, coated with iron, but smaller and swifter and a much more difficult target—she looked, to those who first saw her, not unlike "a cheese on a raft." The *Monitor* anchored on Saturday night amid the vulnerable wooden ships of the Union and was there to meet the rebel ironclad when she steamed out on Sunday morning. While Washington was in a panic, the *Monitor* and the *Merrimack* were blasting away at each other near the shore of Newport News.

This time there was to be little delay in getting the news to Washington, for at 4:00 p.m. on that very day the complete telegraph link via Cherrystone became operational. The first message sent over it was from G. V. Fox, Assistant Secretary of the Navy, to Gideon Welles, his superior in Washington, and it was good news from Hampton Roads: the *Monitor* has met the *Merrimack* and repelled her attacks against the fleet; the southern ironclad is said to be damaged, her northern counterpart "uninjured, and ready at any moment to repel another attack." Fox's message went out as soon as the line began functioning. From Fort Monroe it traveled overland seven miles to Back Creek, then under the Chesapeake to Cherrystone, up the peninsula to Wilmington, and from there southward to Washington, where it was logged in at the Navy Department at 5:30 p.m.[14]

From that day until the end of the war many of the Union's most important military dispatches were routed through Cherrystone. Though geography had dictated that the Eastern Shore of Virginia would be out of the direct line of action, its proximity to one of the most important theatres of the war gave it a vital role to play in the conflict.

As the Union Signal Corps had feared, it did not take long for the telegraphic cable beneath Chesapeake Bay to fail. Already by March 17 the cable was not working, probably damaged by a ship's anchor, and it failed again in May. By then Edwin M. Stanton, Union Secretary of War, had detailed the *Metamora*, "the fastest vessel that could be chartered," to run between Fort Monroe and Cherrystone to guard the cable, and to insure that quick dispatches could be sent through Cherrystone when it was not functioning properly.[15]

Any interruption in the communication between Washington and the troops in the field was a serious matter. When the cable failed yet again in August, General George B. McClellan, head of the Union forces pressing westward towards Richmond, decided that instead of sending dispatches by boat, then waiting hours for the reply, he would go personally to the nearest telegraph office and communicate directly. Finding the telegraph out of order at Jamestown Island, he proceeded to Fort Monroe, only to learn that the cable beneath the Chesapeake was not functioning. So he headed to Cherrystone, and for two days, August 13-14, 1862, communicated with Washington from there.[16]

It was a rare visitation of the war to the Eastern Shore. Though the messages that zipped up the peninsula carried timely and strategic information from the front, on the Eastern Shore itself Union soldiers faced what must have been the monotonous, though safe and easy detail of guarding the overland wires. Regimental companies were stationed along the line—Cherrystone to Eastville, Eastville to Franktown, Franktown to Pungoteague, Pungoteague to Drummondtown, Drummondtown to Temperanceville, Temperanceville to Newtown—all the way to Salisbury, Maryland. The wires were

Union Army Telegraph Office
Back Street, Accomac

guarded day and night by pickets of six men, while officers rode the route daily, and inspectors weekly.[17] The actual route of the line is uncertain, though it probably paralleled the main Bayside Road through Northampton into Drummondtown, then the "Wallop Road" (Route 13) north of Zion Baptist Church. In Drummondtown it undoubtedly passed the little building at 23319 Back Street (later the Parish House of St. James Episcopal Church), for it is known to have been the telegraph headquarters of General Henry H. Lockwood, commander of the Union army on the Eastern Shore of Virginia.[18]

The Confederacy was not unaware of the importance of the Cherrystone connection. In July 1863, John Yates Beall, a rebel "partisan" operating out of Mathews County, sent a small crew to Cherrystone in hopes of seizing a Union steamboat. The *George W. Rodgers* steamed safely out of port before the rebels arrived, so the raiding party contented itself by cutting the submarine cable. Beall triumphantly sent a piece of the cable to the Confederate Secretary of the Navy in Richmond, and direct communication between Cherrystone and Fort Monroe was cut off for at least a month while the cable was repaired.[19]

A more daring and successful raid took place on March 5, 1864, when sixteen men led by Confederate Captain Thaddeus Fitzhugh surprised and overwhelmed the small Union guard at Cherrystone and seized two ships, including the government tugboat *Titan*. Upon hearing the news, Union Captain Robert Duvall hurried from Eastville with reinforcements, only to arrive just in time to see the guerrillas leaving in their captured boats. Gone were $2,000 worth of supplies for the Federal troops—600 barrels of pork, bread, flour, molasses, beans, sugar, coats, and cooking stoves—and in the destruction left behind was the burning guardhouse, the ruined telegraphic equipment, and the submarine cable cut yet again. Telegraph operator W. A. Dunn managed, "by quick moving," to see that no current dispatches fell into rebel hands, but because his equipment was disabled he had to head up the Shore to find a place from which to report the incident to Washington.[20]

The on-again, off-again cable was in operation in June 1863, not functioning in July. By then, the telegraph lines radiating out from Fort Monroe extended as far west as Petersburg, where the major Union offensive against the Confederate capital was centered, and virtually all communication with Washington from that campaign funneled through Cherrystone. In that month Dunn, fearing another Confederate raid, asked for reinforcements for the 18 men stationed at his post, and the value of Cherrystone was attested when his superiors ordered an entire regiment (far more than Dunn thought necessary) to "take post there to guard the telegraph station." By January 1865, there were 346 men "stationed in small squads at the different towns upon the Shore, from Cape Charles to the Maryland line, and also as a patrol along the telegraph line, a distance of eighty miles. Their principal duties [were] to patrol the telegraph line, and to prevent improper communication between this shore and the western shore of Virginia."[21]

It was under the bay and up the peninsula that the news traveled on April 3, 1865: Richmond had fallen. "Probably no other message was ever received at the National capital that caused such rejoicing," remembered one signal corpsman. Yet even more momentous was the news of the following week, when on April 9, 1865, General U. S. Grant telegraphed from Appomattox that Lee had surrendered. The war was over, and once again the dispatch went eastward to Fort Monroe, under the Chesapeake to Cherrystone, and up the peninsula.

With war's end came the swift demise of the once-strategic telegraph line to Cherrystone. By the end of May telegraph wires stretched across the formerly rebel territory between Washington and Richmond, and the Eastern Shore line was suddenly a dead-end. It was discontinued not long afterwards, probably on November 30, 1865, when all Federal telegraph operators "not employed upon strictly military lines and not retained at chief cities...were discharged." It seems likely that the line was soon dismantled, and the materials sold.[22]

The Civil War passed lightly over the Eastern Shore of Virginia, but by supplying the route for one of the most important Union telegraph lines the peninsula played a vital role which is, in our own day, virtually forgotten.

John Yates Beall,
Rebel Raider of the Chesapeake

His appearance on the island that August morning in 1863 aroused no great suspicions in the mind of William Stakes. Though this was wartime, there was little military activity on the Eastern Shore, which had been firmly and peacefully in the hands of the Union for almost two years. Though Smith Island, at the tip of Cape Charles, was a lonely place, visitors were not unknown. Stakes, keeper of the island's Cape Charles Lighthouse, was used to seeing people come and go as the construction of the new lighthouse tower, then 83 feet high and unfinished, dragged slowly towards completion.[23]

This visitor was a young man, handsome and well-groomed with speech and manners suggesting education. Soon Stakes was showing him around the island, demonstrating his work and answering the visitor's many questions.

"My friend," said the visitor at last, "I am greatly pleased with your lighthouse and your management of it. And I have a party of friends belonging to the Confederate States Navy who I think would like to look at it."

At that he gave a whistle, and as if from nowhere eight armed men materialized from behind the bushes and surrounded the astounded lighthouse keeper.[24] The valuable Union light that guarded the entrance to Chesapeake Bay was under attack, and the Eastern Shore was about to meet one of the most colorful figures of the Civil War.

John Yates Beall (1835-1865) was born in Jefferson County, now West Virginia, and attended the University of Virginia. So seriously wounded in the opening days of the Civil War that he could not

Cape Charles Lighthouse
The second lighthouse on Smith Island stood unfinished when raided by John Yates Beall in August 1863

return to battle, he decided instead upon a career as a southern agent behind the Union lines. By the time he moved his operations to the Chesapeake he had already worked in Iowa, been discovered, and made a daring escape in disguise to neutral Canada.[25]

Beall's guerrilla operations on the Chesapeake Bay began in July 1863. His home base was Mathews County, and he had under his command fewer than twenty men, all of whom were "partisans"—irregulars who supplied their own arms and profited from what plunder they could take from the enemy. Two small boats, the black *Raven* and the white *Swan*, which they had seized, were all they had at their disposal. Yet what they lacked in arms, equipment, and status they made up in coolness and daring.

The raid on Cape Charles Lighthouse was the second to the Shore for his men. Only a month earlier his crew had cut the submarine telegraph cable at Cherrystone, cutting communications between Hampton Roads and Washington for a month.

This time Beall himself led the raid on Cape Charles Lighthouse. While Stakes and his wife were held at gunpoint, Beall's men overran the undefended island. What they could they seized—several hundred gallons of valuable sperm oil, reflectors, lamps and other fixtures of the light atop the old tower, an old clock—and all of it they packed into the government boat, which they added to the plunder. What they could not take they destroyed: machinery, lighthouse fixtures, enough to leave the lighthouse dark and unusable. Though they compelled Mrs. Stakes to fix a meal for them, they paid her for it with a five dollar Confederate note. Then announcing that there would be a similar raid on Hog Island Lighthouse, and warning Stakes not to leave the island for 24 hours, they were off as quickly as they had come.[26]

The Union forces then in control of the Eastern Shore were taken by complete surprise. "They threaten to go to Hog Island," telegraphed one general to another. "Every man that can be spared from the line has been forwarded to reach Hog Island before their landing, and to scout both neighborhoods.... [But] one company of local cavalry is all the force left on the Eastern Shore, and with that I can give little protection nor do anything considerable for prevention of rebel depredations."

Beall was not yet known on the Shore, and the raid left both military and civilians speculating who the raiders were. "The mischief is done by rebels who left these counties, aided by friends here," reported one officer. But there were no Eastern Shoremen in Beall's small band. And if Beall's hope was to rally southern sentiment on the Shore, the raid was a failure. "Some of the citizens seem to be incensed against these raiders," wrote Union commander Lockwood. "And I think twelve [jury]men...can be procured who will be disposed to deal with these fellows as their outrages deserve."[27]

Beall waited six weeks before trying again, then on September 18 set out with his two boats and his eighteen men for the southern tip of the Shore. There he divided his forces, taking charge of the *Swan* and putting Roy McDonald, his second in command, in charge of the *Raven*. Beall steered the *Swan* to Raccoon Island, virtually under the gaze of the now darkened Cape Charles Lighthouse, and there succeeded in capturing a sloop named *Mary Ann* and two small fishing scows.

This, however, was mere prelude. The real target was not Cape Charles Lighthouse or even Hog Island Lighthouse, as he had said to put them off the trail. The *Raven* and the *Swan* were headed for Wachapreague Inlet, where Beall hoped to seize the first big Union vessel that came along.

On the night of September 21, 1863, in a heavy northwestern wind, the *Alliance*, a large schooner under Captain David Ireland of Staten Island, sailed into view bound from Philadelphia to South Carolina with a cargo of goods to supply the Union armies in the South. "The night was fearfully dark and stormy," but not enough to cause alarm among seasoned sailors. "The crew had turned in; the captain and mate were playing dominoes in the cabin." Though the ship lay off the coast of Virginia, these were friendly waters, for the Eastern Shore, which lay dark on the horizon, had been peaceful ever since its occupation by the Union army.

The sound of a small boat scraping against the side of the schooner must have gone unnoticed in the ship's rolling. The *Raven* crashed against the schooner in the rolling sea, breaking its tiller and pitching McDonald into the water. Unable to maneuver into position, the *Raven* was forced to withdraw back into Wachapreague Inlet. McDonald swam to the *Swan* and was hauled safely aboard.

After this unpromising start, the plan fell neatly into place. The crew of the *Swan* climbed aboard the ship, and while Beall and his men headed for the forecastle to surprise the sleeping crew, McDonald struck out for the captain's cabin. In a matter of moments, without a shot fired, the ship was theirs. Captain Ireland, suspecting nothing, was interrupted at his game of dominoes and held at gunpoint.

John Yates Beall

Beall had proved his point. With a small band of men and two small boats he could indeed seize larger vessels, harass Union shipping, and perhaps thereby deal a blow to the steady advance of the

Union forces in the South. More than that, the *Alliance* and its contents were now his to plunder.

On the morning of September 22 the crew of the *Raven* was brought aboard, and both of the anchors of the *Alliance* were cast out to keep her steady. That night Beall and his men repeated their successful performance not once but three times, capturing in succession the northern-owned sloops *J. J. Houseman*, *Samuel Pearsall*, and *Alexandria* as they ventured past Wachapreague Inlet.

The next day they faced the question of what to do with so great a booty. Though four large ships (and three smaller ones captured earlier off Cape Charles) and all their contents now lay open before them, the prize was useless to the Confederacy unless it could be transported to southern territory for sale. That meant not only taking it to the Western Shore but also running the blockade past the Union forces that patrolled the coast.

On the night of the 23rd the *J. J. Houseman*, *Samuel Pearsall*, and *Alexandria* were stripped, scuttled, and sent out to sea (the *Pearsall* was later recovered by Union naval forces and taken into Hampton Roads). In the *Alliance*, now laden with extra cargo, a new Confederate crew, and sailors held prisoner, Beall steered south toward Cobb Island. There he set ashore the crews of the smaller vessels, and obtained the services of a pilot willing to try to take the ship through the blockade into the Pianketank River in Mathews County. The force then headed westward across the Chesapeake, Beall in the *Alliance*, McDonald following in the smaller boats with seventeen prisoners.

At Hole in the Wall, near the mouth of the Pianketank, the Federal gunboat guarding the river fired upon the *Alliance*, whose pilot then missed the channel and grounded the vessel on a sand bar. Quick work by Beall and his men succeeded in rescuing most of the cargo, and at about the time that McDonald arrived with the prisoners the captured ship was set afire and abandoned. Once in Richmond, the "sutler's goods" seized in the raid brought Beall a considerable profit.[28]

On the Eastern Shore the Union forces, having been surprised a second time, determined that there would not be a third. A force was detailed to guard Hog Island Lighthouse, and another to guard the lighthouse on Assateague Island.[29]

Meanwhile on the Western Shore, Brigadier General Isaac J. Wistar was ordered to Mathews to catch Beall. Wistar's forces consisted of one regiment of "U.S. Colored Troops," two of white cavalry, and one battalion of artillery, in addition to which he could call upon the services of the ten Union gunboats in the area. That the object of their search was as small as it was would probably have surprised and dismayed them, for as notorious as "Captain Beall" was becoming, his entire force consisted still of only eighteen men and two small sailboats.

While in Richmond dispensing with their plunder, Beall and

McDonald were unaware of these preparations to find them, and upon their return to Mathews on October 5 were surprised by a party of Union soldiers. McDonald and two of the men with him were captured. Beall and the rest narrowly escaped and were forced to lay low for a about a month.[30]

"Nothing daunted" by this setback, Beall set out for his third raid on the Eastern Shore in early November. The raid began well. On or about November 12 he seized a schooner in Tangier Sound, the eighth vessel taken with only the *Raven* and the *Swan,* a considerable prize but still less than the steamer for which he had hoped. Dividing his forces, Beall then sent a party eastward to Accomack County, where they were to attempt a raid on the land.

By now surprise was no longer on his side, and Beall's men found a small band of "coast guard" waiting for them and were quickly captured. (The exact location of his landing is not known today, and accounts vary as to whether the "coast guard" were Union soldiers or simply armed civilians of Accomack.) Back on his captured schooner, Beall waited too long for their return and was surrounded and captured, but not before he was able to scuttle virtually everything of value on board, to prevent its use by the enemy.[31]

His capture was widely heralded. "This is a highly important capture," exulted General Lockwood, who insisted that "this will put an end to these depredations."[32]

But Beall in custody proved to be almost as troublesome as when he had been free. He was taken first to Drummondtown, where he was relieved of some of his personal possessions, then to Baltimore, where he was imprisoned in Fort McHenry. On the boat that conveyed them to Baltimore, Beall kept trying to induce his men to seize the vessel and make their escape.

Once imprisoned, Beall became a *cause célèbre* because of his manacles. Since in the eyes of the Union he and his men were not prisoners of war but guerrillas, or even pirates, he was kept not only in a cell but also chained. Though the routine of the prison was to strike each prisoner's chains for a few hours a day to allow them to exercise, Beall refused this privilege. "No," he objected when they came to unchain him, "let them alone till your Government sees fit to remove them!" The Confederacy learned of his treatment through a letter he was allowed to write to Richmond, and in retaliation placed in irons two commissioned Union officers and seventeen sailors then held as prisoners of war (the same seventeen men that Beall had brought as prisoners from the *Alliance*?). This "taste of retaliation" soon produced its desired effect. General Benjamin F. Butler, commander of the Union military in the Chesapeake, ordered that the "manacled pirates" be released from irons and placed on a footing with other prisoners of war.[33]

Beall spent 42 days in Fort McHenry, and was then moved to the prison camp at Point Lookout in Maryland. From there in March 1864 he wrote to Butler seeking to recover what was taken from him in

Drummondtown. "When I was captured," he wrote, "Capt. Graham, Provost Marshal at Drummondtown, took my commission, other private papers, and money.... He promised to return them, but has not done so [and] I appeal to you that my commission may be returned." The loss of his commission was no small issue, for that piece of paper provided official validation of his claim that he acted under the authority of the Confederacy, and not as a free-lance "pirate."

On May 5, 1864, Beall was returned to Virginia in a general exchange of prisoners at City Point (Hopewell) on the James River.[34] Later that summer he made one last trip to the Eastern Shore, eluding the blockade and journeying "leisurely" overland to Baltimore. From there it was on to New York and Canada and further adventures in behalf of the Confederacy behind enemy lines.

In September 1864 Beall at last succeeded in capturing a steamer for the Confederacy—on Lake Erie, where he hoped to free Confederate prisoners held on an island near the Ohio shore. Even with the captured steamer the plan fell through, and Beall was forced to flee to Canada.[35] He was soon at work again in New York, trying to derail the Cleveland train to Buffalo. When this plan too went awry, he was captured in Niagara, New York, just short of safety in Canada, and conveyed to Governor's Island in New York City.

When one of his band turned state's evidence against him, Beall was convicted of acting as a spy and a guerrilla and sentenced to be hanged. There followed strenuous efforts by friends in North and South to save him, including appeals for clemency directly to Abraham Lincoln. But Beall was by now a public figure, notorious in the North where the newspapers depicted him as callous and hardened, and Lincoln turned a deaf ear.

On February 24, 1865, a crowd of spectators arrived on Governor's Island to witness the execution of the notorious southern spy. With a military band playing popular tunes, Beall walked to the gallows, calm and composed, wearing the same clothes in which he had sat for his photograph only shortly before. When asked if he had anything to say he announced in a low voice: "I protest against the execution of this sentence. It is absolute murder—brutal murder. I die in the service and defense of my country. I have nothing more to say." He died moments later, shortly before his mother arrived on the island in hopes of seeing him one last time.[36]

It was for actions in the North that Beall was executed, not for his earlier career on the Eastern Shore of Virginia. There he had enjoyed, at least briefly, success, fame, and riches.

The Rebel Raid that Never Was

In the waning days of the Civil War, on February 22, 1865, one hundred and fifty four "rebels" set out in several boats from the Northern Neck and headed across Chesapeake Bay for Smith Island in the middle of the Chesapeake. Their goal was to plunder Union supplies, rescue "refugees and deserters" who had escaped to the island from Virginia, and if possible to capture a steamboat with which they could attack Union shipping in the bay.

The first to sound the alarm was Thomas Nelson, Acting Ensign aboard the Union naval vessel *Mercury*. It took him four days to do so, perhaps because the *Mercury*, on patrol in the bay, had been out of touch while out of port. Once back at Point Lookout, on the Maryland side of the mouth of the Potomac, Nelson alerted his superiors, and on Sunday, February 26, the Chesapeake came alive with the alarms, messages, and orders telegraphed back and forth by anxious Union officials.

From Point Lookout, Nelson telegraphed Foxhall A. Parker, Commander of the Potomac Flotilla, then in port at the naval station up the river at St. Inigoes.[37] Parker immediately set out for Washington, after sending the news to two members of Lincoln's Cabinet: Edward Stanton, Secretary of War, and Gideon Welles, Secretary of the Navy. "If the military authorities on the Eastern Shore are immediately informed of this movement, I think the rebels [will] be captured," he suggested to Stanton. "I have nine vessels cruising to intercept them on their return," he assured Welles.[38]

At 9:00 p.m. that night Secretary of War Stanton sent a telegram to General James G. Barnes at Point Lookout: "Keep a sharp lookout and notify the gunboats," he ordered. Barnes responded within half an hour: "I shall take all precautions practicable here, and have given all the necessary instruction to the gun-boats and to our steam-boats"— "already," he might have added, for unbeknownst to Stanton it was from Point Lookout that the initial alarm had issued, and Barnes knew of the raid from the same sources who had informed Stanton.[39]

Parker was also sending messages southward down the bay. To the senior naval officer at Fort Monroe he wired, "I thought it best to inform you of the expedition, that they may not carry your guard-vessel...by surprise." And to Lieutenant Commander Edward Hooker went an order to "send a vessel to Cherrystone without delay."[40] The vital telegraph line that ran through Cherrystone had been cut twice by rebels, in June 1863 and March 1864, and the Union could ill afford to have it happen again.

Hooker was aboard the *U.S.S. Commodore Read* in the Rappahannock River when word of Parker's concern about Cherrystone reached him. Though his orders seemed simple enough, it was he who had to orchestrate the complex maneuvers of re-fueling the ships that defended the southern part of the bay, and thus to determine which one might be available for Cherrystone. His reply to Parker mirrors the complexity of the situation: the *Periwinkle* is already at Norfolk getting coal, and overdue to return; the *Freeborn* needs 20 tons of coal before it can move; the *Yankee* needs 50 tons; the *Commodore Read*, his own ship, has only enough fuel for about 10 days; the *Morse* is already somewhere across the bay cruising the

Eastern Shore, but has only about 10 days worth of coal, and to refuel it would have to cross either to Norfolk or to the Potomac.

Parker, briefing Welles in Washington on this situation, greatly simplified Hooker's report: "I have had a vessel cruising for some time in the vicinity of Cherrystone."[41]

Now from the Eastern Shore came a new spate of messages, as the word spread among the Union army. General John R. Kenly in Salisbury informed Gen. W. W. Morris in Baltimore and Gen. H. W. Halleck, Chief of Staff in Washington, whereupon Halleck informed Morris, who wired back that he already knew, thanks to Kenly. In Eastville, headquarters of the Union army on the Eastern Shore of Virginia, Col. Frank J. White wired his commander in Norfolk that "I do not need any re-enforcements," then immediately asked for exactly that: "I should like two armed boats to patrol the coast from Cape Charles northward, also a small force of infantry to station at

This 1840s cannon at Cherrystone was not fired during the rebel raid of February 1865—with good reason....

Cherrystone." At 7:00 p.m., two hours before Washington got the news, White was wiring orders to subordinates who guarded the telegraph line at Pungoteague, Onancock, and other places up and down the Shore: "I anticipate a guerrilla raid tonight. Have your men all ready for service at any moment. Place pickets along the bayside in order that you may receive notice at once of any landing. Should the guerrillas land in your district, telegraph at once, or if the line is cut send [a] picket." A similar message went to the sergeant in command at Cherrystone, and to General Kenly up the peninsula White hinted, "If you can send to Drummondtown two companies of cavalry I may find them necessary. I have but 250 men, detached at posts over eighty miles of country. I think the rebels will land in this neighborhood."[42]

Monday, February 27, brought further orders that kept the Union warships shuffling in and out of the fueling stations: *Periwinkle* ordered out of Norfolk because "her delay in returning is seriously confusing our plans;" *Freeborn* to refuel at Point Lookout in order then to find the *Morse* to send her to St. Inigoes for coal; *Yankee* on her way to Norfolk for fuel; *Banshee* ordered directly to Cherrystone to "render every assistance in your power;" *Morse* and *Mercury* already somewhere in the waters of the Eastern Shore, but no one seemed to know exactly where.[43]

Meanwhile Frank White had been in the saddle all night, looking unsuccessfully for the raiders. "I have scouting squads in every direction...but can find no guerrillas," he reported. "I do not believe that any are here." Though his forces had been augmented by thirty mounted men dispatched from Salisbury, White continue to plead for help: "I have no boat, and cannot communicate with Hog Island, on which there is a government lighthouse.... Please send 2,000 rounds of cartridges."[44]

At about nine o'clock on Monday evening the sound of heavy gunfire drifted across the bay from Tangier Sound towards the Potomac, and those who heard assumed that the rebels had been cornered at last. On Tuesday, February 28, after ordering the *Anacostia* to Tangier Sound and the *Heliotrope* to guard the Smith's Point Lighthouse, Parker set off down the river from Washington. Cherrystone was by then properly guarded by not one but two steamers: the small *Periwinkle*, and the larger *Banshee*, which was too big to enter Cherrystone Creek and therefore had to anchor out in the bay abreast of the lighthouse that then marked the creek's mouth. Even at that point "I have not yet learned that any rebels have been known to have crossed the bay," wired the Banshee's commander to Parker.[45]

On Wednesday, March 1, the fourth day after first receiving word of them, Parker still did not know exactly where the rebels were, or what if anything was happening about them. "Various rumors are afloat," he wired to Hooker. "Send me all the information in your possession without delay."

But it was only on that fourth day that Hooker, aboard his vessel in the Rappahannock, learned at last the whereabouts of the raiders. They were not on Smith Island or in Tangier Sound, and had never gone anywhere near Cherrystone. In fact, replied Hooker to Parker's inquiry, "the guerrillas are all back [home] again." The locals on the Western Shore had only just reported that the raiders who had crossed the bay had returned without ever landing there, "having become aware [from the first] that the gunboats were there and the people aware of their intentions." As for the gunfire heard on the 27th, it was "from my own guns," reported Hooker," for while in Tangier Sound he had used his ship's guns to answer rifleshots from shore.[46]

The rebel raid on the Eastern Shore occurred, or failed to occur, less than two months before Lee's surrender at Appomattox brought the war to a close.

Richard B. Winder, War Criminal?

On November 10, 1865, the United States executed the only "war criminal" of the Civil War in Washington, D.C. Captain Henry Wirz, commander of the Confederacy's notorious Andersonville prison, was hanged within sight of the U.S. Capitol as curious spectators vied for a glimpse of the proceedings, and companies of Union veterans chanted "Remember Andersonville."

In a prison cell in Washington that day, perhaps within hearing of the chant, sat an unindicted co-conspirator, the man who had served under Wirz as quartermaster at Andersonville, the man whom some considered the next in line for trial and execution. He was a native of Eastville, and a resident of Accomac.

Richard Bayley Winder (1828-1894) was born in "Coventon" in Eastville, the son of a prominent Northampton lawyer. After studying at Princeton and the University of Virginia, he briefly operated a "small mercantile business," then married Elizabeth Custis of Drummondtown and settled down with her in what became Willis Wharf. His wife died two years later, and shortly afterwards Winder married her younger sister Sarah Custis, who had meanwhile come into a considerable inheritance. With his new wife Winder moved to "The Folly," south of Drummondtown, and there lived the comfortable life of a gentleman farmer, indulging especially in racing horses on his own racetrack.[47]

When the Civil War broke out, Winder sided with the Confederacy. He raised two companies of Eastern Shore volunteers, personally

The Execution of Henry Wirz,
Washington, D.C.,
November 10, 1865
...while an Eastern Shoreman sits in his prison cell nearby, probably next to be tried

petitioned Jefferson Davis to defend the peninsula, then ran the Union blockade to the Western Shore to participate in the conflict. By the end of 1862 Winder had been assigned to Richmond as an assistant quartermaster in the Confederate army. He stayed at that post until December 1863, when he was ordered to Andersonville, Georgia, where a new prison for Union soldiers was to be built.[48]

Winder himself oversaw the building of the new facility. The Andersonville prison was not a building but a stockade surrounding sixteen and a half acres of open land. Though his plans included barracks for the prisoners, they were never built, for the Yankee prisoners began arriving from Richmond—400 men a day at first—even before the stockade itself was complete. Within a short time the enclosure was crowded with thousands of men, living in squalid and unsanitary conditions. By March 1864 there were 7,500 prisoners, by September more than 34,000.

Without adequate food, clean water, shelter, or medical care, Andersonville quickly became a place of misery and death. In April 1864, over 500 prisoners died, in July over a thousand, in August almost three thousand. Between March and August of that year 42,686 cases of disease and wounds were reported. No one knows exactly how many died at Andersonville, although there are today almost 13,000 graves at the National Cemetery there.[49]

As quartermaster, Winder was responsible for provisioning the prison, and constantly hounded the Confederate authorities for beef and bacon, corn and meal, baking pans, iron, lumber, nails, horses and mules, wagons and saddles, the countless equipment and supplies needed to house and feed so many prisoners, and always money. "For God's sake, send me [funds]" he wrote in July 1863. "If you only knew what trouble I was in here for the want of funds!" In September he begged, "If I do not get this money, I do not know what I shall do, except to ask to be relieved from this post."[50] Yet the Confederacy was itself strapped for supplies, and the flow of new prisoners seemed never-ending.

Winder was back in Richmond at a new assignment when the war ended. It was there on May 2, 1865, that he received his "parole" and, like thousands of other Confederate soldiers, was free to return home. He returned to Drummondtown in June, reported as required to the Union army officials, and on July 9 took the Oath of Allegiance to the United States. With, he believed, the war behind him, he determined to move to Baltimore and begin all over again in a new career.[51]

Then on August 23, 1865, the court-martial of Henry Wirz began in Washington, and the charges against him read not simply that he had "maliciously, willfully, and traitorously" killed prisoners under his care, but also that in order to do so he had conspired with several others, among whom was Richard B. Winder. Three days after the beginning of Wirz's trial, Winder was arrested by army officers, put in irons, and imprisoned in the jail at Drummondtown, then on August 30 transferred to Washington and placed in the Old Capitol Prison, which stood on the site of today's Supreme Court Building. On November 6 Wirz was sentenced to death. When he was hanged four days later, Winder had been imprisoned over two months, and had "never been informed either by my captors...or by any other person...of the cause of my arrest or of any charge or charges made or to be made against me by the U.S. authorities."[52]

Winder was now in dangerous straits. Public anger about Andersonville was high, and many in the victorious Union wanted revenge. If Wirz had paid with his life for Andersonville, it was only because the man the Union really wanted, the Confederate general who oversaw all Confederate prisons, had died shortly before the war's end. His name was John H. Winder, he was widely despised by Union veterans and officials, and he was related to Richard Winder— a "very distant relative," the prisoner could insist, but it was not a good time to bear the same name. Though Winder insisted that he was never "on the inside of the prison at Andersonville more than half a dozen times in my life," he was guilty by association in the minds of the thousands who had suffered there. To make his situation even more complex, he was now in a kind of legal limbo, because the commission that tried Wirz was dissolved after his execution, leaving it unclear who, if anyone, would pursue Winder's case. The Judge Advocate

Richard B. Winder

General proposed to the Secretary of War that Winder be released, since "no...specific overt acts of violation of the laws of war are as yet fixed upon him." Yet another military judge argued that Winder "ought to be tried for complicity, though there is no evidence of his being a cruel or brutal man."[53]

In November 1865, President Andrew Johnson ordered Winder transferred to another prison in Richmond, and the government began preparing its case against him "for cruel treatment of Federal prisoners." As the legal wheels ground slowly, and Winder waited in prison, Confederate General Joseph E. Johnston interceded in his behalf with Union General Ulysses S. Grant. On December 21 Grant wrote directly to the President recommending "that Capt. Winder either have an immediate trial or that he be released on bonds for his appearance when called on for trial." But even Grant's intervention did not produce immediate results. Winder was still in prison as late as March 1866, while the government was seeking the testimony of Ambrose Spencer, who had been a witness against Wirz and who was said "to be well informed in regard to the criminal conduct alleged against Winder."[54]

But Winder's case never went to trial, and by the end of May he had been released. Exactly when, and whether it was because of Grant's request, is not known; there is simply no surviving record of his release.[55]

By June 1866, Winder was again back in Drummondtown, where his once-prosperous circumstances were now in shambles. His marriage was over. He had filed for divorce the previous year, charging Sarah with adultery, in response to which she counter-charged with a number of accusations about his own affairs with local women. The messy proceedings dragged on until the final divorce decree in October 1867. At Sarah's insistence all the property that had come from her side—most of it, including "The Folly"—was deeded to their children. His own property was sold at auction and brought a paltry $1,100. These affairs settled, he put the Eastern Shore behind him and moved to Baltimore, taking with him their two children, Richard Jr. and Mollie, whom Sarah insisted he "stole away."[56]

Though Winder gained new respectability in his new career in Baltimore, he never regained his former affluence. In April 1868 he married Kate Dorsey, who supported both him and his two children while he studied at the Baltimore College of Dental Surgery. He graduated in 1869, and quickly became a successful dentist "known for his excellent workmanship." In 1873 he earned his medical degree from the College of Physicians and Surgeons at Baltimore, and later organized the Maryland Dental College and helped to establish its faculty, served on the Executive Committee of the American Dental Society and as president of the National Association of Dental Faculties, and in 1879 became Professor of Dental Surgery and Operative Dentistry. Letters from this period suggest that he rarely spoke of his war experiences, even to family and close friends, and that his earlier career was not generally known in his adopted city.

Richard Bayley Winder died respected and lamented, a victim of Bright's disease, on July 18, 1894. He is buried in Baltimore,[57] not at Andersonville, not on his native Eastern Shore—but also not in Washington, where at one time he must have wondered if he would meet his end.

5

A Cast of Characters
Part II

George D. Watson, Evangelist

His career spanned ten countries and four continents. He spoke to audiences that numbered in the thousands, and was one of the most widely heard speakers ever to hail from the Eastern Shore of Virginia. He wrote twenty books and was listed in "Who's Who."

And yet today on the Eastern Shore, as everywhere else, he is virtually forgotten.

George Douglas Watson (1845-1924) was born in a farmhouse on Ames Ridge, between Keller and Painter, the third son of devout Methodists James and Mary Watson. As a child he attended camp meetings at "Nock's Branch" near Melfa, witnessed the dedication of the new building at Garrison's Chapel (the oldest portion of the church still standing in Painter),[1] and at an early age showed such a "serious turn of mind"—he once returned home from church and climbed upon a box to preach to his playmates—that he seemed destined for the pulpit.

He was ten when his family moved to Mount Prospect, just south of Onancock, and at the age of fourteen George was apprenticed to Dr. George O. Tyler, Onancock physician. Still a teenager when the Civil War began, Watson joined the Confederate forces, despite the Union tendencies of his tutor. He may well have been among the rebels who marched north to New Church to repel the Union "invasion," only to flee at the approach of the northern forces when they entered the Shore in November 1861. Shortly thereafter Watson escaped to the Western Shore, hiding out en route for two nights on Watts Island to avoid the Union blockade of the Chesapeake. Under General Henry A. Wise of Accomack he saw service at Yorktown, Seven Pines, Charleston, Johnson's Island, and Petersburg, though he spent much of the war hospitalized in ill health.

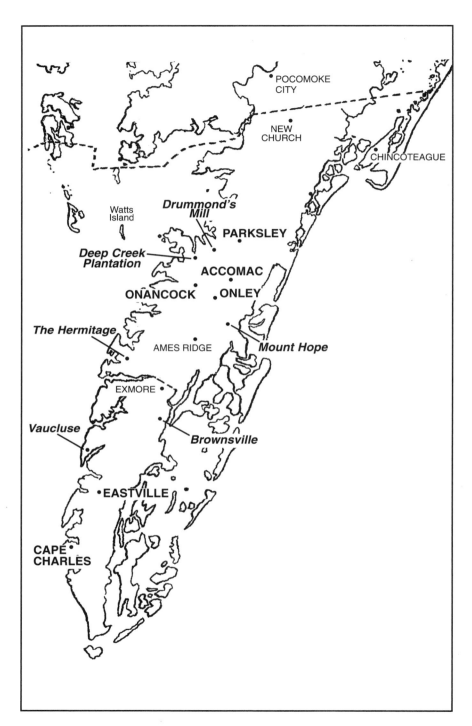

POCOMOKE
CITY

NEW
CHURCH

CHINCOTEAGUE

Watts
Island

*Drummond's
Mill*

PARKSLEY

*Deep Creek
Plantation*

ACCOMAC

ONANCOCK

ONLEY

The Hermitage

AMES RIDGE

Mount Hope

EXMORE

Vaucluse

Brownsville

•**EASTVILLE**

CAPE•
CHARLES

After the war Watson returned to the Shore and worked for some years as a clerk in Onancock and on Watts Island. He joined Cokesbury Methodist Church and was persuaded by the Rev. Levin P. Causey to study for the ministry. After a year at the General Biblical Institute in New Hampshire, he was licensed to preach by the Methodist Episcopal Church in 1866, and for the next several years served churches across the Delmarva Peninsula: Snow Hill (1866), Laurel (1867), Annemessex (1868), Pocomoke City (1869), Frankford (1870), Wilmington (1871), and Dover (1872-1875). While at Annemessex he preached the first sermon ever preached in Crisfield, Maryland. While at Pocomoke City he married Margaret Evelyn Watson of Onancock.[2]

Thus far his career was not unlike that of many another Eastern Shoreman who entered the Methodist ministry. But while at Dover, Watson received a call to the pastorate of the Meridian Street Church in far-off Indianapolis, and with the change in locale came a significant turn in his career. He arrived in Indianapolis in 1875, and was at that time one of a growing minority of American Methodists who were convinced that their denomination was moving too rapidly away from the teachings of John Wesley. In particular Watson held to the Wesleyan insistence, then increasingly de-emphasized, that after conversion the Christian could move on to "perfection," or "sanctification," a second state of grace in which complete

George D. Watson

holiness is achieved. "The truth of Wesleyan theology," wrote Watson, "is that no converted soul can retain the clear sense of justifying grace without going on to perfection." Though he had been preaching "holiness" since 1870, it was not until 1876 in Indianapolis that he himself experienced this "second blessing." Thereafter he led his large city church in a massive revival, and quickly gained a wide renown as a revival speaker and evangelist. Four years later he left the settled pastorate and took to the revival circuit as a full-time evangelist.

With his unique, forceful pulpit style, Watson was well-suited for the evangelist's role. Said one admirer, "When Dr. Watson got through with a text there wasn't anymore to be said on the subject." He possessed a "commanding voice" that enabled him to lead easily in singing. He was unusually adept at Bible study, and when at camp meetings "the bell boy would announce on the camp ground Dr. Watson's Bible Reading, you would see hundreds of people making their way to the tabernacle to get a seat near the front." He buttressed his preaching with the publication of books which had a wide circulation during his lifetime. His preaching was conservative and, after 1892 when he left the Methodist Episcopal Church for the smaller Wesleyan Methodist denomination, full of references to the nearness of the end of the age.

After laboring in Kentucky, Pennsylvania, and Georgia, Watson led his first big successful revival in South Carolina. After that he went wherever called, crossing denominational boundaries if necessary to preach to the Baptists of Philadelphia, the illiterate cotton mill workers of Alabama, or the affluent of Mobile. Soon the calls came from further afield, to Clear Lake, Iowa, and Toronto, Canada, where he filled the largest hall in the city three times a day for ten days straight.[3]

In 1891—by then he was two years beyond the last visit he ever paid to the Eastern Shore of Virginia[4]—he made an evangelistic tour of Great Britain, preaching among the Methodists in rural Yorkshire and in urban Manchester. In London, where his audiences frequently numbered in the thousands, he preached in the slums in the morning and in the afternoon led Bible study in the drawing rooms of the gentry among members of Parliament and their wives.

In 1900 he made the first of three journeys to the West Indies, to Jamaica, where Methodists were holding revivals in Port Antonio and Bowdoin. There followed further missions in Canada, Japan, Korea, Hawaii, Samoa, New Zealand, and Australia. Though everywhere he went he preached in the biggest cities—Honolulu, Auckland, Sydney—typical of his greatest successes were the results in small mining towns like Waihi in New Zealand, where he led a revival that completely transformed the town. By the time he left, miners who before had been a rough and ready lot were holding prayer meetings underground, the churches were packed to capacity, Baptists and Methodists were working together, and conversions were numbered in the hundreds and still increasing.

Upon his return to the United States in 1916, Watson settled in Los Angeles, rented a building capable of seating several hundred, and preached weekly on the "Grand Old Doctrines of the Bible." The crowds came from all over the city and out in the far suburbs, among them large numbers of tourists. By now he was in his seventies, and he had the aura of a grand old landmark of the conservative school. Even so he was still refining the revivalist's technique: experimenting with newspaper advertising, perfecting the methods by which the preacher could keep track of those who answered the altar calls, using address lists to reach potential audiences. And still he was crossing denominational boundaries, eager to attend worship at First Methodist, willing to substitute for the pastor at Tabernacle Baptist, making occasional forays to the Japanese mission in town.

George Douglas Watson made a final evangelistic tour to the East Coast in 1921, preaching as often as twice a day. When he preached in Syracuse, New York, he was physically so weak that he had to sit down to do it. In July 1923 he took finally to his bed, afflicted by old age and diabetes. By then he was 78, and had been preaching steadily for 57 years. He died in Los Angeles in 1924, and is buried in the Rosedale Cemetery there.[5]

At his death a colleague said of him, "I question whether he had an equal in the entire Holiness Movement," and "there is something about Dr. Watson's books that will live forever."[6] But what renown he enjoyed in life evaporated quickly after his death. Today it is not known for certain even how many books he wrote. His wife claimed 14, "Who's Who" lists 10, the Library of Congress 18, and there may be as many as 21. And few people read them anymore, not even on the Eastern Shore of Virginia, where surely a man of his achievements deserves at least to be remembered.

William B. Judefind, Hymnwriter

Had he no greater claim to fame, William B. Judefind might be remembered by some as the man who put Methodism on a firm footing in Parksley. When he arrived in 1900, Methodism in that new town was at a dangerously low ebb. The Methodist Episcopal congregation had sunk so low that it closed the following year, and the Methodist Protestant congregation, of which Judefind was the new pastor, mustered only 58 members and had a total yearly budget of only $453. At the close of his pastorate seven years later, church membership stood at 238, the budget had more than quadrupled, and the Methodist church in Parksley was, as it has been ever since, one of the strongest on the Shore.

Yet Judefind has a stronger claim to fame than his work in Parksley, for this particular minister was also an accomplished musician and composer. His real legacy was the large number of hymns and musical compositions he wrote for church use.

William Burchinal Judefind (1861-1941), pronounced *Jue'di·finned*, was born in Kent County, Maryland, and was 32 years old when he gave up a career as a music teacher to enter the ministry.[7] He served five churches before coming to Parksley, and his earliest known musical composition—"The Snowflakes' Christ-mas, or Santa Claus' Secret"—was published in 1900, the year he came to the Shore. Soon thereafter he and his brother Arlington ("Arly") founded the Judefind Brothers Music Publishers in

William B. Judefind

Baltimore, and began to turn out music for use in churches and schools. One of their first efforts was a hymnbook entitled *On Wings of Love*, published in 1902 while Judefind was still in Parksley. *On Wings of Love* was virtually a family affair. Published by both brothers, it was edited by William and contained 26 hymns for which he wrote the words, 42 for which he wrote the music, 20 for which he wrote both words and music, and four hymns for which Arly wrote the music to accompany words written by William.[8]

It seems safe to conclude that a number of Judefind's hymns were written in the parsonage at Parksley, including the one that became his most famous. In 1905 the Methodist Protestant Church published a new hymnal which contained one composition by Judefind, a hymntune named "Twilight" to which were set the words of a poem by Christopher Wordsworth. Since the 1905 hymnal was frequently reprinted, and was the standard hymnbook of an entire denomination, "Twilight" became the most widely circulated of all Judefind's works.

Judefind served in Parksley from 1900 to 1907 and began there the pattern that marked the rest of his career: long and successful pastorates punctuated by the regular publication of musical compositions. While still in Parksley he produced at least two sacred songs for Christmas, a temperance hymn, and with Arly "Summer Voices," a script with music for churches to use on "Children's Day." After Parksley there followed a six-year pastorate at one Baltimore church, a one-year's leave of absence, and an 18-year pastorate at another Baltimore church. Through it all the music flowed: a sacred song in 1911, a Christmas anthem in 1912, an Easter cantata by 1916, children's day songs in 1923 and 1924. In 1910 Judefind Brothers published *Exultant Praises*, another hymnbook; its over 200 hymns include no fewer than 70 tunes composed by

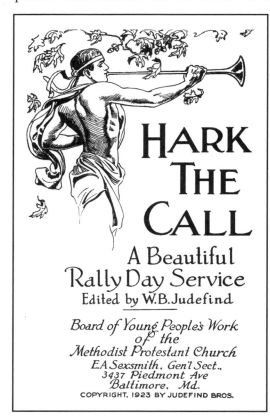

HARK
THE
CALL

A Beautiful
Rally Day Service
Edited by W.B. Judefind

Board of Young People's Work
of the
Methodist Protestant Church
E.A Sexsmith, Gen'l Sect.,
3437 Piedmont Ave
Baltimore. Md.
COPYRIGHT, 1923 BY JUDEFIND BROS.

Judefind.[9]

How could one man produce so much music? When someone put that question to his young son William Lee, born in 1869, the little boy replied, "Oh, he just puts some little black marks on some lines on a page...."[10] Clearly what motivated Judefind was the need for music that could be used in the local church, easily learned and easily sung, written in the musical language of his day. He wrote for rallies, Sunday schools, Mother's Day, and other events of the church. He made use of existing hymns, as in 1904 when his "Crown Him King of Kings" employed "All Hail the Power of Jesus' Name" as a refrain. He wrote new tunes for old texts like "Take My Life and Let It Be" (1902) and "It Came Upon the Midnight Clear" (1919). For words he frequently teamed up with other ministers in the Conference, including J. L. Elderdice (1889-1934) and R. L. Lewis (1847-1899). And his work was used, at least in Methodist Protestant circles. His children's day and Christmas music in particular was sung in Parksley and other local churches on the Shore.

No one knows how many compositions he wrote in all, for his works remain uncollected and uncatalogued. His known songs total 173, 75 for which he wrote both words and music, 82 for which he wrote only the music, and 16 for which he wrote only the words. There were at least eight other compositions, mostly cantatas and children's music, and at least two more hymnbooks. If these unknown hymnbooks contain as many of his hymns as the known ones, his total output may well be over 300 hymns. Yet few if any are used today, and some of his works are known only by name. The very qualities that commended his music to one age—his martial beat, its current idiom—make much of it seem dated today. Yet at least one pastor on the Shore insists that "Twilight" is still used in his churches as a solo for organ or piano.

Judefind retained close ties to the Eastern Shore even after leaving Parksley in 1907. A popular pastor, he was invited to return to dedicate the new church building erected there in 1911, and he and his family were frequent visitors among the former flock. After the death of his first wife Mary Todd Judefind in 1928 he returned to the Shore to claim Stella Scott of Parksley as his new bride, a lady who was "completely unmusical." His three grandchildren, children of William Lee Judefind, were also frequent visitors to the Shore. One of them, Isabelle Eleanor, married Spiro Agnew, later Vice-President of the United States. "Judy" Agnew's nickname is, in fact, a contraction of the family name Judefind.

Only death stopped the remarkable outpouring of church music from William B. Judefind. He died at his home in Baltimore on March 14, 1941.[11] Only a few months before Judefind Brothers had published "The Way of the Cross," a religious drama for Easter containing two Judefind hymns.

How many more hide unaccounted for among the books and memorabilia of Eastern Shore churchgoers?

Robert P. Woodward,
Eccentric Adventurer

One of the most colorful persons ever to call the Eastern Shore of Virginia his home once rode across the continent on a donkey, and did so because he lost a wager.

Robert Pitcher Woodward (1866-1941) was a native of Watkins, New York,[12] an energetic and somewhat eccentric man of no fixed profession. He studied at West Point but was unable to follow a military career because of poor eyesight, so he worked at various times as a "gentleman farmer" and a miner, and was known to family and friends as a "jack of all trades." He always preferred to think of himself, however, as a writer.

Woodward was 30 years old, unmarried, and apparently not tied to a desk when in 1896 he made a bet with a friend on the upcoming Presidential election. William Jennings Bryan was then making his second bid for the Presidency, and Woodward wagered that Bryan would defeat his Republican opponent William McKinley. Bryan lost, and Woodward with him. He faced the prospect of handing over the not inconsiderable sum of $5,000 until his winning friend suggested an alternative form of payment. Though it was offered in jest, Woodward happily agreed to it: to ride a donkey across the United States from New York City to San Francisco.

Robert P. Woodward

The terms of the agreement were quite specific. Woodward was to start with less than a dollar in his pocket and earn his way across the country without borrowing, begging, or accepting gratuities. He was to wear a "plug" hat, a frock coat, and spectacles, and even put spectacles on his donkey. On the route he was to pass through Canton, Ohio, and Lincoln, Nebraska, to call upon President-elect McKinley and his defeated opponent Bryan, respectively. And he had one year from Election Day in which to complete the journey and register at the Palace Hotel in San Francisco, or else forfeit $5,000.[13]

No doubt sensing the possibility of turning the experience into a book, Woodward tackled his assignment with good humor and unfailing resourcefulness. Before setting out he arranged to supply a newspaper with an account of his adventures, proposing a series which he entitled "The Picturesque Pilgrimage of Pythagoras Pod." He cajoled a photographer into printing up hundreds of photographs of him sitting astride his donkey, to be sold en route. Thus armed, he set out from New York City on November 27, 1896, rode his donkey Mac A'Rony up Broadway past the house of his friend (as the agreement required), and began the long trek westward by first heading north up the Hudson Valley.

"Pythagoras Pod" quickly discovered that sleeping outdoors was not nearly as difficult as making ends meet. He sold photographs wherever he could, and wherever possible arranged to entertain the locals with a lecture. But it took both ingenuity and hard work to be self-sufficient. In one New York town he mopped the hotel floor. In Poughkeepsie he shined shoes for the young ladies of Vassar. By the time he got to Indiana he had brewed up a concoction of axle grease, sweet oil and perfume and was peddling it to the crowds as an "eye elixir." In Chicago he profited from allowing his name to be used to advertise patent medicines. When the photographs gave out, he commissioned and sold pins, like campaign buttons, that pictured him and Mac A'Rony.

Gradually, as he journeyed westward, the publicity surrounding him grew. When he attempted to visit McKinley in Canton, detectives, "fearing I might be a malicious crank, would not permit me to see the President-elect." But a few days later in Caledonia, Ohio, "I could not appear anywhere on the street without some rural stranger stopping me to shake hands and purchase a chromo." By the time he passed through Cornville Hollow, Iowa, infant boys along the route were being named "Pythagoras Pod" in his honor. As he moved west he was greeted by the mayors of Elkhart and Chicago (one of whom paid for the privilege of riding Mac A'Rony), entertained by the defeated Bryan in Lincoln, hosted by the governors of Nebraska and Utah, and supplied with lodging by the head of the Mormon church in Salt Lake City. His arrival in Salt Lake City in particular was heralded by much publicity, and whenever there was publicity Woodward managed to cash in on it to sustain himself financially for the journey.

One measure of his success is the fact that what began as one man on a donkey's back soon became a small caravan. In Chicago he picked up a second donkey, christened "Cheese," to accompany Mac A'Rony. A third donkey, acquired in Iowa, came with the name Damfino (for "Damned If I Know"). In Cedar Rapids he was joined by a black man named Coonskin, who accompanied him as valet and companion for the rest of his journey. In time there were two other donkeys—Skates and Coxey—and in addition to the two men the five donkeys carried revolvers, cameras, lanterns, blankets, canned goods, medicines, salves, ink, cow-bells, vegetables, ham, vinegar, old shoes, toilet articles, clothes, soap, flour, salt, cheese, coffee, tea, kerosene, matches, cooking tools, a canvas tent, a typewriter, and a "folding kitchen range." Even with all this paraphernalia it was not unusual for the caravan to cover twenty miles a day.[14]

Woodward's adventures were many. He smoked the peace pipe

with the chief of the Musquaques Indians, and refused the proffered hand of his unlovely and aging daughter. He ate dog soup, and shot prairie dogs, owls, jackrabbits, and rattlesnakes. He was lassoed by a cowboy in Nebraska, treed overnight by a bear in Colorado, and nearly drowned while crossing a river in the Rockies. At various times he walked on stilts, breakfasted on turkey buzzard, and tried (unsuccessfully) to type his newspaper articles while riding on a donkey. He had a narrow escape with a gang of "desperadoes," and was on at least one occasion mistaken for a hobo. Out of water and near death in the Nevada desert, he made it into California only to be arrested for cruelty to animals after the local S.P.C.A. filed a complaint on behalf of the donkeys.

"Pythagoras Pod" and Mac A'Rony

Mac A'Rony, too, had his encounters. Easy prey to pranksters, the donkey was at various times kidnapped and held for ransom, put on ice skates and sent careening across a frozen pond, rolled up into a giant snowball, and carted across the Missouri River in a wheelbarrow. In Rangely, Colorado, local wags used the donkey's tail as a paintbrush to write the town's name on the side of a house.

By the time he reached Sacramento, his fame was such that Woodward was greeted with "handkerchiefs and hats waving from balconies...and newsboys crying [our] arrival." Four days later he arrived in San Francisco, and checked in at the Palace Hotel only 22 hours ahead of the deadline. The hotel courtyard was packed with well-wishers out to greet him, and the crowd grew so large that the police were called to maintain order. He had traveled 4,096 miles in 340 days, gained 33 pounds, and after starting out with only ninety-nine cents ended up with several hundred dollars in his pocket. Upon completing the journey he gave Mac A'Rony to the zoo at the Golden Gate Park, and made the return home to New York by speedier means.[15]

Woodward later described his journey in a book entitled *On a Donkey's Hurricane Deck: A Tempestuous Voyage of Four Thousand and*

Ninety-Six Miles Across the American Continent on a Burro, in 340 Days and 2 Hours, Starting Without a Dollar and Earning My Way. In it were many of the more than 600 photographs taken during the journey. Many of the photographs depict the American Indians, and they became the basis for illustrated lectures which he gave profitably for years to come.

Twelve years after this journey Woodward was a widower with one son when he married Ethel Nottingham (1875-1939) of Eastville. He was in the mining business at the time, a resident of Kansas City, and it is not known how he and Ethel met. To the Woodwards was born one daughter, Maybelle, who spent much of her youth on the Eastern Shore, for during the 1920s Woodward moved his family to Cape Charles and Snow Hill. In 1930, the year in which *On a Donkey's Hurricane Deck* was published for the third time in Snow Hill, the Woodwards moved back to New York City. Woodward died in 1941 and is buried in Kenmore, New York.[16] His Eastern Shore wife died in 1939, and is buried in the Nottingham family cemetery behind the post office in Eastville.

For all his eccentricities he was a man with a remarkable sense of humor, as can be glimpsed by the advice he gives the reader in *On a Donkey's Hurricane Deck*:

"If ever you are tempted to ride a donkey overland, refrain! Rather creep across backwards on your hands and knees, or circumnavigate the globe in a washtub. If you still persist, ride a donkey twenty miles in a pouring rain, then follow your judgment." For, he adds, "There are four distinct distances across the American continent: three thousand miles as the crow flies, three thousand five hundred as the train steams, four thousand by overland trail...and a million miles as a donkey goes."[17]

Carry Nation,
Enemy of Demon Rum

Carry Amelia Nation (1846-1911) was fifty-three years old, a housewife in Medicine Lodge, Kansas, when one night after reading her Bible she had a vision and heard a heavenly voice speaking to her. Shortly thereafter, on June 6, 1900, she filled her buggy with brickbats, drove to the nearby frontier town of Kiowa, marched into Dobson's Saloon, and announced to its startled customers, "Men! I have come to save you from the drunkard's grave!" With that she began hurtling her brickbats at everything in sight, as bartender and clientele scrambled for cover. By the time she rolled out of Kiowa a few hours later, Dobson's and two other saloons were reduced to rubble, and the fame and notoriety of the Kansas saloon-smasher was born.[18]

Kiowa was only the beginning for the complex, fiercely righteous, and sensational Carry Nation. From there she moved on to ever-larg-

Carry A. Nation

er towns in an ever-widening circle: Enterprise, Topeka, Des Moines, Chicago, St. Louis, Cincinnati, Atlantic City, Philadelphia, New York, Washington. Describing herself as a "bulldog running along at the feet of Jesus, barking at what He doesn't like,"[19] she bodily threw off male "bouncers" almost twice her size, intimidated barkeep, customer, policeman, and politician alike, and left in her wake a trail of spilled liquor, splintered counters, fragmented mirrors, and not a few mutilated paintings of scantily-clad women in suggestive poses. At almost every stop the local jail became her lodging, and the local press and admiring followers her companions. In 1901 she switched from brickbats to hatchets, and as women all over the country followed her example "hatchetation," her own term for the destruction of a saloon, became the rage.[20]

It was only after a decade of much publicized saloon-smashing that Carry Nation came to the Eastern Shore of Virginia on a little noticed speaking tour. On October 21, 1910, she addressed a large crowd in Onley, and shortly after that another large crowd in Onancock. Her Onley audience paid 25 cents each, the children 15 cents, to hear her, and assembled in Copes Hall, an old hardware store whose top floor was used, until the 1920s, for public meetings. (Copes Hall burned in the 1971 fire that destroyed much of downtown Onley.) Her Onancock audience gathered in the Town Hall, which stood on the square next to Cokesbury Church. Here "many miniature hatchets were sold" before and after her speech.[21]

It is not unlikely that some of those who heard her on these occasions left a little disappointed, for in Onley and Onancock the sensational reformer wrecked no barroom, created no disturbance, and ran afoul of no law. The local papers described, instead, what must have seemed like just another speech by just another speaker on the lecture circuit. At Onley "her pointed remarks on the evils of the day made a deep impression on the audience," observed the *Accomack News*. Of the speech in Onancock the same paper commented, "At no time was she rude or boisterous, and many of her ideas and claims had much of thought for all." The rival *Peninsula Enterprise*, describing Mrs. Nation at Onancock, wrote, "Her address had but little of the sensational with which she is generally credited, and in the main was entertaining."[22]

When she rose to speak in a Chincoteague church a few days later, Carry Nation was greeted with "warm, pent-up, energized enthusiasm" by "a small, mostly curiously inclined audience." As in Onley and Onancock her standard speech, labeled "amusingly entertaining" by the local newspaper, was politely received, but her audience reacted with "chills" when she veered from her usual topic and condemned the "secret orders." In this she had "reckoned without her host," for Chincoteague Island was proud of its several fraternal lodges, which included Masons, Heptasophs, Red Men, Buffaloes, Woodmen of America, and the Junior Order of the United American Mechanics.[23]

What her local audiences could not have known was that by the time she came to the Eastern Shore this vigorous, animated, ferocious woman was entering the last days of her life, a woman fast failing in health. Having conquered or confounded Washington and New York,

Carry Nation
As usual: in jail, at prayer

Harvard and Yale, London and Glasgow, Carry Nation began a speaking tour in 1910 only to discover that she was at times unable to find the right word or construct meaningful sentences—never a problem before, for the pithy turn of phrase had always been an important part of her public image. Discouraged by this turn of events, Mrs. Nation abandoned her speaking tour shortly after leaving the Eastern Shore and returned home to Arkansas. On January 13, 1911, less than three months later, she arose to speak at Eureka Springs, Missouri, and was felled by a stroke while at the podium. Six months later she was dead.[24]

It was at the invitation of Sadie Savage of Onley that Carry Nation came to the Shore. Though they shared a passion for the temperance cause, the two women were utterly different. Sadie Savage, president of the Accomack County Women's Christian Temperance Union (W.C.T.U.) from 1911 to 1939, was renowned among the local chapters for her gentleness, diligence, and respectability. Carry Nation's own chapter in Medicine Lodge was not so pleased with their famous but not universally respected member. After she began her crusade of hatchetation, they resolved that "we cannot advise the use of force," and that "more harm than good must always result from lawless methods" like Mrs. Nation's.[25] Ignoring such criticism of Nation's methods, oblivious to the saloon smasher's notoriety, Sadie Savage invited her to the Eastern Shore, and was vindicated when Carry Nation's appearance here occurred without incident.

Of course by 1910 the cause of temperance was all but decided on the Eastern Shore of Virginia. For a generation or more the evils of alcohol had been preached about, sung about, prayed about, and promoted from virtually every rostrum across the peninsula. In 1914, just four years after Carry Nation's visit, the Eastern Shore voted 84% in favor of prohibition during a statewide referendum. And when on November 1, 1916, a parade was held in Accomac to celebrate the passage of a statewide prohibition law, Sadie Savage received an ovation when she rose to speak to the crowd.[26]

The late-arriving Mrs. Nation did little to further this cause on the Shore, but on the national scene her influence was greater. On the monument erected over her grave in Belton, Missouri, her admirers carved the words that she gasped as she fell from the podium on that last lecture early in 1911:

"I have done what I could."[27]

Billy Sunday,
Revival Preacher

The cars began pulling into Cape Charles early on Monday, April 6, 1925, and by noon about 2,000 automobiles from every section of the Delmarva Peninsula were parked on the streets and lots across town. On the "potato dock" at the railroad 2,500 chairs set up for the occasion filled up quickly; an equal number of people who could not get chairs willingly stood in place, and some who could not even get within hearing distance "loafed around the town." By the time the 12:20 steamer pulled in from Old Point, between 5,000 and 6,000 people were gathered to see and hear one of its passengers.[28] Billy Sunday, the most famous preacher in America, had come to Cape Charles.

William Ashley Sunday (1862-1935) was an Iowa-born professional baseball player before his conversion in 1886, and in 1895 he embarked on a career as a traveling evangelist that was to last fifty years and to make him the country's most popular preacher. In 1914 he ranked eighth in a nation-wide poll to name "the greatest man in the United States." By the end of his career, Sunday had been the subject of cartoon and painting, hosted at the White House and photographed with the Secretary of State, the leader of over 300 urban "crusades," spoken to a total of over 100 million people (before the advent of the loudspeaker), and brought a million people down the "sawdust trail," as the aisles of his tabernacles were called, in response to his sermons.

Billy Sunday

Though others before him had made revival evangelism first a profession, then a big business, none had Sunday's knack for making it entertainment. The newspapers compared him to vaudeville performers and the Keystone Cops, labeling him the "Mouthpiece for God," the "Calliope of Zion," and a "Gymnast for Jesus." Sunday, who early in his career once hired a giant from the Barnum & Bailey Circus to serve as an usher, could entertain an audience as well as move them, and his sermons were memorable for their simple content and flashy delivery. It was his standard practice when preaching to remove coat and tie, and roll up his sleeves. He moved so quickly to and from the pulpit and around the stage that some estimated that he walked a mile during a typical sermon. During some sermons he was known to stand on the pulpit and wave an American flag. During one sermon he customarily emphasized a point by smashing a wooden chair.[29]

Billy Sunday's four-hour visit to Cape Charles was but a lull in the larger crusade he was conducting at the time in Newport News. On March 31, 1925, a group of Sunday school classes from the Cape Charles area chartered a steamer to Newport News to hear him, and many of these Shore residents shook hands with him after his sermon that night. It was Sunday himself who expressed the desire to visit the Eastern Shore and speak there, and his Northampton admirers returned home determined to make his visit possible.[30] A week later, Sunday stepped up to the pulpit on the potato dock and found waiting the largest crowd that had ever assembled in Cape Charles.

At 1:30 the service began, as Sunday's revivals always did, with a songfest, and at 2:00 he began to preach. His sermon, "The Ready Answer," was standard fare from his repertoire, and lasted about an hour. During it his audience "drank in his truths relating to the average layman of the present day," according to the local papers. "His remarks were full of wit, humor, and laughter, but never missing the opportunity to drive home his subject: Religion." The sermon on the potato dock was actually his second speech in Cape Charles; hosted for lunch aboard the steamer *Pennsylvania* by the local Rotarians, he had earlier spoken to about 60 guests on "The Greatest Need of the Day."

Billy Sunday Mid-Sermon

After his sermon, Sunday was asked if he would consider a full-fledged campaign in Cape Charles at a later date. Professing himself interested and available for October 1926, he rode over to the town park to select a suitable location for a tabernacle, then departed on the 4:30 steamer back to the Newport News crusade.[31]

No sooner were the people from twelve different churches in lower Northampton at work on a crusade for 1926 than they began to encounter the reality of trying to snag a big-name evangelist. Sunday's schedule was, as a rule, fixed as much as three years in advance. Before agreeing to conduct a revival in any town or city, he required that the local Protestant churches unite in support of his crusade, and guarantee in advance that all financial costs would be covered.

Then there was the question of the tabernacle. Billy Sunday simply would not preach in any previously existing building, but insisted upon the erection of a completely new tabernacle. In New York City the tabernacle erected for his 1917 crusade cost $65,000 and took four hundred people two months to complete. Aside from its main auditorium, with seating for 20,000, it contained a post office, a hospital, rooms for "personal workers," ushers, press, custodian, doorkeepers, a book room, and "a retiring room for the evangelist."

And though Sunday had expressed himself eager to return to the Shore, arranging a crusade meant working through the "Sunday party" of specialists and assistants who preceded and accompanied him wherever he went. At the height of his career there were no fewer than two dozen such functionaries who made the arrangements and attended to the needs of the crusade: a business manager (Mrs. Sunday), an advance agent, a research assistant, a soloist, a pianist, a publicity manager, a private secretary, a tabernacle architect, and—when finally the evangelist arrived upon the scene—his own cook, housekeeper, and personal masseur. Among this party was musician Homer A. Rodeheaver, who with his trombone led the singing at the start of each service.

With such an army of assistants Billy Sunday had preached to tens of thousands in the largest cities in the country. And even though by the 1920s his career was in decline, his crowds dwindling,[32] he was still certainly, by Eastern Shore standards, a major-league evangelist. As late as June 1926 the Protestants of lower Northampton were still at work to bring him back to the Shore, but the effort failed when a mutually satisfactory time could not be negotiated with the Sunday organization.[33]

Billy Sunday never returned to the Eastern Shore of Virginia, and when in the summer of 1932 he was the guest preacher at a camp meeting on the Eastern Shore of Maryland, his career and crowds had declined even further. "There are some of us who are a bit curious to know just what Billy Sunday will do," wrote one church editor at that time. "Memories...make us wonder what will happen."[34]

Though he once advertised that he could save the unconverted of any city at the low cost of two dollars a soul, and though he made a million dollars in his work, Billy Sunday died poor and out of the limelight.[35] Today he is remembered more in the "bush league" towns and villages of his earliest and latest days than in the big cities of his greatest triumphs. And among those smaller places to which people flocked to hear him is one town on the Eastern Shore.

Frances Benjamin Johnston, Photographer

She was a small woman, gray-haired and somewhat frail, and when she checked into the Accomac Hotel in the summer of 1934 she was traveling with an unusually large amount of paraphernalia.

The Accomac Hotel was, in those days, *the* place to stay on the

Eastern Shore, and among its guests were long-term boarders who took their meals in a dining room where the tablecloths were crisp and white and the waiters attended to individual diners with old-school civility. One such boarder was Nora Miller, the home extension agent for Accomack County, not yet married or known for her historical writings. Years later Nora Miller Turman (1901-2000) remembered the lady with the luggage as short and pleasant, somewhat regal in her manner, and so energetic that during her two-weeks' stay at the hotel she seemed always on the go.[36]

Her name was Frances Benjamin Johnston, and she traveled with a lot of equipment because she was by profession a photographer, one of the most renowned in America, an acknowledged master in her field.

While still a young woman, Frances Benjamin Johnston (1864-1952), a native of West Virginia, studied art in Paris, then after a brief career in journalism apprenticed at the Smithsonian Institution to learn the new art of photography. Her first camera was given to her by none other than George Eastman, inventor of the Kodak, and by the early 1890s she had opened her own photographic studio in Washington, one of the few women in the field anywhere in the country and virtually the only one for whom photography was not an avocation but a business.

Though she had the

Frances Benjamin Johnston
Self-Portrait

artist's nonchalance about the details of business—she rarely opened and seldom paid her bills, and feuded with the I.R.S. throughout her life—the high quality of Johnston's work consistently assured her both financial profit and critical acclaim. She was probably the first female photographer in the country to master color processing, though she preferred to work in black-and-white and generally spurned the always-newer methods available throughout her career.

Admired for her attention to detail in the composition of every picture, she photographed so many of the rich and powerful of the nation's capital that she was known as the "photographer of the American court." She ventured with her camera into many settings: the mines of Pennsylvania, the factories of the industrial Northeast, the black schools of the South, even the pitch-darkness of Kentucky's Mammoth Cave. Her photographs of Hampton Institute, considered among her best, won the Grand Prix at the Paris Exposition in 1900; her photos of famous men were copied in statues, paintings, and postage stamps (including the one pictured on page 75). Yet throughout her work there is an obvious sympathy for the common people whom she so often photographed at work and play.[37]

After 1910 Johnston turned increasingly to architectural photography, and it was in pursuit of colonial architecture that she came to the Eastern Shore of Virginia. Her first visit in 1930 went unnoticed by the locals, though from it came photographs of Hungars Church and St. George's Church illustrating a book by Henry Brock (*Colonial Churches in Virginia*, 1930). Shortly thereafter she won the first of four consecutive Carnegie grants to photograph the colonial architecture of the South, and armed with one such grant took up temporary residence in Accomac in 1934. This time she came in search of not the grand and prominent homes but, in her own words, "the old farm houses, the mills, the log cabins of the pioneers, the country stores, the taverns and inns, in short those buildings that had to do with the everyday life of the colonists."[38]

Johnston was 70 years old when she came to Accomac, renowned, eccentric, iron-willed, irascible, vulnerable to flattery, and exceedingly proud of her accomplishments as an artist. It was her custom to hire a chauffeur to show her about the countryside, and in Accomac she engaged S. Bayly Turlington (1919-1977), then but a teenager, later an author and professor. She prided herself on her ability to "smell out an old colonial house five miles off the highway,"[39] and for two weeks Turlington took her wherever she wanted to go, up and down the Shore from Horntown to Cheriton. The photographs that resulted from these jaunts down unpaved roads and up isolated farm lanes are today prized for their beauty and artistry as well as for their historic value.

Many of the Shore's great old houses were in less than great shape in the early 1930s. Places that today are much admired during Garden Week—Brownsville near Nassawadox, the Hermitage near Craddockville, Bloodworth Cottage in Accomac—were serving as rental properties, or standing vacant and neglected, or even falling into decay. Vaucluse in Church Neck, once the home of the Secretary of State of the United States, was sorely in need of paint. Hills Farm on Hunting Creek had broken windows, damaged chimneys, and shingles missing from the roof. The porch at Deep Creek Plantation was sagging badly, and Mt. Hope south of Locustville, now restored, was a tenant house in sad disrepair.

Drummond's Mill
by Frances Benjamin Johnston

Undeterred by their condition, determined to preserve what they looked like for posterity, Johnston photographed the inside as well as the outside of many such places. Sometimes she would move the furniture around to compose her picture. Though she had been known to chase the residents out of a house when she was photographing it, there is no record that she did so on the Eastern Shore. It is said that in Williamsburg she once ordered a tree cut down because it blocked her view of a church, but Eastern Shore people remember her as so patient that she would wait for hours for the sun to hit a house a certain way before snapping the shutter. So concerned was she to get exactly the picture she wanted that she climbed out on the roof at Mount Custis, and virtually down into the water at Drummond's Mill. And though the subject might be in disrepair, her photograph of it was likely to be a work of art, emphasizing an unusual angle in an interior, or catching the interplay of sun and shadow on a doorway or roof.[40]

Some of the buildings she photographed have since disappeared: Tankard's Rest near Exmore, Sea View near Daugherty, the old Goffigon House near Wachapreague. At Drummond's Mill she photographed three buildings—the old store, an ancient "cabin," and the mill itself—not one of which remains today. The photographs she took inside Drummond's Mill are the only known pictures of the interior of an Eastern Shore gristmill. And for all the documentary value of such pictures, her photograph of the mill viewed from across the water is lovely as a work of art.

Johnston's photographs of the Eastern Shore—they total about 150, and depict some 42 different places—are but a tiny fraction of her work. In 1947 she donated her life's work of prints, negatives, and correspondence to the Library of Congress, a collection so vast that it has yet to be published except in piecemeal fashion.

She died in New Orleans in 1952,[41] and deserves to be remembered on the Shore for helping not only to preserve some of its heritage but also to foster pride in it.

Aliens in Accomack:
The Visitors Who Never Arrived

In the late 1930s, the Eastern Shore experienced an invasion from Mars—or so it seemed, for one brief terrifying moment.

On October 30, 1938, the evening program on CBS radio's "Mercury Theatre of the Air" was "The War of the Worlds," adapted by Howard Koch from H. G. Wells' science-fiction novel about an invasion of Earth by creatures from Mars. Wells told the story as if it took place in England, but Koch's script moved the locale to tiny Grover's Mill, New Jersey. In addition, Koch rewrote the story as if it were a series of news broadcasts, and as performed by CBS star Orson Welles and cast, the tale came across the airwaves with frightening realism. Before the program was over, panic had broken out all over the country, and hundreds of thousands were convinced that Martians really had landed in New Jersey and were swiftly destroying America with their invulnerable death ray.[42]

Among those fooled and frightened were many people from the Eastern Shore of Virginia. In the corner drugstore in Accomac it was a typical Sunday night, a group of townsfolk, among them the county sheriff and the Clerk of Court, sitting around sipping Coca-Colas. Midway through the broadcast the proprietor entered the room to find them all sitting there strangely quiet, their faces ashen. "We're being invaded!" he was told, and he went immediately upstairs to get out his automatic. Remarkably unperturbed by the news was his wife who, informed of the invasion, quipped, "Invaded by whom? Those little men? We'll handle them!"[43]

Another store near the county seat was also crowded when the broadcast began, and here the merchant himself sat listening. When after a few moments he turned around to comment to his customers, he found the place empty— everyone had fled home. Like them, one couple from the neighborhood no sooner heard the broadcast than they quickly hit the road for Wachapreague to share the impending disaster with their folks.

Orson Welles

In Onancock, meanwhile, the "news" created consternation in home after home. Someone looked in on one lady to find her sitting there moaning, "This is terrible! What in the world will we do? What will we do?" One mother, realizing that her son was not at home, began telephoning among his friends to locate him, and finally succeeded in summoning him home, where he was seated with the rest of the family to await the news of what might happen to civilization and the Eastern Shore. A youngster across town stuck his head out the back door and yelled excitedly, "I can even smell the sulphur, Mother!" Elsewhere in town people woke their children from sleep to join the family in prayer, or to rush outdoors to look for signs of doom in the sky.[44]

A number of people from Craddockville were "considerably wrought up" over the broadcast, and from Chincoteague, Belle Haven, and other communities up and down the two counties came the frightened reactions:

A congregation holding Sunday night services somehow heard the terrible "news," and quickly suspended worship and headed for home.

An Eastern Shore gentleman of the old school was already in his pajamas when he heard the broadcast, and rose from his bed and dressed, the better to face any eventuality.

One man put through a call to New York to find out if the destruction that began in Grover's Mill had reached that far.

One lady sat and listened, expecting the bombs to begin exploding outside her house any minute. "That Hitler," she wailed, "if only someone could stop him. He's responsible for all this!" (She was not alone in that conviction; many across the country were certain that the "invasion" was somehow connected with the gathering storm of war in Europe.)

One young couple, unable to bear such terrible news, turned their radio off.

A number of people heard airplanes overhead during the broadcast, and rushed out to see what was happening. "There they go," insisted one of them. "Those are planes from Langley Field on their way to New Jersey."

And all across the state, college students from the Eastern Shore were starting homeward, or frantically calling their parents to come and get them.[45]

Reactions on the Eastern Shore were mild compared to those in other places. Some cities experienced panic in the streets and near-riots. Frightened citizens besieged radio stations, newspaper offices, and police for information. Crowds huddled in churches, or drowned their fear in drink. One woman in Pittsburgh was only narrowly saved from death when she was discovered in her bathroom clutching a bottle of poison, shouting "I'd rather die this way than like that!"

How could so many have been so fooled, especially since the program began with a disclaimer that the story was entirely fictional? CBS's "Mercury Theatre of the Air" was competing in the same time-slot with the far more popular ventriloquist Edgar Bergan and his dummy Charlie McCarthy on another network. Both programs began on the hour, with undoubtedly far more people tuned in to Charlie McCarthy than to Orson Welles. But then at twelve minutes past the hour Edgar and Charlie completed a sketch, there began a commercial break for Chase and Sanburn coffee, and millions of Americans switched their dials to CBS, where they heard an announcer describing the mysterious landing in New Jersey. The opening disclaimer missed, the program sounded convincingly like a news flash, and not radio drama.[46]

The terror was shortlived, though according to the *Eastern Shore News* "not until the wee small hours [did] some households put away the smelling salts and other old time stimulants."[47] Then began the chuckles and the good-natured stories that Eastern Shore folk began to tell on themselves and each other—and still do, for there are those who still remember that terrifying night.

Many others too young to have experienced it can at least appreciate the fact that it was caused, in part, by one of the least popular of the benefits of modern communications, the commercial.

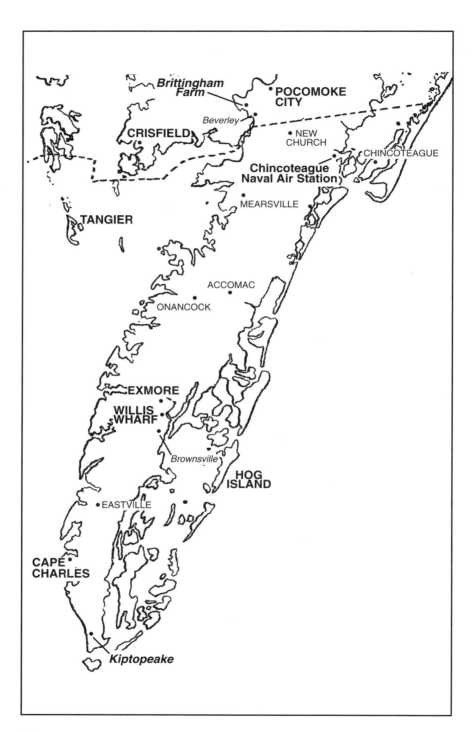

Brittingham
Farm

POCOMOKE
CITY

Beverley

CRISFIELD

NEW
CHURCH

CHINCOTEAGUE

Chincoteague
Naval Air Station

MEARSVILLE

TANGIER

ACCOMAC

ONANCOCK

EXMORE

WILLIS
WHARF

Brownsville

HOG
ISLAND

EASTVILLE

CAPE
CHARLES

Kiptopeake

98

6
Presidential Visitations

The President
Who Loved the Eastern Shore

When Democrat Grover Cleveland was first elected President in 1884, a 23-year Republican hold on the White House ended, and the Eastern Shore of Virginia rejoiced.

In Locustville the townsfolk erected a 65-foot "Cleveland pole" from which wafted a banner proclaiming "Democratic Victory." Residents of Temperanceville, Atlantic, and Mappsville celebrated with music, bonfires, and "illuminations," then descended upon Modest Town to celebrate with 50 rounds of cannon. The parade that formed in Drummondtown wound its the way into Onancock. Chincoteague's parade was even larger: fifty people on horseback, several hundred people on foot, a brass band, over 1,500 spectators, and "for miles along the shore nearly every dwelling was illuminated" for the occasion. In Mearsville merchant A. F. Mears announced that he was changing the name of his store to Cleveland "in honor of the President-elect."[1]

Democrats had good reason to rejoice. In those days before the Civil Service, the party in power controlled thousands of local appointments across the nation: postmasters, inspectors, commissioners, lighthouse keepers. Now that the long Republican control was coming to an end, local Democrats could anticipate filling such jobs, and within days of the election the county papers were reporting that "aspirants for office...are already being heard from."[2]

Though hardly remembered there today, few Presidents have ever been as popular on the Eastern Shore of Virginia as Grover Cleveland (1837-1908). And no President before or since ever loved the Shore more, or visited it as often.

The first President ever to see the Eastern Shore of Virginia was not Cleveland but the Republican he succeeded in office, though he never

Chester Alan Arthur   Grover Cleveland

came until after he left office, and then only passed through on the railroad, probably never actually setting foot on the peninsula. Chester Alan Arthur left the White House on April 4, 1885, abandoned by his party and gravely ill. The following month found him traveling in Virginia where, according to the *Peninsula Enterprise*, "Ex-President Arthur, who is at Old Point Comfort, is suffering from a malarial affection." Arthur's "malarial affection" is known today to have been Bright's disease, a fatal kidney disorder often accompanied by nausea, mental depression, and inertness.

After a brief stay in Hampton Roads, Arthur headed north by way of the Eastern Shore and the New York, Philadelphia & Norfolk Railroad on April 11, 1885. His quick trip up the peninsula was worth a single-sentence notice in the local paper: "Ex-President Arthur, accompanied by his private secretary and a few other friends, was a passenger over our railroad." Eighteen months later he was dead.[3]

By then, in May 1886, Grover Cleveland had spent one night outside Cape Charles at "Hollywood," the home of William L. Scott, the multi-millionaire industrialist and Democratic Congressman from Pennsylvania who was then engaged in developing the new town of Cape Charles. Cleveland, like Arthur before him, traveled by train, and returned to Washington the following day.[4] His one-day visit was the first time an incumbent President of the United States had ever set foot on the soil of the Eastern Shore of Virginia.

The Shore saw no more of Cleveland for the remainder of his first term, but his popularity remained high, particularly in Accomack County.[5] In November 1888 he was defeated for a second term by Republican Benjamin Harrison. Four years later the two men faced each other again, and this time Cleveland won, the only President yet to be elected to two non-consecutive terms. While the chant of "Grover, Grover, four more years of Grover" resounded across the

Shore, his 1892 victory spawned even larger celebrations than in 1884, in Chincoteague, Wachapreague, Harborton, Drummondtown, Mearsville (Cleveland?), Atlantic, Mappsville, and even usually Republican Tangier.[6]

It was during his second term that Cleveland became a more frequent visitor to the Shore, and his several visits began almost immediately. November 1892 found the nation in fiscal crisis, with many people calling for an emergency session of Congress and Democratic office-seekers ready to besiege the new President. Cleveland, who would not officially take office until March, calmly announced that he would consider no applications for offices prior to his inauguration, and set out for some rest and relaxation. His destination was Hog Island, Virginia.

Hog Island was then a popular out-of-the-way spot for wealthy northern sportsmen, and Grover Cleveland loved to hunt and fish. One friend who shared that passion was John S. Wise, an Eastern Shoreman, son of Governor Henry A. Wise, who met Cleveland in New York towards the end of his first term. Though he was a Republican and the President a Democrat, the two men hunted and fished together a number of times, and Wise later described such days spent with Cleveland: "I have known him to sit on a calm sunshiny day in a duckblind for ten consecutive hours, with nothing but a simple luncheon to break his fast and nothing but whistlers and buffleheads coming in to his decoys, and return home at night with nothing but a dozen 'trash' ducks...as content and uncomplaining as if he had enjoyed real sport."[7]

Soon after his re-election, Cleveland pushed business aside, "got out his tackle, and went to Hog Island after bluefish."[8] He arrived on November 23, 1892, and at week's end the local *Peninsula Enterprise* reported that "President-elect Cleveland, accompanied by a few friends, arrived in a special car over the NYP & N Railroad at Exmore station...enroute to Hog Island, where he went, it is stated, to escape the office seekers and to seek recreation and rest in gunning for a few days." Despite his popularity on the Shore, only "a party of fifty Democrats or more who had heard of his coming were on hand to receive him on his arrival at Exmore." The President spent a week and a half on Hog Island, then slipped back to Washington as quietly as he had come, using the private car of the railroad superintendent.[9]

It was the first of several visits. The exact number of times that Cleveland vacationed on Hog Island is uncertain; while still President he was there at least once more, in June 1893, and possibly also a third and even a fourth time.[10]

On at least two such occasions Cleveland was met at the railroad station in Exmore by Henry Clay Johnson (1845-1919), who then drove him to the boat awaiting him and his party at Willis Wharf. Johnson lived in a big house overlooking the waterfront at Willis Wharf,* and once took his small daughter Lucie along to meet the

---

* Johnson's house now stands elsewhere; see pages 149-150.

"President-Elect Cleveland's Vacation
at Broadwater Island on the Virginia Coast"

The national publication *Once a Week* carried this full-page article, "specially photographed and drawn by Frank H. Taylor," on December 3, 1892. Pictured (from the top) are (1) a Broadwater fishing boat, (2) landing at Willis Wharf, (3) "one of the natives," (4) Broadwater Club House, (5) cottage on Hog Island, (6) Rum Hill and Hog Island Lighthouse president. As Cleveland settled his large frame into the rear seat of Johnson's surrey, he leaned forward, patted Johnson's daughter on the head, and asked "And what pretty little girl is this?"

"I am Lucinda Joyce Johnson," replied Lucie firmly, one of the few times in her life that she ever used her full name, which she detested.

That ended that conversation, but for a long time Lucie Johnson (1884-1941) was envied by her classmates because "she had met the President."[11]

At least two Eastern Shoremen served as guides to the President during his visits to Hog Island: Henry Warren Doughty (1867-1960) and Thomas Major Doughty (1836-1925). On one of these visits, the Presidential party returned from a day of fishing and walked up the lane to their lodging, leaving Thomas Doughty to secure and tidy up the boat. Among the party was Frank H. Taylor, an artist-reporter for the *Boston Advocate*, and when he later saw Doughty trudging up the same lane, wearily carrying sails and water jug and trident from the boat, he made a hasty sketch of the man and gave it to him; it is still preserved in the family, as is also the bed in which Cleveland is said to have slept. On one of Cleveland's visits islander Mary Anna Doughty came out of the house to call her four young sons to dinner only to find them shooting marbles in the lane with the President. When she called them in, Cleveland is said to have asked if he too could come, and happily joined the family for a meal of fried pies and milk.[12]

Tom Doughty of Hog Island
by Frank H. Taylor

Cleveland's connections to the Eastern Shore did not cease after he left office in 1897. While still a young man, William F. D. Williams (1872-1956), later a Justice of the Peace in his native Northampton County, operated a seafood restaurant on the waterfront in Washington, where Cleveland was a frequent guest. "Judge Billy" loved to tell about the time the former President slipped away from his entourage, got into a scow, and went rowing on the Tidal Basin. "When he came back to the restaurant," recalled Williams, "he was tickled to death, like a boy playing hooky."[13] Cleveland visited his friend John Wise at least twice after his retirement, once in November 1901 when he was accompanied by several affluent friends. Wise lived at "Kiptopeake," a large frame house which was demolished to make way for the Administration Building of the Bridge-Tunnel in the 1960s.[14] Cleveland may also have known Thomas T. Upshur (1844-1910), local genealogist and historian, for he is known to have spent the night at Upshur's home "Brownsville;" it seems likely that any stay with Upshur would have been during a trip to Hog Island.[15]

He was so admired on the Eastern Shore that people went out of their way to shake hands with him[16] and named their children after him: Grover Cleveland Harris of Exmore (1907-1987), Grover Cleveland Tull of Pocomoke City (1914-1990). Also of Pocomoke City was Grover Cleveland Brittingham, but therein lies another story....

A Tale of Two Presidents

The farm is still there, just outside of Cedar Hall below Pocomoke City, about three miles west of Route 13 where it crosses from Virginia into Maryland. It backs up to the Pocomoke River, a more modest place than the venerable "Beverley" next door downstream.

According to the family story there were only two people at home that spring day in 1892. John E. Brittingham (1830-1909) was down in the gully pruning fruit trees, his eight-year-old son up at the house. Mary Ann Brittingham, wife and mother, had gone into Pocomoke City. Though there were other children in the Brittingham household at the time, family tradition says nothing about their whereabouts on that day.[17]

When the two surreys pulled up at the house, the boy recognized one driver as W. Ulysses Schoolfield, whose larger farm lay halfway up the road to Pocomoke City. "Boy, where's your father?" asked Schoolfield.

"Down in the gully pruning trees."

"Well, go get him and tell him that the President of the United States is here and would like to meet him."

The boy sped towards the gully, as fast as his feet could carry him, found his father, and tried to persuade him of what he had seen and heard. "Boy, what's the matter with you?" his father scolded. But the boy persisted, and at length his father laid down his tools, picked up his coat, and hurried back to the house. There the party was still waiting, and Schoolfield introduced John Brittingham, Eastern Shore farmer, to Benjamin Harrison, twenty-third President of the United States.

Benjamin Harrison (1833-1901) was in the third year of his presidency when he stepped off the train at New Church on April 8, 1892. He was on a quick trip to do some hunting, with no advance notice, and the only person there to greet him was a local farmer who happened to be in the station when the train pulled in. John Brittingham

(1823-1898) of New Church—the same man who had led the Union troops astray to Horntown in 1861,* a distant cousin of the other man by the same name, the first of the two John Brittinghams the President would meet that day—boarded the train and welcomed Harrison with an "impromptu address." Shortly thereafter Harrison set out to hunt, accompanied by Brittingham's son Hiram and neighbor Schoolfield, both "skillful sportsmen."[18]

It was the President's request for a home-cooked country meal that brought them to the doorstep of the second John Brittingham. John E. Brittingham's home had a local renown for its informal hospitality, the frequency and number of its guests, and the excellence and quantity of Mary Ann's cooking. "The President has expressed a desire for a real country dinner," Schoolfield told Brittingham. So the farmer invited them in, opened the doors and windows that afforded a view of the river, and sat peering anxiously out of the other side of the house awaiting the return of the cook, his wife. When at last her black mare trotted into view, Brittingham greeted her with the news: "Mary Ann, we've got company—and

Benjamin Harrison

you're going to cook dinner for the President of the United States." A few minutes later he went into the smokehouse and cut the heart out of nine hams, and Mary Ann whipped up a country supper of ham and biscuits.

Before the President's party left there occurred a few moment's conversation between Harrison and Brittingham's eight-year-old son.

"What's your name?" asked the short bearded man.

And the boy answered truthfully, "Grover Cleveland Brittingham."

One can only guess at the President's reaction. Grover Cleveland was his chief political opponent, the man he had defeated for the presidency, the man he was about to run against a second time, the man who would defeat him at the polls in November. Benjamin Harrison had found his way into a den of Democrats so enamoured of his rival that they had named their son after him![19]

Strictly speaking, Grover Cleveland Brittingham (1884-1962) was not named for a President, for Grover Cleveland was not yet President when John and Mary Ann Brittingham's ninth child was born on July 3, 1884.[20] Cleveland was then Governor of New York, widely heralded as presidential timber by those advocating reform and clean government. The Brittinghams were staunch Democrats,

*See page 55.

but why name a Maryland farm boy after a New York governor?

The name is easily explained if one family tradition is true: Grover Cleveland Brittingham was so named because not simply Benjamin Harrison but also Grover Cleveland himself, before him, happened to visit John Brittingham's house. Though this would certainly account for little Grover's name, the story cannot be substantiated. There is no written record that Grover Cleveland ever visited the Brittinghams, and in 1883 and 1884 Governor Cleveland vacationed not in Maryland but in the Adirondacks of New York. Grover C. Brittingham's name remains, then, something of a mystery. Clearly the result of his father's politics, his name is that of a man who did, but who also might not have, become President.

Grover Cleveland Brittingham
and his parents, c. 1889

Benjamin Harrison never enjoyed the kind of popularity that his opponent Grover Cleveland did on the Eastern Shore. Quite apart from his being of the wrong political persuasion for most Shoremen, Harrison was personally cold and stand-offish. John S. Wise wrote of him, "He was not an approachable man and had few intimate friendships.... There was a coldness and indifference in his manner in private which was very repellant."[21]

Still Harrison, pursued by the name of his rival to the very edge of the Pocomoke swamps, pronounced himself pleased with his brief visit to the Eastern Shore, and politely assured his guests that he would make another visit (though he never did).

Grover Cleveland Brittingham liked to tell the story of his encounter with the President, but never let it affect his politics. True to long-standing family persuasion, the Eastern Shore farmer voted Democratic until his death in 1962.

Presidential Spy

World War I was already blazing in Europe, the United States cautiously watching, when on Saturday, April 1, 1916, a large and unknown vessel appeared off Tangier Island. Early that morning the mystery ship dropped anchor in Steamboat Harbor, at the southern end of the island, and sent out a small vessel filled with uniformed officers. The little boat landed briefly at Banty's Wharf, then quickly returned to the mother ship.

Tangier had neither telephone nor telegraph in 1916, and because the weekly steamboats had already come and gone there was no way to communicate with the mainland, and no way to know who the visitors were. If they were Germans, coming to blow up the island, or to occupy it as the British had a hundred years earlier, there was no defense, decided the islanders, except to gather the family into the house, shut the door, and pray.

Later that morning a larger party emerged from the vessel, rowed over to Banty's Wharf, and started up Main Ridge, and the islanders, true to their plan, scurried into their homes.

One of the visitors later described that day from their vantage point:

"We transshipped to the tiny boat, landed on a wooden 'dock' and made our precarious way over a single plank which led to dry land at one end of the small street that composed this quaint little town. On either side were neat little one-story houses, each with a tiny front garden, surrounded by a picket fence. The yards contained the family graves marked by simple headstones.

"We walked the entire length of the village, and, although by this time it was nearly noon we saw only closed doors and drawn blinds; not a person in sight. It truly seemed a city of the dead."

Puzzled by the eerie quiet, the visitors returned to the dock, but were unwilling to leave without solving the mystery of the missing inhabitants. "Let's go back again and see if we can find out what this means," said their leader.

As they walked again up Main Ridge, "about the nearest houses we found no sign of life as before, but at the far end of the street our return had taken the inhabitants by surprise. The people were all outside. But the moment they saw us they sped back into their houses and closed and locked the doors. Only one man stood his ground, peering at us through his glasses.

"My husband lifted his cap. 'Good morning, sir,' he said. 'I hope we are not disturbing your quiet homes here.'

"The old fellow stood agape and, slowly removing his own hat, he said, 'Isn't this the President?'"

It was indeed. The unknown ship was not from Germany but was the Presidential yacht *Mayflower*, all the way from Washington, D.C. The uniformed men were not German but American officers, some of them Secret Service staff. The leader of the group was no foreign invader but Woodrow Wilson, President of the United States.

The following week the *Accomack News* described the remainder of that day on Tangier:

President Wilson and Party
Visit Tangier Island
*On Saturday, April 1st, the yacht Mayflower arrived in this port
and about 3 P.M., President Woodrow Wilson and Mrs. Wilson
were seen on the streets of Tangier, Va. The streets were crowded so
no one could hardly get by. Old Glory was displayed on most every
building and the school children sang many songs of cheer for our
President.*[22]

Over eighty years later two Tangier residents could still recall that
day. Annie K. Parks was 15 when the President came to Tangier, Ruth
Wallace Clarke was 9, and both had vivid memories of the hearty wel-
come the townsfolk gave him, even where they stood when they saw
the President and shook hands with him. Neither, however, remembered the earlier part of the day, when the doors of the town were
closed to him because his entourage was thought to be German.

That part of the story comes from the autobiography of Edith
Bolling Wilson, the President's second wife. She alone records the
conversation with the old man who recognized the President:

"'...Isn't this the President?'

"When Mr. Wilson replied, 'Yes, I have that honour, sir,' the old
man broke into a hearty laugh and then told us that early that morning they had seen a big ship anchor outside in the [harbor], then some
men in uniform put out in small boats for their island. This gave them
great alarm, for they decided that the officers were coming to blow up
the island. They had been greatly relieved however, when the men
did not land and thought they were safe—until a second time the
same boat put out and headed for their
abode.

"The old fellow added: 'Well, sir,
when I saw your lady with you I kinder
felt she wouldn't be with Germans; so I
thought I'd just stay out here and she
would see there was no harm in me.'
Then he begged to go and tell his
friends. In a moment the street was
filled and every one wanted to shake
hands with the President."

What brought Wilson to Tangier was
his own curiosity. While taking a brief
holiday aboard the *Mayflower* he saw "a
tiny speck" called Tangier on the ship's
maps, and asked to go there. As Mrs.
Wilson reports, "Captain Berry said...he
would send the launch over to see what
the conditions were." So the "German

Woodrow Wilson

officers" whose appearance so unnerved the islanders were simply
scouting out whether there was a way for the President to come
ashore.

Three days after his return to the capital, the *Washington Post* carried an article about the "quaint" and "odd" little island which had "interested the President immensely." Of particular interest to Wilson were the graves and tombstones in the yards of the island's homes. "The yards are small," reported the *Post*, "not larger than two good-sized rooms. But in each of them are graves, here four or five and there nine or ten, with elaborate monuments and customary headstones. The lawns are green and well-kept, with neat walks and fences."

The *Post*'s account of Tangier almost certainly derives from a description given reporters by Wilson himself. The world's notice of and fascination with Tangier's graves—for years a source of some discomfort for the islanders, for such burials are hardly unique to the island, and are not uncommon on the Eastern Shore—may well have begun with no less a person than the President of the United States.[23]

Piscatorial Presidents

In the early twentieth century Tangier Island was heavily Republican, and in the 1928 Presidential election voted for Herbert Hoover 55-11 over his Democratic opponent Al Smith. Though many in the country blamed the Great Depression on Hoover and his policies, Tangier's opinion of the President remained high even during the hard times that followed. After all, when the stock market crashed in September 1929 only one man on the island owned stock, and during the lean days that followed Tangier lived "close to the water," as many rural communities lived "close to the land," so that no one actually went hungry.

Herbert Hoover was in the declining days of his increasingly unpopular term when he took a three-day fishing trip on the Chesapeake Bay and on August 16, 1932, went fishing in the waters off Tangier Island. This time the entourage accompanying the Chief Executive included a Cabinet officer—Patrick J. Hurley, Secretary of Commerce—two well-heeled and high-powered friends, businessman

Herbert Hoover

Clarence Woolley and author Will Irwin, and a bevy of photographers and newspapermen.

The President and his party were aboard the Commerce Department vessel *Sequoia*, and Hoover, an avid fisherman, rose early that morning and indulged in his favorite recreation long before his friends joined him for breakfast. After fishing from the *Sequoia*, he boarded the smaller motorboat of islander John Crockett, whom he had engaged as a guide, and fished even more. Crockett's boat was more approachable by the press corps than the larger *Sequoia*, and as a party of journalists drew near they glimpsed the President pole in hand, attired in white trousers, blue coat, and Panama hat.

"Any luck?" one of them shouted out across the waters.

"Good catch," the President replied with a smile.

Later that day Hurley, Woolley, and Irwin toured the island with Crockett as their guide, and here at last the press corps could get close enough for an interview. Most of their attention was directed to Crockett, whom they labeled a "tall, grizzled fisherman" who "drawled" when he spoke. "Mr. Hoover is a good fisherman," Crockett answered obligingly to their inquiries. "He caught more than anybody else. I'll be glad to go out again if he comes down here any more."

The President himself, meanwhile, was apparently still back on the *Sequoia*, probably still fishing. It is not clear from the Associated Press reports of the event whether he ever actually set foot on Tangier Island.

After one day at Tangier the Presidential party departed "for an unannounced destination," and was back in Washington in three days.

Altogether they snagged about 40 fish from Tangier waters. The President caught 15 trout, one of them three feet long.

Crockett got a $10 tip.[24]

The two Democratic administrations that followed Hoover provided the Eastern Shore with two Presidential near-misses.

Less than a year after Hoover's fishing trip, on July 15, 1933, President Franklin D. Roosevelt alighted from the *Sequoia* in Crisfield, Maryland, accompanied by Henry Wallace, the Secretary of Agriculture and his wife. There, by pre-arrangement, they were met by a small fleet of automobiles dispatched from Washington, and conveyed inland for an impromptu sightseeing tour of the region.

After a stop at "Makepeace," an old 17th century home near Crisfield, the President's party drove into Pocomoke City and pulled to a stop on Market Street to purchase cigars and soft drinks. The visit was completely unannounced, and among the small crowd who were lucky enough to be on hand to greet the President were George T. Littleton and Mark Costen. When one of the Secret Service let it be known that the President wanted to see "Beverley," the handsome old mansion on Pocomoke River, Costen agreed to escort them to it. When Franklin D. Roosevelt alighted from the car at Beverley, he was less than a mile from the Eastern Shore of Virginia.

But that's as close as he came. After returning to Pocomoke City, the Presidential tour headed for Snow Hill to see old All Hallows Episcopal Church, then motored back to Crisfield, having spent a grand total of six hours on the lower Eastern Shore of Maryland.[25]

Pocomoke City welcomes Franklin D. Roosevelt on his second, much more heralded visit to town

Roosevelt, however, came closer than Truman.

On July 23, 1946, President Harry S Truman's yacht *Williamsburg*
anchored for the night in Chesapeake Bay, about two miles west of
Cape Charles. Truman was on his way back to Washington from
Hampton Roads, where he had reviewed the naval maneuvers of the
Eighth Fleet.

None of the Presidential party came ashore, but a group of about
fifteen press representatives who had been aboard the *Williamsburg*
came to Cape Charles to file their reports. The *Williamsburg*, meanwhile, weighed anchor the next morning, and continued up the
Chesapeake.[26]

When the *Williamsburg* returned to the waters off Cape Charles on
May 16, 1953, the President of the United States was again aboard, this
time Dwight D. Eisenhower.

This time the Presidential yacht created a good deal of attention
among the fishing boats working the area, and thanks to attorney
Otto Lowe of Cape Charles, who helped to set up the brief fishing
visit to Latimer Shoals, those on land knew who was just offshore.
Bryan Travis, a veteran fishing guide, accompanied by Bob
Rittenhouse of the Chamber of Commerce, steered his cabin cruiser
Petunia towards the Presidential party to deliver a gift of bait to the
distinguished guests, but to no avail. Not only were there no nibbles,

even with the bait, but also one fisherman in the President's party momentarily laid down his baited rod only to have a big drum come along and make off with it all, rod and tackle included. And no sooner had the yacht departed for Annapolis, insisted the local fisherman, than the fish began biting "like hungry lions."

President Eisenhower, through it all, was not to be seen; he was in his cabin working on a speech to be delivered later that week. He was the fourth President in a row to come close—within eyesight!—of the Eastern Shore of Virginia, without ever setting foot on it.[27]

An Elephant Stampede

In early 1942, shortly after America's entry into World War II, the Navy began to acquire land in upper Accomack County, on the mainland opposite Chincoteague Island, for use as an auxiliary air station. Chincoteague Naval Auxiliary Air Station was officially commissioned on March 5, 1943, its purpose to provide an outlying field for the support, maintenance, and training of carrier squadrons.

Today "the Base," as it became known locally, is the Wallops Facility of the Goddard Space Flight Center, for the Navy abandoned it and turned it over to the National Aeronautics and Space Administration (N.A.S.A.) in 1959—but not before a generation of young naval aviators strutted their stuff with such bravura antics and stunts as flying distressingly low over the houses of Chincoteague, or even under power lines.

The most famous, or notorious, such incident occurred in the fall of 1943 when an aviator training at Chincoteague decided, on a lark, to "buzz" the house of a young woman he had met at a U.S.O. dance. Jackie Sterling, the young lady, lived in Crisfield, Maryland, a good distance away by land but only twenty miles by air. Whether she was favorably impressed by her flyer's attention is not recorded; many of her neighbors were most assuredly not.

Crisfield, at the time of the "buzzing," happened to be hosting a small traveling circus at the fairground near the Sterling house, and the low-flying airplane frightened one of the circus elephants, who escaped and found his way into a residential neighborhood. When a local housewife looked up from her kitchen sink to find an elephant eating peaches from a tree in her back yard, she called the mayor, who called the police, who called Lt. Frederick M. Smith, commander at Chincoteague, who, eventually, found out who the culprit was, called him in, and sternly reprimanded him.

The flyer was "unofficially grounded" for, as he later recalled, "causing an elephant stampede."

His name was George Herbert Walker Bush, and in 1988 he was elected President of the United States.[28]

7

Murder, Mayhem, and a Ghost or Two

Epitaph in Bullbegger

One of the most enigmatic tombstones on the Eastern Shore lies aside the road that passes through Bullbegger.

Of course, Bullbegger itself is an enigma. Lonely and remote, it is reached by a single road heading north out of Jenkins Bridge through Jolly's Neck to Pitt's Neck. It has borne its strange and unexplained name—in old English dialect it means "bugbear" or "hobgoblin"—since at least the late 1600s,[1] though why the place received that name is unknown. Early in the twentieth century Bullbegger could boast a scattered collection of houses and a country store with a post office. The post office closed in 1935, and though the name still appears frequently on maps published since then, the only thing to be seen there today is farmland, one large old house, and a few old gravestones, one of which is that of Julia Dix.

Julianna Taylor Dix (1819-1861) was the second wife of Thorogood Dix (1811-1861), who in 1847 purchased the largest and oldest farm in Jolly's Neck and moved his family out of the Guilford area into the big house in Bulbegger. The Dix family consisted of six children: John, Isaac and Anna (Nancy), children of Thorogood's first wife, and Mary, Elizabeth, and James, children of Thorogood's second wife Julia. The 1850 census reveals that Julia's adult sisters Nancy and Eliza Taylor also lived with them.

Though not a great deal is known about Thorogood Dix, he seems even across the years a hard and stern man. Like many of his contemporaries he was a slave-owner, and it is said that he was a harsh taskmaster who broke his slaves as if they were horses. According to family tradition it is at his own request that his grave is located at the roadside, not at the house or back in the field, so that he could hear the sound of slaves being marched off to work.[2] That he was a hard man is also suggested by his will. Thorogood Dix died in the summer of 1861, bequeathed money and slaves to sons and daughters, directed that his possessions be sold and the profits divided among his chil-

113

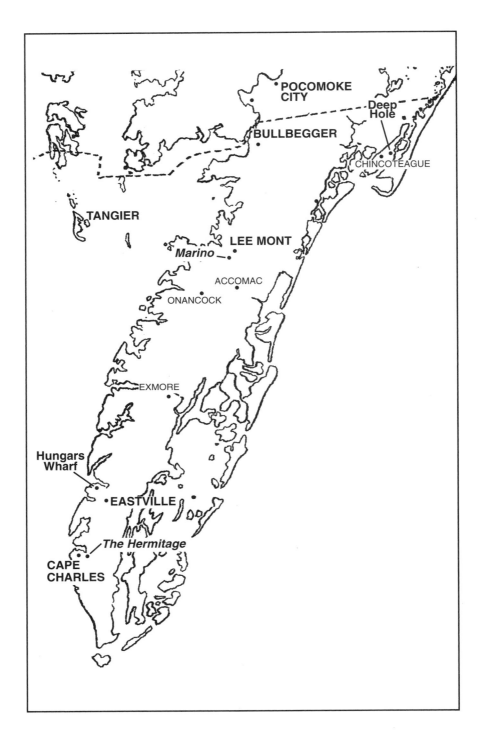

POCOMOKE
CITY

Deep
Hole

BULLBEGGER

CHINCOTEAGUE

TANGIER

LEE MONT

Marino

ACCOMAC

ONANCOCK

EXMORE

Hungars
Wharf

EASTVILLE

The Hermitage

CAPE
CHARLES

dren (although not "until a set-tlement of the present existing difficulties between the North and South"), and to Julia, his wife of eighteen years, left not one thing.[3]

Even so, the widow Julia was not destitute. Though she owned no property, she was guaranteed by law a widow's right, or one third "dower inter-est," which could, if she wished, hold up the sale of a third of Thorogood's land for as long as she lived.

Was it this dower interest, or some smoldering family jeal-ousy, that proved her undoing?

The sale of Thorogood's per-sonal property was scheduled for Christmas Day, December 25, 1861. Five days before the auction, one day after her 42nd

The Dix Graves at Bullbegger

birthday, Julia Dix sat rocking in her chair next to a window in a "nook" in the old house when a shot rang out. A bullet crashed through the window, splintered off part of the chair, and struck and killed her. An inquest was held—in those days a certain sign that the death was considered suspicious—but no suspect was named or iden-tified. On Christmas Day the public descended upon the place for the auction, and the sale netted $5,781.49.[4]

They buried Julia next to her husband's new grave at the side of the road, and carved upon her flat horizontal stone an inscription that neither family nor community has ever successfully explained:

> Farewell, my children, my sisters
> and my brother dear.
> I had not long to stay with you here.
> It was not sickness that hurried me
> away from here.
> It was my enemies and the Balls
> and my enemies without a cause.
> I have gone to rest in heaven to share.
> I am not dead, but sleeping here.
> Prepare for death, for die you must,
> and with your mother and sister sleep in dust.

For over a century one line in that epitaph—"It was my enemies and the Balls"—has puzzled virtually everyone who has read the stone. To add to the puzzlement, many insist that the stone reads not Balls but Bulls—"It was my enemies and the Bulls"—and that the inscription cryptically identifies someone by the last name of Bull as Julia's murderer. Those defending "Balls" can cite the rhyme: "Balls" rhymes with "cause" and is consistent with the rhyming couplets throughout the inscription. Those defending "Bulls" can cite the fact that in all the inscription this one word alone, apart from those at the beginnings of sentences, is capitalized, consistent with its being a proper name. And if to the modern eye the carved word looks more like "Balls" than "Bulls," there is the family tradition that the proper reading is "Bulls" and that there was once more lettering on the stone than appears there today. In fact, one passer-by is said to have been so indignant that the Bull name was indicted in the epitaph that the inscription was later surreptitiously altered.

But if it was the Bulls who killed Julia Dix, which Bulls, and why? Bull is a common name on the Eastern Shore, but there were no Bulls in Bullbegger, nor (at that time) in either Thorogood's or Julia's families. Five men named Bull showed up at the Christmas Day auction, but exactly where they came from is not clear.

According to one story passed down through the family of Julia's daughter Mary Ann, an old black man, once a slave on the Dix farm, confessed on his deathbed many years later that the only thing he did wrong was to kill "Miss Julia." He was, he insisted, told to do it and was paid by one or more of the stepsons. Descendants of Julia's stepson Isaac had their own family tradition: that an "unhappy" slave had fired the shot that killed Julia, without the instigation of either of the brothers. From Bettie Dix, Julia's younger daughter, there descends no story at all—strangely, for eleven-year-old Bettie was there in the house when her mother died.

Though the old house on the Dix farm in Bullbegger has been restored, there are persistent local traditions that it is still occasionally frequented by the ghostly presence of "Miss Julia." The chair in which she sat when she was killed, missing the spindle that was shattered by the bullet, was preserved in the family until destroyed by fire in the mid-twentieth century. In recent years the descendants of Thorogood have restored the small family burial plot, even adding a simple footbridge across the ditch from the road to the site.[5]

But the questions remain: who killed Julia Dix, and why?

What, if anything, did the Bulls have to do with it?

And no less intriguing: since it was almost assuredly not Julia herself who wrote it, who spoke for her when they carved the stone, and left us that most mystifying inscription?

Shootout in Eastville

Eastville seems to have been quiet that March morning in 1878. Though John Cragen had the bar open inside Taylor House (today's Eastville Inn), most of the day's activity was outside in the street. "Buzzard's Roost," that favorite meeting and gossiping place on the

A Typical Day at Eastville
Ringing the dinner bell at Taylor House (today's Eastville Inn), from *Harper's New Monthly Magazine*, May 1879

steps of the old drugstore, was apparently empty,[6] but a number of village men—among them Major S. Pitts, R. W. Nottingham, and George Toy—were talking together out in front of the store on the opposite side of the street. A typical morning in a sleepy county seat, at least until attorney Alfred P. Thom walked past on his way to his office.

As Thom passed, young Major Pitts called out and asked if he could speak to him. "Certainly," replied Thom, and the townsfolk barely noticed as the two men talked briefly in the street in front of the courthouse. But soon heated words wafted back to the sidelines.

"You are a damned rascal and a scoundrel!" said Pitts to Thom, and when Thom drew a pistol, "If you shoot me, I shall shoot you!"

Within a matter of seconds shots rang out, Thom firing first, then Pitts, four shots in all. Both men fell, and as the villagers rushed upon them, Pitts lay already dead, a bullet in his chest. Thom appeared also to be mortally wounded, a bullet having torn across his lip and into his mouth, knocking out teeth, breaking his jawbone, and lodging somewhere in his neck.[7]

It was not, in the formal sense, a duel. But it was one of the last and most sensational episodes on the Eastern Shore from that era when upstanding men of the community carried weapons and wielded them readily for points of honor real or imagined.[8]

That both of the participants were highly regarded citizens from prominent families only made the affair seem all the more shocking. Major Sydney Pitts (1857-1878) was the son of a judge and grandson of a general. His father Edward P. Pitts (1816-1875) had served in both the House of Delegates and the State Senate.[9] Alfred Pembroke Thom (1854-1935) was the son of Dr. William A. Thom (1820-1899), a physician who lived at "Stockley" just south of Eastville. He had been practicing law in Eastville for about two years.[10] Both men were natives of Northampton County, and both seemed to have promising careers ahead of them.

The cause of the shooting turned out to be a trivial amount of money, a confused set of legal circumstances, and an exaggerated sense of personal honor.

Some weeks prior to the event Pitts, who was about to head west to study law under a friend of his father, borrowed $20 from Eastville postmaster Elijah Brittingham. When he attempted to visit Brittingham to repay the loan the postmaster lay seriously ill and was unable to transact business. In fact, Brittingham died shortly thereafter, and R. V. Nottingham, acting unofficially in his behalf, soon called upon Pitts to repay the sum, stating that Brittingham had taken the money not from his own pocket but from post office funds. Upon advice from his brother, Pitts refused to pay Nottingham, insisting that Nottingham was not a legal representative of the deceased, that another person would ultimately have to be appointed, and that he could end up having to pay the sum back twice.

In the midst of these proceedings Pitts left Eastville for Hungars Wharf to book passage by steamer to Baltimore, prelude to his upcoming journey to St. Louis. No sooner did he leave town than Thom qualified as curator of Brittingham's estate, and no sooner did he qualify than he swore out a warrant for Pitts' arrest as an absconding debtor. Since sheriff L. J. Nottingham lay ill, Thom set out for Hungars Wharf with jailer W. E. Colonna to serve the warrant. They accosted Pitts there, but Pitts refused to accept the warrant, arguing that Colonna was not legally sworn in as deputy sheriff. Though Colonna and Thom called upon bystanders to help them make the arrest, none would assist them, and Pitts successfully boarded the steamer *Maggie* and left.

A short time later Pitts' brother followed him to Baltimore and advised him to return and settle the debt. Pitts returned to Eastville on Monday, March 25, and encountered Thom there the following Thursday. Their fatal encounter in front of the courthouse began with Pitts' demand for an explanation for the insult of having been labeled an absconding debtor.

Pitts was buried on March 30 in Norfolk, while in Eastville a coroner's inquest concluded that "Major S. Pitts came to his death on Thursday morning, March 28th, between the hours of 8 and 9 o'clock, by a bullet fired from a pistol in the hand of Alfred P. Thom." The following month Thom, still carrying a bullet in his neck and "quite weak from the effects of the wound," came before three Northampton justices, who after hearing testimony from twenty witnesses and deliberating for about a quarter hour discharged him, deciding not to send the case to jury. Once acquitted, Thom left for Richmond, where his father had arranged for a consultation with "an eminent physician."[11]

Alfred P. Thom survived his wound and went on to a distinguished career in law. He moved to Norfolk and became a partner in several law firms: Ellis & Thom (1878-1882), Tunstall & Thom (1883-1900), and White, Tunstall & Thom (1900-1905). He was a member of the convention that rewrote the Virginia Constitution in 1901-1902, and there made a statewide reputation as "a strong debater and a learned Constitutional lawyer."[12] In 1904 he was elected president of the Virginia Bar Association. He married Jennie Tunstall Baylor in 1881, survived her to

Alfred P. Thom

marry again in 1916, and was the father of Alfred P. Thom, Jr., who was also an attorney. Thom served as legal counsel for several railroads, and eventually moved to Washington. He died there in retirement in February 1935, honored by "many of the most prominent personages in the official, professional, and social life" of Washington, New York, Philadelphia, Baltimore, Cleveland, Chicago, Richmond, and Norfolk.

Like his adversary Major Pitts, he lies buried in Norfolk.[13]

The Ghost of Marino

"Marino" stood, until a few years ago, just south of Lee Mont, visible back in the field towards Drummond's Mill. A small story-and-a-half house known to some as Peach Brandy Farm, it was built about 1796, had brick ends, dormer windows, and a small front stoop.[14]

Marino also had a ghost.

In or about 1880, Marino was the home of George Parker Parks (1845-1911), who rented and farmed the property to support his family. In addition to his wife Elizabeth Grinnalds Parks (1845-1915), the family at that time consisted of five children: Henry, Marcelline, Otho, Elizabeth, and Ella Grace. The youngest two children, Oscar and Everette, had not yet joined the family and—because of the ghost—never lived at Marino.

During those days George Parks worked hard around the farm and his children played hard around the old farmhouse, until dinner time would find the entire family seated around the table. There, occasionally, the children's conversation would turn to the "lady in black." And though at first the parents paid her no mind, eventually they began to notice how often this lady in black recurred in the chatter of their children.

Finally one evening the parents inquired about her: "Who is this lady in black?"

"The woman who comes to visit us," came the answer.

"Oh?"

"Yes, she comes up the lane from the main road every day."

"Really? When?"

"In the afternoon, about four o'clock."

"Then why haven't we met her?"

"Because when she gets to the top of the steps of the front porch, she disappears."

No amount of parental reasoning could shake the children from their story: there really was a lady in black, who really did come up the lane every day. And no amount of arguing or scoffing could persuade them that they must be imagining things: she really did disappear when she got to the top of the steps. This, insisted every child, really was true—they had all seen her.

Marino

The lady in black remained a fixture of conversation around the dinner table for many meals, the children apparently not at all perturbed by her strange behavior, the parents utterly convinced that it was childish nonsense. But finally George Parks grew tired of hearing about it, so one day he took off from work early and lay in wait, hiding, determined to prove when she did not appear that the alleged visitor did not exist.

But then at about four o'clock he saw her, just as the children had said: a lady in black coming up the lane from the main road, quiet and slow. He watched as she reached the edge of the yard, and watched her head straight for the front porch, and then, as he watched, she reached the top of the stairs and just as she was about to enter the house she vanished.

George Parks was convinced. That night he packed up his wife and children and moved them out of Marino into a house in Lee Mont.

Who, supposedly, was the lady in black? If the explanation of a ghost requires a graveyard, Marino had one. A dozen people lie buried in a small burial plot on the farm, and one of them, by gender and chronology, could qualify as the lady in black. Levin D. Lewis (1818-1886) purchased the farm in 1857 and lies buried there next to his wife Mary Ann (1831-1908), though both of them were still living at the time Parks farmed the property. Near their later graves are those of three of their children, all of of whom died in the 1860s before reaching the age of nine, and near them is the grave of Annie F. Willett Melson (1798-1872), Mary Ann's mother, Levin Lewis' mother-in-law, grandmother of the three children. Was the lady in black the grand-mother returning to visit the three little boys whom she had loved?

Without any such attempt to identify her, the Parks family kept alive the story of the ghost of Marino. The seven Parks children— Henry (1868-1931), Marcelline Parks Melson (1870-1958), Elizabeth Parks Custis (1873-1955) Otho (1875-1951), Ella Grace Parks Wescott (1877-1943), Oscar (1881-1969), and Everette (1888-1947)—passed the story on to the next generation, the five oldest of them insisting that they were eyewitnesses to the ghost. Ella Wescott's daughter Marguerite Whitehead (1902-1998) lived for many years in Nassawadox, and a century after the event was still recounting the story told to her by her mother and attested by her aunts and uncles.

Does the lady in black still come up the lane at four o'clock in the afternoon? If so, these days she has to perform her vanishing act before reaching the top of the porch stairs, for Marino burned to the ground on June 26, 1982, the victim of an arsonist.[15] Today only the graves remain for sure—and the story.

Love and Death in Deep Hole

The house is still there at the end of Deep Hole Road, sturdy and comfortable and silent about the events that stunned the community more than a century ago. Even the little burial ground next to the yard looks like many another on the Eastern Shore, as ordinary as the next, with no story to tell. But here occurred the first murder on the island of Chincoteague, and one of the most tragic love stories of the Eastern Shore.

In 1885 this was the home of Timothy and Zipporah Hill. The house was then a farmhouse, for Timothy Hill owned a good deal of land and still engaged in a little farming, as once almost everyone on the island had done. He was a prominent man in the community, suc-cessful in business, a pillar of the local Methodist church, with a fam-ily well-known and respected.

Another resident of the farm was Thomas W. Freeman, then a young man of twenty. Except for those times when he served as a deck hand on the lightship off Winter Quarter Shoal, Freeman worked around the Hill place doing odd jobs.

And then as fate would have it, Tom Freeman fell desperately in love with his employer's daughter Emma Virginia. "Jennie" was "a

Jennie Hill

perfect blond of a bright and happy disposition, in every sense the pet of her entire family." She was also just barely into her teens.

It was soon obvious that Tom Freeman could be persistent. When Jennie spurned his offer of marriage—she was too young, she told him—Freeman stated his case to her parents, who let it be known that they found the whole idea completely unacceptable.

What was not so obvious was that Tom Freeman was also a very troubled man. He spent his spare time pouring out his feelings in letters which he then did not mail. To Timothy Hill he wrote: "I am going to kill myself on a count of Jennie Hill. Wee have been corting about 8 mounts and this is the last." And to Zipporah: "You are the caues of me doing so. You sid you would not let no one go with Jennie."

On the morning of June 18, 1885, Jennie and her mother stepped out of the house to go to the dressmaker's, and they were met suddenly at the gate by Tom Freeman. When Tom inquired if Mrs. Hill had changed her mind about the marriage, she replied angrily, and tempers flared. Suddenly and without warning Freeman drew a 32-calibre pistol and began firing.

He aimed first at Zipporah Hill, but his shot went wild and merely grazed her head. Though she fell to the ground, she scrambled quickly to her feet, shouting at him not to shoot again. He fired a second time, with aim more accurate and deadly, and the bullet struck her in the head.

Tom then turned the gun upon the horrified Jennie and fired twice. The first shot grazed her head. The second lodged in her neck.

Incredibly the two women ran a hundred yards to the door of a neighbor, where they fell exhausted and bleeding. As neighbors rushed to the scene, Freeman turned the gun to his own forehead and with his last cartridge pulled the trigger. Now at last his aim was good, and he fell dead almost at the door of the Hill's kitchen.

"Excitement was at fever head" as the news of the shootings spread. "On our streets, in the stores, on the boats and in the fisherman's cabin, all conversation has reference to the terrible tragedy," wrote the local correspondent to the county paper. Meanwhile Jennie Hill lingered, at times conscious and coherent and "in the most excruciating agony." She died at eleven that night, having never once uttered "a murmur of complaint against the murderer."

Methodist preacher J. D. Reese conducted Jennie's funeral in the parlor of the Hill house even as her mother lay in another room "hovering between life and death." The mourners bore her body a few yards to the family burial ground at the northern edge of the front yard. Her gravestone is still there today: "E. Virginia Hill, born Feb. 25, 1872, died June 18, 1885."

Zipporah Hill recovered from the shooting, and four years later when the Methodists built a new church on the island (the old frame building opposite the present stone church) she and her husband placed in it a stained glass window dedicated to their daughter's memory.

Tom Freeman died unmourned. So great was the "lack of sympathy for the assassin" that neither friend

Tom Freeman

nor relative would claim his body. The day after the shooting the local undertaker buried him in a "rude pine box" without ceremony or benefit of clergy, with only "a few gaping boys" in attendance.

And then, later, they found the letters Tom had written and never mailed, and caught a glimpse into the tortured soul of the troubled man. "My dear friend," Tom had written to one of the crew in the lightship, "I will tell you about my trubel. I am in love with a girl and hear name is Jennie Hill. I think to much of her. I will die for love, so good by my old friend take warning from this, don't go to far with the girls, this is my last letter from me so I will die for love."[16]

Years later Freeman's grave, along with others in the small burial ground behind 4211 School Street, was moved to the burial ground of the Methodist Protestant church. Frank Bradford was then a young boy as from a distance he watched the gravediggers uncover, lift, and then open Freeman's coffin, but fled when they remarked aloud (probably for his benefit) that the bullet hole was still visible in the skull. Freeman lies today in his new unmarked grave in what is now the churchyard of St. Andrew's Roman Catholic Church.[17]

Who Shot the Shooter?

In May 1920 a "movie camera man" arrived on Tangier Island, and had no sooner begun filming than he was so roughly handled by the islanders that he had to be rescued by the Methodist preacher. He had the misfortune to discover that the recent incident he had come to publicize was not one that the island wanted broadcast abroad.

On Sunday, April 11, 1920, Charles "Bud" Connorton, Town Sergeant and Deputy Sheriff, shot and wounded 17-year-old Roland Parks while trying to enforce a town ordinance that forbade "loafing on store porches and streets on Sunday." Tangier then as now was a remarkably religious community, and citizens were required "either to be in church during the hours of service, or in their homes." According to the report that made the local newspapers, Connorton discovered Parks on the streets when he should not have been, was cursed by Parks when he tried to arrest him, and fired during a scuffle after Parks resisted arrest.

Many islanders insisted, however, that the newspapers had it wrong. Parks, they contended, had gone to the store which his family operated to get some ice cream for his invalid mother when Connorton saw him open the store, and warned him against it (stores were, of course, closed on Sundays). Angry words were exchanged as Parks entered the store, got the ice cream, and walked home with it, the Town Sergeant at his heels. When he got to the door of his home at 16338 Main Ridge, Parks turned before entering it and taunted Connorton, daring him to shoot. Connorton fired, and the bullet passed through the boy's chest and lodged in the front door.

Front Door of the Parks House
Young Roland Parks was shot here, and the bullet lodged in the front door

The shooting electrified the community, and as news of it spread many islanders became concerned that the publicity surrounding it gave a false impression of their community. So when "a representative of a motion picture company" arrived a few weeks later to film the island where the shooting had occurred, "he was warned...against taking any pictures, and when he ignored the warning was handled roughly. His camera was taken from him and destroyed, along with the reels of film he had taken," and "but for the intervention of Rev. W. F. Godwin, pastor of the only church on the island, [he] would have fared worse." The cameraman was given until midnight to leave, and promptly secured a boat to take him to safety on the mainland.

Connorton surrendered to the county authorities the day after the shooting, and on June 18 was sentenced to a year in prison. Despite his appeal to the State Supreme Court, he was taken to the state penitentiary in October, but served only a brief time before being pardoned by the Governor. He returned to Tangier, and resumed his old position as Deputy Sheriff.

Roland Parks, meanwhile, had survived his wounds. He spent the rest of his life on the island, and for many years ran the family store that still operates at 16315 Main Ridge. He served on the Town Council, and died peacefully in 1973 at the age of 70.

Connorton had much less time on the island. Months after his return from prison, he was seated in an oyster house (located in the front yard of 16126 Main Ridge) when he was fatally shot through an open window.

His murderer has never been identified. His is one of the few murders ever to occur on Tangier Island, and the only one still unsolved.[18]

Murder by Mail

At "the Hermitage" near Cape Charles, the noises and dangers of the modern world seem far removed.

The old house, built prior to 1783, stands at the end of its own private lane half a mile east of Cape Charles, a handsome structure with a gambrel roof and dormer windows.[19] The front yard is studded with shade trees and lined by a white wooden fence, while at the back the house commands a lovely view of Kings Creek. To the many visitors who have trooped around and through it during Garden Week the Hermitage conjures up enviable visions of the quiet country life.

But the modern world once intruded upon this pleasant spot with a horror such as the world had then seldom seen. It was here that, for one of the first times in the world, a man was murdered by the very modern means of a bomb sent through the mail.

In 1936 the Hermitage was owned by Curry S. Thomas, 47 years old, well-to-do gentleman farmer. His first wife died in 1934 when her car was struck by the train at the crossing nearest

The Hermitage, Cape Charles

the house,[20] and he was a widower when he met Elsie Dickinson Salmons, who first came to Cape Charles to visit her brother, attorney W. A. Dickinson. Mrs. Salmons was by then divorced, and had for three years been employed as an assistant to Harvey R. Hege, a dentist in Mount Airy, North Carolina. After several visits back and forth, Curry and Elsie were married on June 10, 1936, at her mother's home in her native Hillsville, Virginia,[21] and the newlyweds promptly took up residence in the Hermitage.

On July 22, the 41st day of their marriage, the Thomases stopped by the post office at Cape Charles on their way home from a golf game at the local country club. Waiting for them there was a small package wrapped in brown paper, tied with ordinary string, and bearing a Richmond return address.

"A wedding present!" exclaimed some friends who happened to be in the post office at the time, and they urged the couple to open it right then and there. But the Thomases resisted, and hurried home. After pulling his sedan to a stop at the Hermitage, Curry Thomas took the package into his lap and broke the string around it.[22]

The explosion that followed could be heard for a mile, and sent parts of the automobile hurtling 100 yards across the property. Elsie Thomas was blown out of the car with shrapnel in her left side and arm, and with injury to one eye. Curry Thomas was killed instantly.[23]

The explosion occurred about 6:30 p.m. on Wednesday. By the end of the day S. Thomas Nottingham, postmaster and former police chief at Cape Charles, had notified Federal authorities of the bombing, and the scene of the crime had been roped off to protect if from the curious.[24] By noon Thursday investigators from the postal service, flown

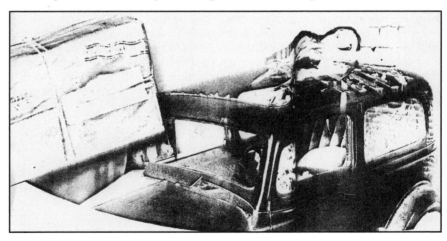

The car in which Curry Thomas was seated when he was killed by a mail bomb; on the left: the package containing the bomb, as reconstructed by Federal authorities to show to postal clerks as they sought clues to the crime. From *True Detective*, February 1941.

in by Navy plane from Baltimore, were taking charge of the case. Among them were 6-foot, 250-pound B. B. Webb and "a little fellow with a black moustache" named J. B. Sentman; together the two were said to resemble the comic strip characters Mutt and Jeff.[25] By Friday some of the inspectors had been dispatched to Mount Airy and Hillsville, and to Galax, Virginia, where Mrs. Thomas' first husband lived. Curry Thomas was buried on Friday. His widow, meanwhile, lay in the Nassawadox hospital in serious condition, often delirious.[26]

For weeks the investigation moved too slowly for a community frightened and incensed by so horrible and senseless a crime. After four days in the Western Shore towns, the investigators moved on, veiling their work in secrecy and promising a public statement only when an arrest was made.[27] By September, Eastern Shore citizens were growing impatient. "Why have we any reason to believe that we are being protected against this criminal or others of his like?" demanded the *Northampton Times* of Cape Charles. The county sheriff, his deputies, and the Cape Charles police all stood ready and eager to take up the case, but had been told by the Federal officials that "We'll handle it." "But what about results?" stormed the *Times*.[28]

It took less than three months for the investigators to get their man. At 10:00 p.m. on Monday, October 6, two men from North Carolina walked into the Bluemont Hotel in Galax, unaware that the people in the lobby included three postal investigators (including Mutt and Jeff), an array of local police and state troopers, and, from Northampton County, sheriff George T. Turner and Commonwealth's Attorney C. M. Lankford. Sheriff Turner presented them with warrants, arrested and handcuffed them, and promptly left for Eastville with his culprits. Charged with the crime were Elsie's old employer Dr. Hege and his friend and "alibi" Edward Banner.

The investigators had done a thorough job of connecting the bombing to Hege. Through remnants at the scene of the crime they had learned that the bomb had been built from a mousetrap, a small battery, a fuse, and dynamite in a piece of pipe. They traced the battery to its factory of origin in Canada, then to Mount Airy, the typewritten return address to Chicago, then back to the dentist, and even the string that bound the package to Hege's supply house. There were witnesses from Richmond who placed Hege and Banner there the day the bomb was mailed. As for motive, there were letters from Hege who strongly objected to Elsie's leaving his employ to get married,[29] and Elsie's statement that Hege, though a married man with children, had become infatuated with her to such an extent that she had considered giving up her job—though later, upon meeting Curry Thomas, he had expressed a high regard for him, and wished them both well.[30]

In Eastville, Hege and Banner were lodged in separate cells in the county jail and the considerable evidence against them placed in the hands of Lankford. Within hours, Deputy John R. Womble found Hege in his cell bleeding from the wrists. When Dr. Holland Trower was summoned to stitch up the wound, Hege insisted he must have broken the crystal of his watch as he rolled over on it while sleeping.[31] During the next several days Hege engaged a local attorney, summoned another from Mount Airy, asked his wife to visit him, and steadfastly maintained his innocence. "I may have been indiscreet," he told his attorney, "but as God is my witness I had nothing to do with that bomb." On Saturday night, October 10, he complained of headaches and asked that his eyeglasses be returned to him. The following morning he was found dead in his cell, the eyeglasses broken and the glass used to slit his wrists and throat.[32]

Dr. Harvey Hege was buried in Mount Airy on October 14. Elsie Thomas left the Nassawadox hospital on October 20. Before the end of the month Edward Banner had been cleared of conspiracy in the murder, and charges against him dropped. On November 8, Federal authorities announced the closing of the case.[33]

The Cape Charles mail bombing, picked up by the Associated Press and United Press International, was news from coast to coast. It was covered in detail by the *Richmond Times-Dispatch*, and was front-page news in the *Washington Post* and the *Los Angeles Evening Herald & Express*.[34] Five years later it was featured in *True Detective* magazine, complete with a photograph of Thomas' bombed sedan.[35]

Elsie Thomas fully recovered from the bombing incident, and later remarried and moved to Amarillo, Texas. She died in 1981, and is buried there.[36]

Dr. Hege's house in Mount Airy, built about 1925, was at one time listed in the National Register of Historic Places. It was demolished in 1992 to make room for the future expansion of, ironically, the local post office.[37] Curry Thomas' house still stands overlooking Kings Creek, as quiet and peaceful as if nothing bad had ever happened there.

8

Almost Forgotten
Little Places That Are No More

Wagram

Through an exclusive neighborhood of Paris, France, within sight of the Arc de Triomphe, runs a street named Avenue de Wagram. And on the Eastern Shore, a mile west of Route 13 at the Maryland boundary, is—or was—another place called Wagram.

Today a single house is all that remains of the once thriving village of Wagram. The millpond around which the village clustered has long since been drained, and the several old stores have disappeared. There is not even a roadsign to identify the spot.

Before the mill there was only Pitts Creek, flowing southwesterly out of lower Worcester County in Maryland through Accomack County in Virginia towards the Pocomoke River. Just across the line from Virginia, the Reverend Francis Makemie established a Presbyterian church on the bank of the creek sometime before his death in 1708; today that congregation still worships at the same site, in a much later building. For many years before her death in 1788 the founder's daughter Anne Makemie Holden worshiped at this church, and to reach it she probably went by water, boating from her home in Jenkins Bridge, up the Pocomoke into Pitts Creek, past the future Wagram to the church.[1]

Today no boat could travel this far up Pitts Creek, but in those days the creek was naviga-ble up to the church, though the southernmost of the two smaller branches just beyond the church was even then known as Impassible Branch. The church is still visible on the left heading north on Route 13, and just to the right is the confluence of the two small branches, Impassible Branch coming in from the south from behind the Maryland Information Center.

Who established the mill that became known as Wagram, and when, is not certain today. It was in existence by 1802, and was almost

Paris Street Sign

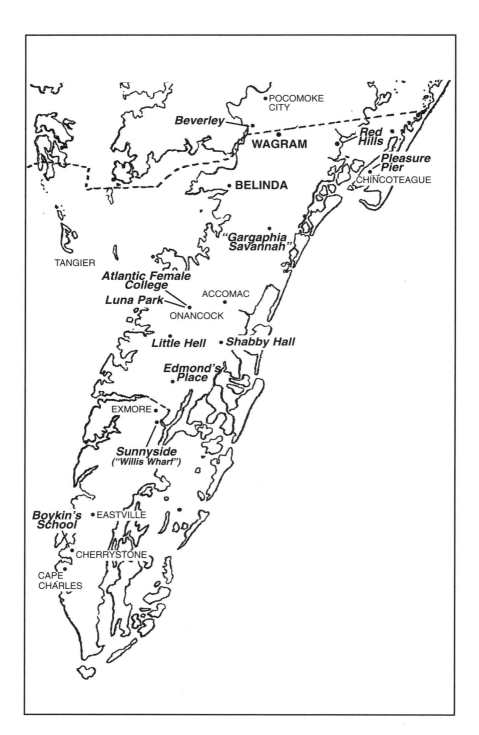

POCOMOKE
CITY

Beverley

WAGRAM

*Red
Hills*

*Pleasure
Pier*

CHINCOTEAGUE

BELINDA

*"Gargaphia
Savannah"*

TANGIER

*Atlantic Female
College*

ACCOMAC

Luna Park

ONANCOCK

Little Hell •*Shabby Hall*

*Edmond's
Place*

EXMORE

Sunnyside
("Willis Wharf")

*Boykin's
School* •EASTVILLE

CHERRYSTONE

CAPE
CHARLES

130   Little Places

certainly built by someone in the illustrious Dennis family of Worcester County,[2] but how much before 1802 and exactly which Dennis is not certain. The Dennises were the most prominent family in the lower part of Maryland. They lived at "Beverley," the handsome and much admired house of 1774 that still stands overlooking Pocomoke River just north of the Maryland-Virginia boundary.

It is possible that the mill was established by Henry Dennis, seventh in the Dennis line, son of Littleton Dennis who built the big house.[3] But Henry Dennis died at sea a young man, only one year after the birth of his only son, and a more likely candidate is that son, Littleton Purnell Dennis (1786-1834). Born at Beverley, Littleton P. Dennis was educated at Yale, admitted to the Maryland bar in 1804, and throughout his life lived up to the prominence of the family name. He served twice in the Maryland House of Delegates, was five times a presidential elector, and in 1831 was elected to the Maryland Senate. Two years later he went to the U.S. Congress, but there his promising career was cut short by an early death on April 14, 1834.[4] Although it is not certain that this is the Dennis who established the mill on the home property on Pitts Creek, it is also not unlikely.

Wagram
From an 1870s Maryland Atlas

South of the creek, just across the line in Virginia, a family by the name of Bayne began acquiring substantial acreage in the early 1800s, and in 1806 Littleton P. Dennis, retaining only his mill and the two acres around it, sold 110 acres near "Dennis' Mill" to William Bayne. It was apparently William Bayne who named the village that grew up around the mill, for in 1811 he bequeathed to his brother John the "land at my New building called Wagram," the earliest known use of that name.[5]

Wagram was an unlikely name for an Eastern Shore village. The original Wagram is in Austria, northeast of Vienna, and it was there in 1809 that Napoleon Bonaparte defeated the Austrians in his attempt to maintain control over Europe. Just why Bayne should name his holdings after a Napoleonic victory is yet another of the unknowns surrounding the founding of Wagram. Was he an admirer of Napoleon? Did he hold some special grudge against the Austrians, or against Napoleon's greatest enemy, England?[6]

Wagram Mill sat astride both the state boundary and the 38th parallel. The Bayside road leading from Accomack to Worcester ran along the top of its earthen dam,and the mill house stood west of the road, opposite the pond, just barely within Virginia. The shallow millpond backed up to within half a mile of the Presbyterian church, and from it ran a sluice, or "flume," which carried water under the road to the small wooden building where two giant grist stones ground corn into meal. By 1813 there were two such flumes and two separate mill buildings, the newer of which was one of the earliest water-powered sawmills on the Eastern Shore of Virginia. There was also an icehouse, in which, in those days before refrigeration, ice cut in large chunks from the millpond could be stored and sold in warmer weather.[7]

Wagram Mill

There is no record of how and when the several houses and establishments of Wagram came to be clustered around the mill. An 1820 map of Accomack County shows the village already in existence. A post office was established on July 14, 1843 (the French "Independence Day," 54 years to the day after the storming of the Bastille), and it seems safe to assume that the post office was located in one of the several small stores in the village. In those days the postmaster's position was a political appointment parceled out by the party in the White House, and Wagram's postmasters changed frequently over the next 20 years, giving us the names of the families in the village: Wishart, Dennis, Fletcher, Bayne, Merrill. In February 1860 John O. Selby became the village's seventh postmaster, and the following year, on June 6, 1861, the post office was moved out of Accomack County, Virginia, into Worcester County, Maryland. It could be that Selby simply relocated his store a few yards away in Maryland, taking the post office with it. At any rate the post office at Wagram, Maryland, was not long in existence, for it closed altogether on August 10, 1861.[8]

Sometime between the 1850s and the 1870s a merchant named Levi C. Tull (1810-1872) moved to Wagram; indeed, he may already have lived on the Maryland side of Wagram and only moved across the line into Virginia. By 1870 his son William T. Tull (1834-1900) had taken over his father's store. The following year the younger Tull purchased over 200 acres around the village, including the mill itself, and four years later on June 8, 1875, he became the postmaster of the re-established post office, which was located in his store. All of this made Tull the most prominent man in the village, and his big house, which stood across the road from the store, sported a large Palladian-style window befitting his prominence. Though the village at that time consisted of only about ten houses, Tull's was one of no fewer than three stores. One old map shows his store located in Maryland, but the state boundary was resurveyed in 1883, and maps after that date place it clearly in Virginia.[9]

Wagram Store

Towards the end of the 1800s improved technology spelled the end of the Shore's dependence upon water-powered mills. No longer was it necessary to haul timber to the mill, for a boiler could be erected right in the middle of the timber and the lumber cut by steam. At about the same time flour, already ground and conveniently packaged, began to appear on the shelves of local stores. No longer needed either to grind grain or to cut lumber, the old watermills began to decline all up and down the peninsula. Wagram declined with its mill, while only a few miles away the village of New Church, bolstered by the coming of the railroad in 1884, experienced a boom, and soon far outdistanced it.

The last days of Wagram were not dignified. In 1891 the mill was vandalized by "some malicious person [who] sawed into the capsill of the waste gatebridge, and did other injury to the property."[10] When a man named Griffin Callahan visited the mill three years later, he labeled it the "old mill on the Virginia-Maryland boundary," and took a photograph that shows a roofed but open-sided structure that appears to be in an advanced state of disrepair. Callahan also photographed Tull's store, and the two photographs are the only known pictures of the village.[11]

William T. Tull died in 1900. The post office was discontinued, permanently, later that year, and the store ceased to operate soon afterwards. The mill continued in operation until about 1910, and when it closed there was no longer any reason for anyone to come to Wagram. The mill house collapsed within a few years, and by the end of the 1930s the millpond was drained. By mid-century only three houses were left, two of them abandoned. Tull's home burned in the 1960s, the victim of arson. Within a few years what had been the south bank of the millpond became the site of a county dump.

The last operator of the mill at Wagram was Alonzo Matthews, who upon closing it moved to New Church and ran a boarding house. Matthews took with him the large old millstone from Wagram, and it rests today, broken into two large pieces, behind the home that was later erected on Matthews' lot at 30525 Depot Street.[12]

The originals of Griffin Callahan's old photographs of Wagram are located in the library at Accomac. Further afield, in Congressional Cemetery in Washington, D.C., stands the tomb of Littleton Purnell Dennis, the mill's founder. Much further afield, in the building that houses the tomb of Napoleon in Paris, hangs a painting by Edouard Detaille of the battle from which Wagram took its name. Outside Paris, in the palace of Versailles, is another more famous painting of "The Battle of Wagram" (pictured on the stamp on page 129) that shows Napoleon astride his horse, using a telescope to follow the course of action on the plains of Wagram below him. The original European Wagram lies even further afield in eastern Austria, and is known today as Deutsch Wagram.

It was an auspicious name for a tiny and insignificant Eastern Shore village. In Europe the name is recognized and remembered today, but on the Shore it is all but forgotten.

The College on the Creek

The site lay, at that time, east of Onancock, well outside of town.[13] Here from 1832 to 1858 lived Samuel C. White, operator of a ferry between Onancock and Norfolk, in a large home called "Whitely" overlooking a creek then known as White's Branch. White sold his house in 1858, and the following year it became the site of Atlantic Female College,[14] the first college ever located on the Eastern Shore of Virginia.

Today White's Branch is known as Joynes' Branch, and the town of Onancock completely surrounds the old college campus. Atlantic Female College has been gone for more than a century, and in its place stands the Onancock Learning Center in the former high school on a street still known as College Avenue.

While never officially a Baptist school, Atlantic Female College was founded and patronized largely by Baptists. The five trustees who actually owned the property—George Bradford, Louis Drummond, Tully Joynes, George Rogers, and Edward Waples—were all Baptists, and the school's president, Rev. J. H. Phillips, was a member of Onancock Baptist Church who in 1861-1862 served as pastor of Red

Bank Baptist Church in Marionville. The college was founded because "female education had...so deeply interested the [Accomack Baptist] Association and the Baptists generally on the Eastern Shore." Yet the college advertised no churchly connection, required none for admission, and invited ministers of all denominations to enroll their daughters tuition-free.[15]

Opened in 1859, the college very quickly grew to contain three buildings. In addition to the original house in which Samuel White had lived ("parlor, sitting room, reading room, dining hall, kitchen and a number of chambers") a second building was erected "expressly for College purposes, containing a handsome study hall, recitation rooms, piano rooms, and eleven chambers." In 1860 a third building was added containing four rooms for the "Music and Ornamental" departments.[16]

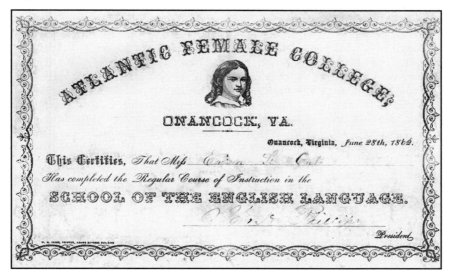

The girls of Atlantic Female College came from all up and down the Eastern Shore of Virginia, from Worcester County, and from as far away as Smithfield and Baltimore,[17] and they studied Latin, Greek, French, Spanish, Italian, mathematics, natural sciences, history, geography, English, music, painting, and physical education. They were expected to attend lectures on anatomy, physiology, hygiene, and "Evidences of Christianity." They could choose instruction in piano, guitar, voice, watercolor, oil painting, and embroidery, or make use of a library of "appropriate Historical, Scientific, and Literary books" or the "chemical and philosophical apparatus" on hand.

Campus life on the outskirts of ante-bellum Onancock was less than uproarious. At night the girls slept on comfortable featherbeds, but during the day they lived highly supervised lives. Students were not allowed to leave campus without permission from the president or the teachers, and then had to be accompanied by a teacher. They could not "make bills" in the stores of the town without permission, or receive visits except by assent of the president.

All correspondence into and out of the college passed through the president's office, and "suspected impropriety" was duly noted. Daily study halls were supervised by teachers, and report cards were sent home monthly. There were religious services every morning and evening, and on Sunday students were expected to attend one of the churches in town; if their parents failed to designate which one, the president chose for them. Parents were assured that even though the campus was within five minutes walk of Onancock, it was also "so retired as to prevent intrusion."[18]

The college began with a faculty of five, three women and two men, one of whom was President Phillips. By 1862, when enrollment had increased, at least four other people had served on the faculty at various times.[19] Romance could bloom among the faculty, if not the student body, and in December 1861 Henry Battaile, instructor in Ancient and Modern Languages and Mathematics, married Adelaide Rogers, daughter of one of the trustees and teacher of Ancient Languages, English, and Instrumental Music. Battaile, a native of Caroline County who came to the Shore to teach at the college, became a prominent educator and farmer on his adopted Eastern Shore, served on the Accomack County Board of Supervisors, and after "Addie's" death in 1881 married her sister Susan.[20]

After a very promising start the college found itself thrust suddenly into the turbulent years of the Civil War in a community much exercised by the conflict. A significant number of Onancock's citizens were pro-Union, and in 1864 one of them described the college and its president as the place where "more mischief has been concocted in the way of blockade running and general...disloyalty than in any other place of equal dimensions within our region."[21] Perhaps because of the unsettled times in general or the politics of its faculty in particular, attendance began to drop, and within a few years the school was closed. The actual date of its closing is not known, but it was certainly by the early 1870s.[22]

In 1877 the "College Property" was sold and from it lots for homes and businesses were created. Tully A. T. Joynes bought the college buildings themselves, then in 1893 sold them with seven acres to the trustees of Margaret Academy. Margaret Academy had, until then, been located down the county in Bobtown, but then merged with two other earlier schools, Onancock Academy and Eastern Shore Academy, and occupied the old college site. In 1920 the property became public school land, and the present Onancock School was built just a few feet from the foundations of the original college building.[23]

Today no part of old Atlantic Female College stands. But not without reason is one street in modern Onancock still known as College Avenue.

Mr. Boykin's School

The big house that stands at the entrance to Cherrystone is "Huntington," built "only" around 1800 and thus hardly old by the standards of this vicinity. But in this house occurred a little-known chapter in the African American history of the Shore, yet another of those events that make this corner of the peninsula historic.

In 1895 Huntington was owned by William A. Kimberley of Hampton, and in that year he sold it to another Hampton resident named Arthur L. Boykin. Tall, thin, dark-skinned, distinguished and well-dressed, Boykin was a graduate of Hampton Institute and was given to wearing the uniform of that school which had been established for blacks at the close of the Civil War. It was not as a home but for a school that he purchased Huntington, and for about six years at the turn of the twentieth century this historic old ground was the site of the private school that he operated for the African American children of Northampton County.

Modeled after Hampton Institute, Boykin's school is in one old record called Cheriton High School,[24] and no doubt he envisioned that it would ultimately become a high school. He had first, however, to provide an elementary education, then to graduate students to the high school level. When the school opened in 1896, there were about 50 elementary students. Most of them attended daily from home at a cost of $2 per month, but some of them boarded at the school from Monday through Friday at the cost of $8 per month. Hattie Spady taught first and second grade, Nora Bull and Sally Trower the higher grades—they were all local African American women—and "Major" Boykin and his wife Esther rounded out the faculty.

Huntington
The old house that was the site of Arthur Boykin's school for black children was photographed from across the creek by Griffin Callahan in the 1890s

At Boykin's school there were classes in reading, writing, arithmetic, geography, history, English, music, cooking, sewing, carpentry, and a class in Bible every Friday. At daily devotional exercises in the big room the students memorized Biblical passages. On weekends Sunday school was held in the main room, often attended by parents as well as children. And on Wednesdays occurred the "parades" that were the high point of the week, when the Major taught the boys to march and drill.

Huntington was hardly a fancy schoolhouse. Fireplaces in every classroom provided the only heat. There were few desks and chairs. Students usually sat on church pews rescued from an abandoned Baptist church adjacent to the farm. Blackboards in the dining room were simply boards painted black on which the students wrote with chalk or crayon. Purchase of textbooks was the responsibility of the students and their parents. "Miss Hattie" often took her students outdoors, and taught them from nature from the bridge over the creek at the side entrance to the farm.

Nor was time out of the classroom easy. Boarding students lived upstairs and downstairs in various rooms around the house, and some even in the smaller out-buildings on the property. Most of the boarders worked to help pay their way, the boys outside at the many chores around the farm, the girls at cooking, laundry, and cleaning. Food was prepared in the old kitchen that stood apart from the house in the yard, and with student help was carried into the dining room in the main house. Though Major Boykin enjoyed wearing his, there was no required school uniform. There was not much time for play, but the students made games around the trees and buildings on the old estate, and were known to scamper among the tombstones in the side yard where old Obedience Robins (1600-1662), member of the Governor's Council, lay buried.[25]

Boykin's school was at least unofficially a Baptist project. Its faculty were Baptists, as were most of the families from whom the students came, and the local churches of the African Baptist Association frequently helped with food, money, and supplies. It is apparent that Boykin began the school with the understanding that the Association would ultimately purchase it from him. The property cost him the hefty sum of $19,500, to be paid in ten annual installments, and with tuition so low he was necessarily dependent upon local support. However a number of Baptists in the Association were unclear whether Boykin or the Association would own the property once it was paid off, and there developed some degree of resentment between the locals and some of Boykin's Hampton contacts.

By 1902 it was apparent that the anticipated local support would not be forthcoming. When the Association met in the summer of that year there were not sufficient funds to buy the property, and Boykin was already behind in his payments. After much juggling of mortgages, sales of a few lots, and other attempts to keep the project afloat, Boykin abandoned the effort and the school closed. The property was sold back to Kimberley in 1903, and Arthur and Esther Boykin and their two children moved back to Richmond. Their students then had to walk as much as five miles to attend the nearest public school for blacks on the Cheriton-Oyster road.

The black Baptists of Northampton were undeterred by the failure of the school. In 1903 George E. Reid, pastor of Cheriton's African Baptist Church and friend of Esther Boykin, led in the incorporation of Tidewater Institute nearby in the little railroad village of Chesapeake. With the support of the local Baptist Association, this school opened in 1907 and for the next 28 years was a major force for education among an entire generation of Northampton's black population.[26]

Today a state historical marker indicates the site of Tidewater Institute. Its predecessor a few miles to the west is unmarked, and all but forgotten.

Belinda

The Belinda who left her name on the map of the Eastern Shore of Virginia was at least the third woman in her family to bear that name.

Her mother, also, was named Belinda. This first Belinda Broadwater (1827-1898) was already a young widow when in 1851 she married her second husband William Robinson Drummond (1826-1917). The daughter that was born to the Drummonds in 1858 was the second Belinda, but she died in 1863. Another daughter was born in 1870, and once again the favored name was bestowed. It was this third Belinda Broadwater Drummond (1870-1934) whose name is still found on the map between Sanford and Messongo in upper Accomack County.[27]

In 1888, when Belinda Drummond was a popular young belle of the region, a local merchant named Walter J. Hall obtained permission to operate a post office in his store near Marsh Market. The menfolk of the area, gathered as usual in the store to pass the time of day and to rule on local affairs, began conferring on what to name the new post office. No doubt several names were tried and rejected before someone suggested: why not name it for one of the pretty ladies in the neighborhood—why not name it "Belinda"? Belinda it was. The Belinda post office commenced operations on September 6, 1888, with Hall as postmaster. Some years later Hall's store burned, and the post office was moved up the street to another location, but the name remained.[28]

The popular young Belinda, whom the family called "Bin" to distinguish her from her mother, became Belinda Broadwater Drummond Drummond in 1894 when she married Herbert A. Drummond (1872-1971). The newlyweds settled down near the village named for Mrs. Drummond, a well known and respected couple. Mr. Drummond engaged in the oyster business, owned and operated a cannery, served as a trustee of the Atlantic District School Board, and even ran (unsuccessfully) for the county Board of Supervisors. Mrs. Drummond taught Sunday school at nearby Pocomoke Methodist Church, and was active in many civic affairs. A daughter Avalon was born in 1899.[29]

Belinda Drummond
c. 1910

On a Sunday night in August 1934—by then they had been married for forty years, and daughter Avalon, married to Milton Bodley, was a schoolteacher living in Oak Hall—the Drummonds went to bed at their regular hour only to be awakened by a fierce thunderstorm. Belinda Drummond rose from her bed and went up to the attic, kerosene lamp in hand, to inspect the roof for leaks. She returned shortly to her bed and the two went back to sleep, unaware that a spark from her lamp had landed somewhere in the attic—or was it that lightning later struck their home?

When the Drummonds awoke a second time, the fire had already spread across the attic and roof and into the second story where their bedroom was located. Upon seeing the fire all around her, Mrs. Drummond became disoriented and quickly fled into the back part of the house, where her husband could not reach her because of the flames. Herbert Drummond got safely out of the house and ran to get a ladder, hoping to climb up to a rear window to rescue her. But by the time he reached the window the second story of the house caved downward into the first, carrying his wife with it.

By now neighbors had arrived upon the scene, and one of them rushed into the house and brought Mrs. Drummond out, badly burned and bruised from her fall but still alive and conscious. They took her to her daughter's home and summoned the doctor. It was two o'clock in the morning, and Belinda Drummond died at eight that evening.

As befitting a respectable lady, and according to the custom of the time, the county newspapers eulogized Belinda Drummond solemnly: "She was of a kindly disposition and was helpful in all civic and religious activities...a fine Christian lady popular throughout upper Accomack.... Mrs. Drummond will be greatly missed by everyone in the community." Among those who called at Avalon Bodley's home as her mother lay dying were "five old colored women" who came "to inquire of one whom they said they loved," for the community's respect was real, and transcended the racial barriers of that day.

Herbert Drummond's home was a total loss,[30] but his was hardly the only home in Belinda that has disappeared. Never a large place, the little village dwindled slowly away in the years following the death of its namesake. Today only a few houses remain, no post office, no distinguishing landmarks, only "Belinda Road" through an isolated and lonely part of the Shore.

Little Hell

If you live on the Eastern Shore you've probably been to Little Hell but just didn't know it. It's not much to see, but the story behind its name is one of the better tales from the lore of the Eastern Shore—and is just possibly true.

Little Hell is located on the main Bayside Road, exactly 2.8 miles below the intersection of the Onancock-Cashville road and the road to Savageville, exactly 1.5 miles above the Pungoteague Elementary School. It has no sign, no store, no landmarks, just three small and unremarkable houses, all of them on the west side of the road. Between the largest house (27488 Bobtown Road) and the road itself there once stood a fourth house. In the late nineteenth century this fourth house, long since gone, was a tavern, and it was the site of the incident that gave Little Hell its name.

An old black preacher, so the story goes, had to pass that way regularly between his two churches in Onancock and Pungoteague. A man widely known for his sanctimoniousness, never one to miss an opportunity to try to convert a sinner, the preacher almost always let it be known that he disapproved of the riotous goings-on that were usually issuing forth from the tavern whenever he passed by.

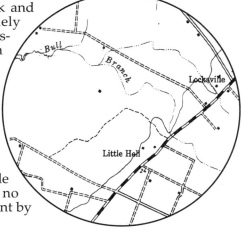

One day the tavern clientele could take his criticisms no longer, and as the preacher went by they invited him in—forcibly.

"Drink with us," they offered, but he refused. So they bodily held him and poured liquor down his throat.

"Dance with us," they insisted, and he would not. So one of them pulled out a gun and shot bullets on the floor at his feet until he "danced" to escape them.

"Sing with us," they commanded, and he refused. So one of them twisted his arm behind his back and he "sang" to keep it from being broken.

Then they let him go, safe and sound but not a little shaken.

When he arrived at his church in Onancock he preached an unusually forceful sermon, with more than the usual hellfire and brimstone. In it he told his flock about his experience. "I don't know what Hell is like," he added, "but I sure have been to Little Hell!"[31]

Is it just a story, or did it actually happen? At least one detail of the story rings true. There are indeed black churches in Onancock and

Little Hell

Pungoteague, both of them African Methodist Episcopal (AME), Bethel and St. Paul's respectively. And for some years in the late 1800s and early 1900s these two churches were on the same "circuit" and shared the same pastor.[32] Thus it is a fact that week after week, year after year, an African American Methodist minister would have had to pass this way as he made his rounds from one church to the other.

As for who is the hero of this story, let it be noted: both of the preacher's two churches are still alive and well today. Of the infamous tavern at Little Hell, only the name remains.

Luna Park

When W. D. Caldwell arrived in Onancock from Chicago in the spring of 1906, it was with enough fanfare to gain the notice of the town's newspaper. Caldwell settled his family into a large house belonging to Henry Crockett overlooking the town wharf from the north bank of Onancock Creek. And in June the *Accomack News* observed that "W. D. Caldwell...is making extensive improvements...preparing to entertain quite a number of expected city guests."[33]

For the next two years Caldwell was very much in the local news, and very much visited by very many guests. For he turned his extensively improved home into "Luna Park," Onancock's own amusement park.

Luna Park opened during the first week of July 1906 and for the next four months operated every day except Sunday from 2:00 in the afternoon until 10:00 at night. The first "entertainment" offered at Luna Park was "box ball," a "genteel, lively amusement for ladies and gentlemen and older boys and girls. Each player rolls three balls in an inning, and there are 10 innings in a game." At five cents a game the park was an immediate success. Within a matter of weeks prominent ladies of the town were including a visit to the park in the activities of their summer parties, and people were coming from miles around to sample the "nice shade, cool breezes, and novel entertainments at Luna Park."

Two Postcard Views of Luna Park

For two summers Luna Park was the "mecca to which all pleasure-seekers" flocked. The first customers were met at the Onancock Wharf by rowboats which conveyed them across the creek, but soon a "new and substantial ferry boat" was placed in use, and Caldwell was insisting that he would eventually build a footbridge to the wharf. By August 1906 guests could dance to the happy sound of the "orchestrian," a steam-operated instrument on the order of a calliope. By September the park could boast both a concert grand and a player piano, and a "Big Dance"—admission $1 per couple—was likely to feature an orchestra imported from Cape Charles or even further away. On the night of the "Tasley Fair Ball" in August as many as 75 couples crowded the dance floor. Labor Day featured picnics, boat races, tub races, fireworks, and booths that sold ice cream and soda water.[34]

The most popular item at Luna Park proved to be the roller skating rink which Caldwell opened in August. To promote its use he secured the services of "Professor" Kelley of Annapolis, who instructed the locals in the fine points of skating, free of charge. The following week he advertised the first of his several "Masked Carnivals," and offered prizes to the male and female skaters who wore the "best" and the "most comical" costumes. Over the next several weeks there were skaters dressed as Uncle Sam, Satan, Little Boy Blue, "Aunt Dinah," Irishmen, Dutchmen, and clowns. The winners of the prize for best female and male skaters on September 24 were "Indian Maiden" and "Russian Jew." The next Monday a greased pig was loosed on the rink, and younger skaters scampered to catch it.

The first season drew to a grand close on October 22, 1906, and among the large crowd in attendance was one lucky lady who walked away with the doorprize of a monkey. "Any amount of innocent amusement and pleasure has been derived from Luna Park since it was opened," lauded the *Accomack News*. "We predict another successful season for Mr. Caldwell next spring when he proposes to open again."[35]

Luna Park opened for its second season in late April 1907, and throughout the summer the amusements continued much as before: a "fun factory," more masked carnivals, a "mammoth fireworks display" on July 4th.

Luna Park,

Onancock, Va.

Soloists from Tangier will sing comic songs,

SATURDAY NIGHT.

September 29th.

Catching a Greased Pig.

Monday Night, Oct. 1st.

PRIZE—ONE PIG.

Male Quartette from Parksley will sing

Monday Night, Oct.. 1st.

This is a celebrated quartette for fine music and comic songs.

Accomack News, September 29, 1906

Labor Day began with a parade on roller skates, the skaters wearing "comical hats made of paper." The *News* urged patrons to break all previous records by turning out in a crowd of 1,000.

But Caldwell and his amusement park were not long in Onancock. By the end of his first season he was already negotiating for another such establishment in Cambridge, Maryland. The second season appears not to have lasted as long as the first, and in early fall the park closed for good. It did not re-open in 1908, and in July of that year Caldwell left town—not for Cambridge but for New York (or perhaps for Mexico, the local papers differ in their reports). A tentative plan for continuing the skating rink under Frederick Pryor did not materialize. In August, Henry Crockett placed an advertisement in the local papers attempting to sell the remaining equipment: a "gas light plant used for lighting grounds around Luna Park," "a complete Box Ball Alley and equipment," 250 pairs of roller skates, "some never been used."[36]

Eventually Crockett moved back into his house, which stood for years afterwards, fully visible from the wharf. Long after the house had disappeared the site was remembered as "Luna Park," and many a local could point to it and speak with pleasure about the good times that had been experienced there.

The Pleasure Pier

If you had traveled to Chincoteague in the days before bridges joined the island to the mainland, if you had taken the train to Franklin City and boarded the steamer for the five-mile journey across the bay, you would probably have landed at the Railroad Dock, behind the restaurant at the foot of Church Street. And if you had come to Chincoteague for vacation or relaxation, as a number of people did in those days, chances are you would have noticed, as your boat was about to dock, the unusual pier that jutted into the bay just north of your landing. For like Atlantic City and Virginia Beach and other resorts larger and more famous, Chincoteague Island also, briefly, had its own amusement pier.

On May 13, 1905, S. Burton Dennis and Nathaniel S. Smith, Jr. opened a new business on a pier on the waterfront at 4153 Main Street, where an insurance company is located today. The site was owned by Smith's father, who lived at the corner of Main and Smith Street in a big house (now part of the Island Manor House) that enjoyed an unobstructed view of the bay, for in those days the water ventured, at high tide, almost up to Main Street itself. The new business was unlike any other in Chincoteague, and the islanders did not know quite what to call it: the "amusement palace," the "playhouse," the "entertainment hall." Mostly they called it simply "the Pier."

Chincoteague at the turn of the century was a town of many amusements: a dozen ice cream parlors, ten milk-shake stands, a race track, a merry-go-round, and an auditorium that hosted concerts, plays, and—a major form of entertainment in that day—speeches. As popular as these establishments were, none had as much to offer as

The Pleasure Pier

the new pier. At the end of the pier was a small playhouse, roofed but open on all sides, where minstrel shows and vaudeville played nightly. The pier itself served as a bowling alley, around which clustered food stands with "refreshments in abundance." But its crowning glory sat on the shore's edge near the street: a merry-go-round whose handsome wooden horses circled to the tune of a steam calliope.[37]

The pier was well into its second successful season when it was struck by fire on a Sunday night in July 1906. Flames spread from the playhouse towards the street, destroying everything above the pilings, sparing only the merry-go-round. The owners began rebuilding immediately, and in less than a month re-opened an enlarged and improved establishment. When the third season began, on May 18, 1907, they added a roller skating rink. By 1908, the fourth season, Smith and Dennis were offering not only plays, skating rink, merry-go-round, and refreshment stands, but also moving pictures, the first on record on the island. One of the last events of that season occurred in October when local Republicans used the pier to host a speech by former Congressman John S. Wise.[38]

In March 1909, Smith traveled to Philadelphia to book "songsters and vaudeville artists" for the pier. The entertainment season of that year opened not at the pier but just down the street at Redmen's Hall (where the Methodist parking lot is located today), when the two-act live comedy "Three Hats" played to "a large and enthusiastic audience" in April, starring local actors O. M. Jones, Asa Conant, and Alice Burton. The pier opened the following week with an orchestra from Philadelphia, and thereafter the acts changed almost nightly. In May players from Bloxom presented "Brookdale Farm," a "medley of action and fun," admission 15¢ to 35¢. The other performers of that season included pianist Professor Schemmerhon of Philadelphia, the Chincoteague Cornet Band, the singing and dancing Delmar Sisters, and a child duo known as the Hanges Sisters. When there was not live entertainment, there were moving pictures. "The entertainment

Concession Stand, Red Hills
Red Hills, on the mainland opposite Chincoteague, offered a beach, and was the Pleasure Pier's main competition

appeals to all who can enjoy a clean, wholesome and amusing hour of solid fun," commented the *Accomack News*, which assured the public that the comfort and pleasure of the patrons, especially that of women and children, was "uppermost in the minds of the management."[39]

Yet competition for the entertainment dollar remained keen in Chincoteague. Across the bay, on the shore just east of Signpost and in full view of Chincoteague itself, the summer crowds at Red Hills sometimes numbered as many as 3,000 a day, lured by something the island waterfront could not offer: a beach. Smith and Dennis moved their merry-go-round from the pier to Red Hills for the month of August 1908, then in 1909 leased Red Hills outright, offering merry-go-round and movies to crowds larger than the pier could attract or accommodate. By that year there was new competition back on the island itself, where James T. Powell opened Chincoteague's, and the Eastern Shore of Virginia's, first movie theatre early in 1909.[40]

The pier's sixth and last season was brief. In March 1910 Smith and Dennis advertised the merry-go-round for sale—"good as new, a bargain for a hustler"—probably because they were dissolving their partnership. The pier opened on schedule on April 2, but thereafter all mention of it drops from the newspapers. That summer Dennis operated the merry-go-round not at the pier but at Red Hills. That fall he brought "Madam Mora, Queen of Clairvoyants," to the island, who performed not at the pier but at his home. In April 1911, Smith's parents sold the waterfront where the pier was located to William C. Bunting for $1,500. For a number of years afterward Dennis continued to operate the merry-go-round and moving pictures, but never again in partnership with Smith and never again at the pier.[41]

Today no sign of the pier remains. In fact, the site is now dry ground, occupied by a number of buildings, for here as in many other places on the island the land west of Main Street has been built up artificially over the years. A warm night no longer brings the sounds of orchestra or calliope, and it is hard to imagine of a site so prosaic that it could once be said: "If you were in Philadelphia, you would be eager to drop in and see the same pictures and artists that are nightly exhibited at Dennis & Smith Pier."[42]

Alive and Well and Living in Maryland

Just north of Locustville there once stood a handsome old house of the late 1700s with the unusual name of "Shabby Hall."

The story goes that in this house there once lived a handsome bachelor who went to Baltimore in search of a wife. There he wooed a pretty girl with talk of his southern plantation, married her in a whirlwind courtship, and brought her to Locustville. Upon first seeing her new home his bride remarked, "Southern plantation, humph! Shabby Hall!" And the name stuck, even though they lived there happily the rest of their lives.[43]

Shabby Hall
in its original location in Locustville (top);
in its new location in Maryland (bottom)

For many years Shabby Hall stood vacant and falling into ruin, but today it is handsomely restored, and once again a home. However, to see it one needs to travel over a hundred miles from Locustville, across Chesapeake Bay to Calvert County, Maryland. For it is one of several old houses from the Eastern Shore of Virginia that were rescued by being relocated.

Perry B. Van Vleck (1912-1986) was by vocation a builder and by avocation an *aficianado* of old homes. Over the years he built thousands of new houses in and around Washington, D.C., but he himself lived in an old house which he had restored, and he enjoyed purchasing and restoring other old houses. Because of his intervention, a number of old Eastern Shore homes that would undoubtedly have fallen completely into ruin are still standing today.

Van Vleck had already accomplished several restorations when, on a trip up the Virginia Shore in the early 1970s, he was struck by the number of abandoned old houses that could be seen from Route 13. "You know," he said to his wife, "I could move those houses, if people would sell them." Within a matter of weeks realtor Johna Davis had found five such houses for him, and Van Vleck bought four.[44]

Thus began the long and curious journey of some of the old houses of the Eastern Shore of Virginia to new locations on the Western Shore of Maryland.

The first to make the trip was "Gargaphia Savannah" (a name supplied by Van Vleck, not to be confused with an earlier house that once stood nearby). Built by the Bundick family in the late 1700s, it was, when Van Vleck found it, standing vacant and abandoned on the east side of Route 13 at Littleton Road, between Gargatha and Nelsonia. He had the house cut into large sections and hauled away, and by September 1971 it was being reassembled on a new site near Huntingtown, Maryland.[45]

Shortly thereafter its neighbor became Shabby Hall, reassembled right next door. Both houses were relocated through a process Van Vleck called "flaking": the main beams holding the house together were sawn apart, and the house was disassembled in large pieces, its facades intact.

Van Vleck's most ambitious restoration project was Lower Marlboro Towne, an entire community of 18th century homes, gathered from various parts of the region, relocated and restored on a lovely site overlooking the Patuxent River. The first house to rise in the new "towne" he moved overland from Upper Marlboro, Maryland, seventeen miles away. The second came not by land but by water, from over 200 miles away in Willis Wharf, Virginia.[46]

The Willis Wharf house, known by generations of Eastern Shore folk who had lived there as "Sunnyside," was the original old house around which the village of Willis Wharf grew up. The earliest part of it was built by Arthur Downing in 1743, when the neighborhood was known as Downing's Wharf. Zerobabel Downing built the second section in 1762, and Edmond Downing the third in 1795. By the late 19th century Sunnyside was the home of Henry Clay Johnson, Grover Cleveland's sometime chauffeur. Johnson's house sat on a rise facing the waterfront at the end of Terry Lane, but in time other buildings sprang up in front of it. As the modern village of Willis Wharf took shape, the old house that was its nucleus fell into disuse. In the early 1970s Perry Van Vleck found it, and determined to rescue it.[47]

On September 30, 1971, the big old house—it totaled 85 feet in

Sunnyside traveled over 200 miles by barge (top) to its new location in Maryland (bottom)

length—was loaded on a barge, and began its long journey. Powered by the tugboat *Rebel Steele*, which was small enough to fit into just one of the big house's three sections, it was floated down Parting Creek, into the channel behind the Barrier Islands, through the Great Machipongo Inlet and out into the Atlantic. The house had just rounded Cape Charles when Hurricane Ginger blew up the coast, so to protect it the movers pumped water into the barge and sank it in shallow waters near Smith Island, the house itself jacked up just above the water. Ginger passed lightly by, and once the barge was refloated, the rest of the passage up the Bay and into the Patuxent was uneventful. The house was landed at Lower Marlboro in mid-October, the only damage to it the loss of three shingles from the roof.[48] There it was restored and renamed, appropriately, "Willis Wharf."

Soon another Eastern Shore of Virginia house was relocated almost in sight of it. The "Edmond's Place" had, until then, stood at the southeast corner of Edmunds and Alexine Streets in Painter. Built about 1797, it had already been stripped of some of its interior paneling when Van Vleck bought it, but it still had its original siding, shutters, mantel, and doors over two inches thick.[49] Van Vleck dismantled both the frame section and its two brick ends, and had it all reassembled just behind Willis Wharf. It is known today as "Edmond's Choice."

There are four Eastern Shore houses that stand today in Calvert County, but Eastern Shore folk remember that Van Vleck took a total of six old buildings from the two counties. He also purchased the "Northam Place," which stood on Route 13 north of Accomac, and an old house from the Downing property on Red Hill Road south of Keller. Though these houses, also, were dismantled and removed, they are nowhere to be seen today in their old identities. It seems likely that they have been incorporated into other structures, for Van Vleck would often "dismantle an old building just to get materials."

At the back of Edmond's Choice he erected a gambrel-roof addition which was not a part of the original structure, no doubt part of some other old house, and it seems likely that these two other houses from the Eastern Shore were used in other structures.

For each of the houses that he moved to Calvert County, Van Vleck paid an average of $1,000 to $1,500, and to move them cost him about $25,000 each. Once restored, the homes became luxury properties—Willis Wharf was offered for sale at $299,000 in 1986—but Van Vleck always insisted that the restorations were principally "a labor of love," given the "time, personal effort, and money invested in them."[50]

For those who lament the disappearance from the scene of the old landmarks of the Shore, a trip to Calvert County may be reassuring. There, at 981 and 951 Bowie Shop Road, one can see the restored Gargaphia Savannah and Shabby Hall. Edmond's Choice stands several miles away in Lower Marlboro, at 3920 Chaneyville Road, just around the corner from Willis Wharf at 4000 Chaneyville Road.

These old houses may be a long way from the Eastern Shore, but thanks to Van Vleck they are once again exactly what they were always intended to be: "home."

Part of Edmond's Place in Painter (above) became Edmund's Choice (left) when it was moved to Maryland

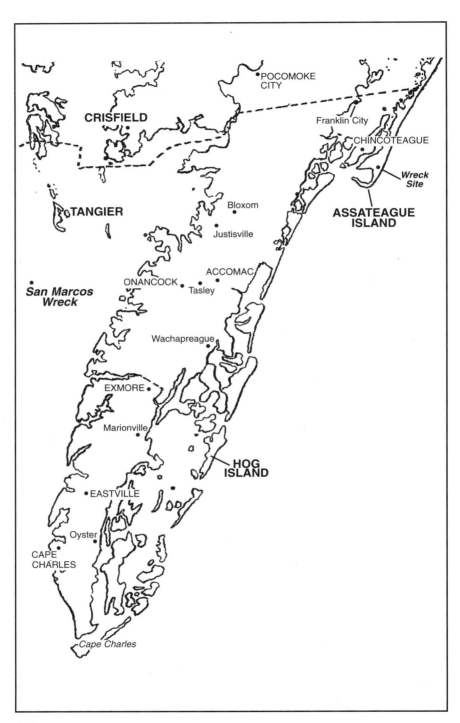

POCOMOKE
CITY

CRISFIELD

Franklin City

CHINCOTEAGUE

*Wreck
Site*

TANGIER

Bloxom

Justisville

ASSATEAGUE
ISLAND

ACCOMAC

ONANCOCK

Tasley

*San Marcos
Wreck*

Wachapreague

EXMORE

Marionville

HOG
ISLAND

EASTVILLE

Oyster

CAPE
CHARLES

Cape Charles

152

9

As the World Watches
Brief Moments in the Limelight

The Wreck of the Despatch

The weather was foul and the seas "disagreeable and dangerous" when the *Despatch* steamed out of New York, yet by early morning of the following day the ship had traveled as far south as the Virginia end of Assateague Island. There the officer on duty, mistaking the beam of the Assateague Lighthouse for that of the Winter Quarter Shoals Lightship, miscalculated that the vessel was miles further off the coast than it was. At 3:00 a.m. on Saturday, October 10, 1891, the *Despatch* ran aground on a sand bar about 75 yards off the beach of Assateague Island, and began to break into pieces.

Many a ship had met its demise in these waters, but few came to that end amid such publicity. The *Despatch* was no obscure vessel but the Presidential yacht, on its way to Washington, D.C., where it was to take on board the President of the United States and members of his Cabinet.[1]

Like many other vessels of that day, the *Despatch* was a steamship rigged with the sails of a schooner. Built in 1874, it was 174 feet long, over 25 feet wide, and said to be the "largest and most handsome yacht afloat." During its years of service to five Presidents—Hayes, Garfield, Arthur, Cleveland, and Harrison—it had hosted not only American officials and celebrities but also a British duke, the Emperor of Brazil, and the King and Queen of Hawaii. Its furnishings were elegant and included china and silverware said to have cost $30,000. Even its two life-boats were renowned, one used in the Arctic expeditions of A. W. Greeley, the other named for Queen Kapilolani of Hawaii, who was one of the first dignitaries to sail on the ship.[2]

The ship had a crew of almost eighty, most of whom were asleep when it went aground. Though "each man expected that in a short time...he would be left choking in the breakers," there was no panic as the disciplined procedures of the U.S. Navy clicked into gear. The anchor was lowered, stress flares fired, and the ship's single cannon discharged three times. Shortly from down the beach came an

The *Despatch*

answering signal—a patrolman from the Assateague Beach Life
Saving Station had seen the flare, and help was coming!

By the time the patrolman was able to report the wreck to the station, and Capt. James Tracy and his crew were able to drag their rescue boat more than two miles across the marshes and the beach, it was
5:00 a.m., and the ship's stern was under water, its bow looming
above the angry surf. It took Tracy and his men six hours and ten trips
out to the wreck to rescue the sailors; ten of the sailors got safely to
shore in the *Despatch*'s own whaleboat. Saved in addition to the entire
crew were a Maltese cat, two collies, and "Docksey," a small dog
owned by the Secretary of the Navy. The last to leave the ship was its
commanding officer, Lt. William S. Cowles. By 11:00 a.m. all hands
stood safely on shore, as pieces of the vessel and its contents came
crashing in on the surf: planks and moldings, a box of cigars, a can of
ham, tables and chairs, candles and boxes.[3]

Though safe, the crew of the *Despatch* were nonetheless in dire
straits. Most had escaped with little more than what they were wearing in their bunks, and were without food, clothing, medicines, and
necessities. At the site of the wreck (approximately where today's

road ends at the beach) half of the men made camp under a makeshift shelter improvised from sails and two life-boats. The other half, including the captain and most of the officers, were quartered at the Life Saving Station (on today's Pony Trail in the National Wildlife Refuge). The sailors held "want and wretchedness" at bay by retrieving anything that floated to shore, until Paymaster S. L. Heap was able to make arrangements with a merchant on Chincoteague Island, and an ox-cart full of provisions came lumbering across the sand from that direction.[4]

By late Saturday the word of the wreck had been telegraphed to Washington and Wall Street, and this corner of the Eastern Shore leapt quickly into the national limelight. From the Brooklyn Navy Yard sped the steamship *Atlanta* to retrieve the crew, and from Norfolk the wrecking tug *North America* to survey the damage and salvage whatever possible. From the big city newspapers came the reporters, hot on the trail of a good story. From Chincoteague and Assateague flocked the locals, most of them to see the sight, some of them hoping to "reap a rich harvest" of materials washed ashore, for centuries of maritime tradition allowed "wreckers" to keep what they could find or salvage from shipwrecks.[5]

The Wreck of the *Despatch*
Harper's Weekly, October 17, 1891

By Monday readers of the *Baltimore Sun, Richmond Dispatch, New York Herald,* and *New York Times* were following the events of the disaster on the Assateague shore. First on the scene may have been the reporter from the *Sun,* who was in Chincoteague by Sunday, but by Monday morning it was the reporter from the *Herald* who was out on the cold Assateague beach, interviewing sailors under their makeshift shelter. On Tuesday the *Herald* crowed that it was the first to interview Cowles, and that it alone had kept a correspondent in "the most inhospitable place on the Atlantic seaboard." For three days its reporter, unidentified by name, filed lengthy reports to New York, cataloging the hardships of the crew, the continuing destruction of the ship's hulk just offshore, and the frustrating delay in the arrival of the *Atlanta* (which meanwhile, unbeknownst to Chincoteague and Assateague, had been damaged by an explosion in its engines off the Delaware coast).[6]

The Sailors' Camp at the Wreck Site
New York Herald, October 14, 1891

The *Herald* was read not only in New York; it was also the second most popular newspaper in Chincoteague, and as they read about their island, the locals grumbled. The *Herald* described Assateague as "barren" and "desolate," even though the island had a number of inhabitants, a village, even a school. The Life Saving Station was "a ramshackle old building," though built as recently as 1875, and it was located in a "suicide-inspiring and desertion-prompting place" that was "only fit for a doghouse or a pony stable." As for the islanders themselves, they were strange and rustic, an "odd people" who spoke in "high pitched tones" and had only a generation ago "laughed at civilization."

Worst of all, the *Herald* described the people of Chincoteague and Assateague as "born wreckers" who thought "robbing the crew of the *Despatch* no offence" and had to be restrained from snatching what floated ashore. Unimpressed by the long tradition of "wrecking," the *Herald* insisted that the *Despatch* and its contents were U.S. government property that would have been stolen outright by the locals if not for the intervention of the sailors and the help of Capt. Tracy. Even so, reported the newspaper, one islander managed to sneak at night into the tent of one of the sailors and steal his rations. Another pulled abreast of the wreck in his boat to bargain with Cowles for the purchase of some of its equipment—even while the ship was going down, and the rescue of its sailors taking place.[7]

Chincoteaguers were quick to rebut such accusations, but had only the local weekly in which to do so. It was not until a full week after the wreck that the *Peninsula Enterprise* was able to inform its readers of the event. In that issue the Chincoteague correspondent noted that "since the disaster many reporters have appeared on the scene of action and some of them, notably some of the New York correspondents, have shown themselves the possessors of vivid imaginations. Assateague is not a barren island, as they reported, nor did the *Despatch* have to be guarded against Chincoteaguers, the same being a lie out of the whole cloth."[8] Yet the day after the *Enterprise* carried this rebuttal, the *Herald* produced an even lengthier article about "odd, old-fashioned Chincoteague" and its "uncouth and daring watermen."[9]

Meanwhile Cowles, though instructed by Washington to return his crew to New York by the *Atlanta*, grew increasingly concerned about the plight of his men as the wait for that ship lengthened. After scanning the horizon for the rescue ship one final time, he ordered the bugle sounded (it had washed ashore the previous day) and on Wednesday, October 14, the crew of the *Despatch* broke camp. With bare feet and trousers rolled up, they tromped single file across the marshes toward Chincoteague, caught a boat to that island, then marched through town singing "The Girl I Left Behind Me." A crowd gathered at the railroad wharf to watch as the men posed for photographs and offered last-minute speeches and cheers for Capt. Tracy and his Coast Guard crew. The steamer *Widgeon* whisked the men to the railroad at

Sailors of the *Despatch* at the Railroad Wharf prior to departing from Chincoteague

Franklin City, and that night—by which time the *Atlanta* had at last limped into Delaware Bay for repairs—they slept in naval barracks in Philadelphia.

Cowles and four others were left behind to guard all that had been salvaged from the *Despatch*: its small boats, the gilt eagle from the prow, flags, furniture, a life buoy, and a few blankets. They left for Washington by train on October 19.[10] By then the disaster, and the "inhospitable" islands, had received another burst of publicity in *Harper's Weekly*, one of the most popular publications of that era; still to come was yet another in the national monthly *Illustrated American*.[11]

Capt. James T. Tracy (1835-1925), the acknowledged hero of this event, served at the Life Saving Station for another five years after the wreck. A native of New York, he lived in retirement in Chincoteague and lies buried in the Redmen's Cemetery on Taylor Street. By the time of his death the Assateague Beach Life Saving Station had been replaced by a new Coast Guard Station on "the hook" at the southern end of the island.[12]

Despite the loss of his ship, Lt. William S. Cowles (1846-1923) went on to a highly successful career. A court-martial only weeks after the event ruled that his orders had been "safe and proper," and labeled the accident a result of the fact that the light on the Winter Quarter's Lightship "must have been entirely out, or was burning dimly." The following year Cowles was promoted to Lieutenant Commander, in 1902 to Captain, and in 1908 to Rear-Admiral. His advancement may have been aided by his excellent family connections: in 1895 he married Anna Roosevelt, whose brother Theodore became President in 1901.[13]

As for the *Despatch* itself, its demise was only slightly premature. The ship was "old and in much need of repairs," and its voyage from New York to Washington—to pick up President Benjamin Harrison and Secretary of the Navy Benjamin Tracy to convey them down the Potomac to witness a test in new naval armaments—was to have been its last one. It was slated then to be de-commissioned and sold.

Instead, its remains were sold at public auction in Washington on November 10, 1891, and several "parties" came to Assateague to view her before the sale. Except for some brass items valued at $165 that washed up on the beach in 1905, there is no record or memory of what happened to the rest of the ship's contents.[14] Its valuable silver and china, upon which presidents and kings had dined, were never recovered from the crashing surf at Assateague Island.

The "Battle of the Chesapeake"

In 1921 a war—a war of sorts—raged in the Chesapeake Bay, and while the country watched with interest, the Eastern Shore hardly even noticed.

The "war" was not between nations, but within the United States government, its adversaries two branches of the military, its cause the uses of air power. World War I had demonstrated the military possibilities of the airplane, but now the Army and the Navy were at loggerheads over whether and how to use it.

Foremost among the Army's advocates of the military usefulness of the airplane was General William "Billy" Mitchell (1879-1936). Colorful, vocal, and able to command the nation's headlines, he contended vigorously that the airplane could destroy any battleship, thus rendering the conventional Navy obsolete. So relentlessly did Mitchell pursue this idea in military circles and in the press that at last the government agreed to arrange an experiment to test his theory. The Navy was ordered to make ready a series of target ships and give Mitchell the chance to destroy them from air.[15] The tests were to be held in two locations: in the Atlantic off the coast of the Virginia capes, and in the middle of Chesapeake Bay.

The Navy was itself already an old hand at target practice in the Chesapeake. In 1911 the battleship *San Marcos*, which began life in 1895 as the *Texas*, was towed to a location a few miles southwest of Tangier Island. There, in a carefully orchestrated demonstration, it was reduced to rubble by shelling from the newer battleship *New Hampshire*.[16] Later a second ship, the *Indiana*, joined the *San Marcos* near Tangier as a target ship, and in 1920 as Mitchell's boasts became headline news, Captain (later Admiral) Chester Nimitz bombed it in a secret test for the Navy, using not live but "dummy" bombs. The Navy's announcement that this test on the *Indiana* proved the "improbability" of a battleship's being sunk from the air satisfied neither Mitchell nor the public, and did not forestall the "Battle of the Chesapeake."[17]

General Billy Mitchell

In February 1921, Mitchell and his crews, based at Langley Field in what is now Hampton, began making practice flights up and down the Chesapeake in preparation for the demonstration. The old *San Marcos* was again subjected to shelling, this time from the air. When hazy Chesapeake weather sometimes made it impossible for the Army flyers to orient themselves, Mitchell prevailed upon Lawrence Sperry to solve the problem. Sperry quickly created the "artificial horizon," a device that has aided aviation ever since.

The first phase of the "battle" began in the ocean off Cape Charles on June 21, 1921, when the targets were German ships captured during the war. The plan called for flyers to attack first a submarine, then work their way upwards through a destroyer and a cruiser to a battleship. On the first day the German submarine *U-117* was bombed by three waves of planes and immediately sunk. A month later it was the turn of a destroyer, the cruiser *Frankfurt,* and the battleship *Ostfriesland.* Though the giant *Ostfriesland* was supposedly unsinkable, it too, with the others, was quickly dispatched. The significance of its sinking was not lost on those who witnessed this demonstration. "A bomb has been fired that will be heard around the world," commented one bystander.[18]

In the month between these two tests, Mitchell and his crews continued their practice runs up and down the Chesapeake, and in late June two of his flyers, Captain Howard T. Douglas and a Lieutenant Plumb, died in a midair collision of their aircraft. Plumb's body was quickly recovered, but Douglas' was not found until two weeks later; it was then taken to Tangier and transferred to the authorities from there.

In September the second phase of the test opened in the Chesapeake, where the battleship *Alabama* had been moored not far from the *San Marcos.* On September 23, Mitchell watched from the motor launch Dodd as his flyers covered the ship with a smokescreen and then bombarded it with small phosphorus bombs and tear gas. At 11:00 p.m. there was a night attack, the first of its kind in the history of aviation, and this time 300-pound bombs struck the ship and set it afire. After each bombardment observers went aboard to survey the increasingly devastating damage. Finally on September 26, one-ton bombs were dropped from 2,500 feet, and within half an hour the *Alabama* was resting on the floor of the Chesapeake, it upper parts still visible.[19]

Though military and government officials were slow to understand the lesson, Mitchell had proved his point, and there in the bay southwest of Tangier opened a major chapter in the technology of modern warfare. Curiously, however, the Eastern Shore of Virginia seemed little aware that anything was happening. On September 30, the *Accomack News* of Onancock reported that "the battered hulk of what was once the proud battleship *Alabama* rocked gently in shallow water in Chesapeake Bay, off Tangier Island, today—victim of airships." This was the only notice of the "battle" in the local newspapers of Virginia's Eastern Shore, and it was from a national syndicated column, bearing the headline "Washington," not "Tangier."[20]

It was not only from the air and motor launch that Billy Mitchell saw the Eastern Shore. During the days when the *Alabama* was being shelled, he came ashore several times to Tangier. Islander Frank Dize (1914-1991) remembered him as "a very friendly man [who] passed out candy to the local kids."[21]

In 1924 the remains of the *Alabama* and the *Indiana* were sold for salvage and removed, but the old *San Marcos* proved immovable. Ownership of the *San Marcos* reverted to the government, and there off the coast of Tangier it sat for a number of years, resting on the bottom with its superstructure jutting above the surface of the water.

With the advent of World War II, the *San Marcos* was again used for

A Direct Hit on the *Alabama*

target practice, and shortly before the United States entered the war she claimed a victim of her own. The last steamboat to serve the Eastern Shore of Virginia was the freighter *Lexington*, still plying between Onancock and Baltimore. On March 27, 1940, the *Lexington* was pulling abreast of Tangier Island when she struck the hulk of the partially submerged wreck and sank, a total loss. Nor was the *Lexington* the last; two other shipwrecks, caused by the *San Marcos*, followed in 1948 and 1949. Built prior to the Spanish-American War, the *Texas/San Marcos* never sank a ship in battle, but managed to take down three vessels in the Chesapeake before it was finally reduced to further ruin and rendered harmless, a safe twenty feet beneath the surface of the bay, in 1959.

The *San Marcos* is still indicated on navigational charts of the bay, but the "battle" that happened around it in 1921 is little known or remembered on Virginia's Eastern Shore.[22]

The Graf Zeppelin
Makes Its American Debut

When commercial air passengers crossed the Atlantic Ocean for the first time, they traveled not by airplane but by dirigible. And the first place those first passengers saw when they reached this side of the Atlantic was Virginia's Eastern Shore.

On the morning of Thursday, October 11, 1928, the giant *Graf Zeppelin* left Friedrichshafen, Germany, turned south toward the Mediterranean, and sailed out over the Atlantic bound for New York. The *Graf Zeppelin*—"Graf" is German for "Count"—was named for Count Ferdinand Adolf August Heinrich von Zeppelin (1838-1917), inventor and pioneer of the rigid, lighter-than-air airship. It was 776 feet long, 100 feet in diameter, and capable of carrying a cargo of over 33,000 pounds at a cruising speed of between 59 and 68 miles per hour For its first transatlantic flight it carried high-value freight, 66,000 pieces of mail, and 20 passengers who expected to reach New York in a little more than three days.[23]

The world watched with interest and excitement. Newspapers carried daily reports of the zeppelin's progress, ships wired the mainland when they sighted it, and U.S. Navy radio stations as far south as Florida attempted to track is location. By Sunday, thousands of people hoping to see it had gathered outside of New York at the Naval Air Station in Lakehurst, N.J., where it was to dock. On Monday, by which time it was a day behind schedule, fully half the front page of the Norfolk Virginian-Pilot was devoted to the latest news about the *Graf Zeppelin*.[24]

While Americans waited on tiptoe, the airship's passengers enjoyed luxurious accommodations in their gondola beneath the giant balloon. The views were magnificent, the noise of flight mini-

The *Graf Zeppelin* in the US Navy Airship Hangar
Lakehurst, New Jersey

mal. There were private staterooms, and elegant public rooms fitted with large windows set at angles so that they could watch the world pass below them from their easy chairs. The dining room rivaled that of an ocean liner, with monogrammed china and silverware, attentive service, a good wine list, and cuisine by a first-class chef.

Yet even the passengers began to grow weary as the ship's progress across the ocean turned out to be slower than expected. Dr. Hugh Eckner, the ship's commander, avoided the more adverse winds of the direct northern route and steered a longer, more southerly route over Madeira and Bermuda. Even there adverse winds slowed the vessel down to as little as 35 miles per hour, and the vessel once had to slow its speed for repairs to a damaged stabilizer. By Saturday morning the *Graf Zeppelin* was still 1,800 miles out at sea. The Sunday newspapers, in giving her location, placed her closer to Bermuda than America.

The Monday newspapers, less clear about her location because of an intervening break in communication, speculated that the food supply in the gondola was diminishing, that "plainer foodstuffs were probably exhausted," and that passengers were facing the prospect of subsisting on champagne and caviar.[25] By then one person in the crowd of would-be witnesses at Lakehurst had dropped dead, victim of "heart shock incident to excitement." Thousands of others, after giving up on seeing the ship, abandoned their vigil, packed into their cars to head for home, and promptly created a massive traffic jam that left thousands sleeping in their cars overnight. By Saturday night Lakehurst's two restaurants were so besieged by stranded motorists that they had run out of food, and the canned goods supply in the town's grocery stores was almost depleted.[26]

When at last came "the flash that America has been awaiting," it was at 9:30 a.m. on the morning of Monday, October 15, and the news read: "*Graf Zeppelin* sighted off Cape Charles." The vessel at last made landfall in America at 10:15 a.m. on the Eastern Shore of Virginia about six miles north of the cape, then immediately turned north-northwest. The long-awaited first report of its arrival went out from the Coast Guard Station on Hog Island.

A few watchers, hoping to see the vessel, had been waiting at Virginia Beach. When the word spread that it had been sighted, schoolchildren were let out of class to try to catch a glimpse. But from that far south the *Graf Zeppelin* appeared so small that "she scarcely could have been picked up by the naked eye except by accident." J. Frank Newsome, an observer for the U.S. Weather Bureau, trained his "glass" upon the ship from further north at Cape Henry, and even from there, and with a full broadside view, he was unable to read the ship's markings, and could only conjecture that it was the *Graf Zeppelin* because he knew no other dirigible was scheduled to be in the area at that time.[27]

The first people in America to enjoy a full-fledged view of the *Graf Zeppelin* were residents of Virginia's Eastern Shore. "The *Graf Zeppelin*, of Germany, passed west of this place Monday morning," wrote the Hog Island correspondent to the *Eastern Shore News*. "The German Zeppelin 'Graf' passed over here...about 10:30 o'clock," came another calm report from Oyster. Marionville's correspondent was more enthusiastic: "It was a thrilling experience to get a fairly good view of the giant zeppelin as it flew over the Peninsula on Monday morning, and almost impossible to realize that a number of people were on board at that very time who had come all the way from Germany on this wonderful ship of the air."

From his home near Cape Charles nine-year-old Edwin Jacob could see the ropes that dangled from the vessel. Bernice Finley Sigreon was also nine when she saw it pass directly over her back yard in Tasley. It seemed, at that point, to be following the highway northward, but by the time it came into the view of E. Thomas Crowson in Justisville it was clearly following the straight path of the railroad tracks. In Cape Charles, Eastville, Exmore, Wachapreague, and Onancock people watched as the giant ship passed quietly up the peninsula. Yet, reported the *Eastern Shore News*, "while thousands of curious eyes searched eagerly for glimpses" of the vessel, "there were hundreds who were disappointed in not locating the great dirigible."[28]

Leaving Virginia, the zeppelin passed Crisfield at 11:18 a.m., then "sailed lazily out of sight." An hour later it paid a courtesy call on the nation's capital, where President Calvin Coolidge left his desk and stepped outside to see it, while Mrs. Coolidge viewed it with friends from the roof of the White House. (The vessel also managed somehow to drop a mailbag, by mistake, into a Washington schoolyard, where it was found by a student and whisked on its way by more down-to-earth transportation.) From there it moved up the coast, passing over Baltimore, Wilmington, Philadelphia, and Trenton. After overshooting its destination to make a brief circling flight over New York City, the *Graf Zeppelin* docked safely at Lakehurst at 5:38 p.m. on Monday, eight hours after making landfall on the Eastern Shore. It had been in the air 111 hours and 44 minutes; the trip that was to have taken three days had consumed four and a half.[29]

With this journey, transatlantic passenger flight service was born. Though the *Graf Zeppelin*'s crossing was much slower than anticipated—another zeppelin, the *Los Angeles*, built in Germany and flown to the United States in 1924 without passengers or cargo, had taken only 81 hours to cross the ocean—it was even so at least 12 hours faster than the swiftest ocean liner then in operation. As for the airplane, transatlantic crossings were still a novelty. Lindbergh's famous solo flight from New York to Paris in May 1927 had taken only 33 hours 30 minutes, and when Clarence Chamberlain duplicated the achievement the following month he carried one passenger. Yet passenger service by airplane was still years away, and in the late 1920s the future of long-distance travel seemed to rest with the zeppelin. By 1935, the *Graf Zeppelin* had made 505 flights covering more than a million miles.

In 1936 a new and even larger zeppelin was launched for the passenger trade. The *Hindenburg* dwarfed the *Graf Zeppelin* at 804 feet long, 135 feet in diameter, a payload of 41,900 pounds, a cruising speed of 84 miles per hour, and a maximum range of 10,250 miles per flight. By the end of 1936, the *Hindenburg* had completed eight trips between Europe and America, carrying 3,530 passengers; eighteen further trips were scheduled for 1937.

On May 6, 1937, as the *Hindenburg* approached its dock at Lakehurst, a small burst of flame (its origin never fully explained) appeared on the upper part of the hull. The giant balloon exploded,

The Explosion of the *Hindenberg*

and in 32 seconds the airship went down in a mass of flames. Of the 61 people aboard—an unusually small number; only 36 were passengers, many of the rest were trainees for another zeppelin then under construction—thirty-six people died. It was a very public disaster, caught on film while a horrified radio reporter described it for his live audience.[30]

At the time of the *Hindenburg* disaster, the *Graf Zeppelin* was nearing the Canary Islands on a return flight from America, and once landed safely in Germany it was permanently grounded. It had completed 590 flights, flown 1,054,000 miles, and carried 13,100 passengers, but the passenger-carrying days of the zeppelin were over. The *Graf Zeppelin* ended its days as a museum exhibit in Frankfurt; the *Graf Zeppelin II*, still under construction when the *Hindenburg* burned, made only 30 test flights and was never used otherwise. Both vessels were reduced to scrap for salvage in the early part of World War II, and their hangars and construction facilities later destroyed by Allied bombing. When transatlantic passenger service became commonplace after the war, all flights were by airplane.[31]

Yet for a few years the zeppelin seemed to blaze the way for a new era in long-distance travel. And for a little over an hour in 1928 the residents of Virginia's Eastern Shore enjoyed an envious nation's first view of what seemed to be the future of commercial aviation.

An Elephant for Tangier

Toward the end of her life Vienna Crockett grew increasingly confused, a cause of great concern for her family and her many friends in the close-knit community of Tangier Island. One afternoon in the summer of 1977 she woke her husband Hobson from a nap to report that she had just seen an elephant walk past their house. Later that day Hobson Crockett called their son to report that "You're mother's gotten worse. Today she thought she saw an elephant."

Undoubtedly she did, her age and confusion notwithstanding. An elephant did walk past her house on Long Bridge Road on Friday, July 15, 1977, when for the first and only time in the island's history the circus came to Tangier.

Tangier's date with the circus was born in the mind of Stan Mulford, publicity manager for the Roberts Bros. Circus. Based in Sarasota, Florida, Roberts Bros. was a small circus, fairly new and in need of publicity. Mulford, of Norfolk, was aware that many big-city newspapers had a "love affair" with isolated Tangier Island, and would readily print any "copy" they could find about it. If, he reasoned, he could get the circus to the island, it would undoubtedly generate publicity and increase bookings. Mulford also had another more personal motive: he himself had always wanted to see Tangier.

Roberts Bros. wintered that year in North Carolina, and come summer would normally have headed straight north for the lucrative regions of rural Pennsylvania and New York State, but to justify the trip to Tangier, Mulford scouted out a route up the Delmarva Peninsula, the first for Roberts Bros. and the first for the Eastern Shore since the Hunt Bros. Circus had closed some years earlier. The week of July 10 found them scheduled for Chincoteague on Monday, Bloxom on Tuesday, and Cape Charles on Wednesday, and then three days were set aside for Tangier—one each for going and coming, and one for the show itself. With island Mayor Robert Thorne he arranged for two shows on Saturday, July 16, to benefit the local fire department's effort to build a proper firehouse.

The greatest challenge facing Mulford and his sponsors was, of course, how to get over to the island the equipment and personnel that constituted the circus: one 15,000-pound "big top" with seats, 3,570 pounds of electrical equipment and props, 30 performers and crew, two ponies, five dogs, and—most challenging of all—one 8-year-old elephant weighing 2,775 pounds. It was the elephant who presented the biggest problem and generated the most excitement. "Pasha"—Mulford had bestowed that name on her for the event; she was really named "Mona"—was not a permanent part of the circus, but rented for the season from a supplier of exotic animals in Oklahoma. Mulford, having recruited her, knew from his own experience that Mona/Pasha was "an escape artist;" she was also, he insisted, "nosey, no pun intended."

There were challenges on the island too. While the Homecoming Ground was available for the circus, the bridges to it were at that time limited to a two-ton capacity. "If the elephant [fell] through," predicted one islander, "they'd have a devil of a time getting him out of the salt mud, and that'd be it."

On Friday morning Freddie Pruitt's 65-foot crabbing boat *Anthony Kline* arrived at the Crisfield dock for what one local wag dubbed "the Great Chesapeake Bay Elephant Float." Equipment was loaded first, then the animals, and when her time came Pasha stepped somewhat

Roberts Bros.
CIRCUS
TANGIER ISLAND
Home Coming Grounds
SPONSOR: VOLUNTEER FIRE DEPT.

PERFORMANCE: 3:00 & 6:00
SATURDAY
JULY
16

nervously but calmly aboard—unlike the ponies Bullet and Flicka, who had to be lifted on. The waterborne circus train set out at 4:00 p.m., escorted by the Coast Guard cutter Highland Point. Pasha stood crossways in the *Anthony Kline*, one leg chained to either side, and with the help of Life Savers candies behaved quite well. The ponies rode over on the bow and two of the dogs in cages while the third, Tanya, roamed and barked excitedly.

The sight of an elephant juxtaposed against the afternoon sun and the flat Chesapeake gave pause to all who saw it. As spectators in Crisfield watched it fade into the distance, watermen returning from

Pasha Poses with Capt. Freddie Pruitt aboard the *Anthony Kline*

work stood in their boats in disbelief. And when, two hours later, the *Anthony Kline* pulled into Tangier harbor, the reception was unlike any other ever seen there: the harbor was alive with the small boats of excited youngsters, people viewed from windows and rooftops, and a solid phalanx of curious islanders crowded the County Dock and lined Main Ridge Road. As the circus crew unloaded the equipment into waiting trucks and vans, locals volunteered to help with the wheelbarrows. And when at last Pasha stepped ashore, a host of children swarmed around to accompany her down Main Ridge Road, past Vienna Crockett's house, and over the Long Bridge to the Homecoming Ground at the northern end of the air strip—a spontaneous "parade" like those that had once, but no longer by the 1970s, greeted the circus in hundreds of small American communities.

Once at the Homecoming Ground, dozens of island children watched as the crew erected the big (60' x 150') white tent and hurried to open the "midway." Soon the islanders were enjoying refreshments, concessions, pony rides, elephant rides, and a "moon walk," but not yet the performance under the big top, which was still almost 24 hours away. The crew, bereft of the trucks and the pile-drivers that they used on the mainland, worked for more than four hours to erect the tent, driving the stakes by hand into the sandy soil. By the time all

Pasha Arrives at the County Dock

was ready it was dark, and most of the crew, which usually slept in their own trailers, spent the night in the new Community Center; Mulford himself stretched out to sleep on the kitchen counter.

Saturday afternoon found the circus tent filled to capacity with an excited crowd, a great many of them children, some of them tourists from one of the daily boats, but not until 4:00, an hour behind schedule, did the ringmaster blow the opening whistle (some parts of the tent had been left at Crisfield, and had to be retrieved). The sights were such as had never before been seen on the island: Gabriel Flores on the trapeze and Rudolpho on the tightwire, Segunda the Magnificent on the Rolla Bolla, and Bob and Edna high above the center ring on roller skates. Bullet and Flicka performed as Earl's Military Ponies, and the dogs as the comic Bullfight Boxer Dogs with El Toreador. Mulford, the all-purpose advance man, served as Ringmaster in a tuxedo. There were jugglers and clowns, among them 76-year-old Max Bertel, a parrot who could sing "Rule, Brittania," and of course music and refreshments and souvenir stands. A second show, scheduled at 6:00 p.m. so that the island watermen could attend after a day's work, was also sold out.

At a time when Tangier's population was about 900, the circus tent, which held 1,200 people, was filled to capacity at both shows by people who had paid $1 (children) and $2 (adults). For Roberts Bros., which frequently played to a half-capacity crowd, the event was an unexpected financial windfall. And for once, the well-traveled circus crew was as impressed with the community where they performed as the community was with them. "Something out of a storybook," said circus member Cleo Miller. Edna, of Bob and Edna the aerialists, was from England, and was fascinated by the distinctive island accent. "Love," she asked Mulford, "where did you find all these Cornishmen?"

Sunday morning found the islanders getting ready for church as the circus crew packed up, took down the tent, and prepared to leave. With little fanfare and attention Pasha and her companions marched back to the county dock, where they were loaded aboard Homer Pruitt's *Bessie L*. The return trip was uneventful, except that Pasha was less cooperative in disembarking than before. A Maryland waterman is said to have arrived back at Crisfield that day somewhat in his cups, insisting that he must have been drinking too much because he thought he saw an elephant floating across Tangier Sound. Meanwhile the story of the circus' coming to Tangier had been picked up by the newswires of AP and UPI and televised on CBS News, and the newspaper clippings that eventually filled Mulford's scrapbook came from all over the country.

Today a fine modern firehouse stands at 16344 Main Ridge Road in Tangier, erected in part with some of the funds that came from sponsoring the circus. The fire engines inside are full-size, no longer the golf-cart-size engines once used by the firemen, and the bridges and roads of Tangier have long since been widened and strengthened to accommodate them. If Pasha ever returned to the island, the traditional circus parade through the town could now be had without fear of an elephant falling through into the water.

It could happen, for the Roberts Bros. Circus is still playing the small towns of the eastern seaboard. And Pasha is still alive and well at 33, dividing her time between her two homes in Florida and North Carolina.[32]

Pasha and Her Admirers Cross the Long Bridge

Notes

Notes to Chapter 1: Definitely Not Maryland

1 Charles B. Clark, ed., *The Eastern Shore of Maryland and Virginia* (New York: Lewis Historical Pub. Co. Inc., 1950), vol. 1, p. 192. Hulbert Footner, *Rivers of the Eastern Shore* (New York: Farrar & Rhinehart Inc., 1944), p. 27.

2 Clark, p. 202. Nathaniel C. Hale, *Virginia Venturer: A Historical Biography of William Claiborne, 1600-1677* (Richmond: Dietz Press, 1951), pp. 158, 187. Donald G. Shomette, *Pirates on the Chesapeake* (Centreville, Md.: Tidewater Publishers, 1985), p. 10. George Schaun, "Isle of Kent," *Chesapeake Bay Magazine* 11 #3 (July 1981), p. 42.

3 Clark, pp. 203-205. Footner, p. 27-30.

4 Footner, pp. 30-31.

5 Hale, p. 201-202.

6 Clark, p. 207.

7 Hale, p. 297.

8 Kirk Mariner, "The Eastern Shore of Virginia in 1608: Examining John Smith's Map," *Eastern Shore News*, 6 March 1991.

9 James R. Perry, *The Formation of a Society on Virginia's Eastern Shore, 1615-1655* (Chapel Hill: University of North Carolina Press, 1990), p. 31. Louis N. Whealton, *The Maryland and Virginia Boundary Controversy, 1668-1894* (New York: Albert J. Leon, 1897), p. 15. *Communication from the Governor of Virginia Transmitting Report of the Commissioners to Arbitrate the Boundary Line Between Virginia and Maryland* (Richmond: Senate Document XII, 1877), pp. 14, 26.

10 Perry, p. 35. Whealton, p. 14.

11 Whealton, pp. 15-16. Scarburgh's report of his "Expedition into Maryland" is reprinted in Ralph T. Whitelaw, *Virginia's Eastern Shore* (Richmond: Virginia Historical Society, 1951), pp. 1414-1418.

12 Whealton, pp. 18-19, 24.

13 This is the position taken in 1877 by James B. Beck of Kentucky, who dissented from the majority report of the commissioners appointed to arbitrate the boundary. Beck argued that in early deeds and local transactions what is today known as "Watkins' Point" was then known only as "Cedar Straits," that there is significant local evidence naming Janes Island as "Watkin's Point," and that the several instances in which the records refer to the "river Pocomoke within the limits of Virginia" are meaningless unless the east-of-the-river line continued westward to the Janes Island site. See *Communication from the Governor of Virginia*, pp. 24-25, 38, 40, 42-45, 49-50, 52-53.

14 *Communication from the Governor of Virginia*, p. 8. Russell Morrison et al., *On the Map: Maryland and the Chesapeake Bay* (Chestertown, Md.: Washington College, 1983), pp. 27-28.

15 Jenifer's map, in the Virginia Historical Society collection, is described in *Virginia Magazine of History and Biography* 87 #2 (April 1979), pp. 236-237.

16 Morrison, pp. 27, 70, 72. Even Thomas Jefferson perpetuated the Maryland version in a map of the state published in 1787. An official map of Virginia published in 1825 by the order of the legislature did not even indicate a boundary with Maryland on the Eastern Shore, although this same map did indicate Watkins' Point in Maryland, at the Janes Island location; see E. M. Sanchez-Saavedra, *A Description of the Country: Virginia's Cartographers and Their Maps, 1607-1881* (Richmond: Virginia State Library, 1975), p. 64. A folio of reproductions containing the "Nine-Sheet Map" accompanies this publication.

17 "Lieut. Michler's Report" in *Virginia House of Delegates,*

1859-60, Document #40 (Vol. 6), p. 16. Whealton, p. 36. Even though Michler "discovered" the WSW-ENE tilt of the boundary, Baltimore mapmaker Fielding Lucas Jr. had drawn it thusly as early as 1832; see Morrison, pp. 93-94.

18 Whealton, p. 44.

19 Beck in *Communication from the Governor of Virginia*, pp. 38, 40.

20 Quoted in James C. Mullikin, "The Separatist Movement and Related Problems," in Clark, vol. 1, p. 481.

21 Mullikin, pp. 454-457, 458-460, 463-466.

22 Mullikin, pp. 465-466. Edward Noble Vanlandigham, *Delaware and the Eastern Shore* (Philadelphia: J. B. Lippincott Co., 1922), pp. 27-28. There were no newspapers on the Eastern Shore of Virginia at this time, so it is difficult to determine what the citizens of Accomack and Northampton thought of the proposal, or even the extent to which they knew of it.

23 Mullikin, pp. 467-469, 471-472, 474-475, 476-480.

24 Mullikin, p. 481. *Richmond* [Va.] *Times-Dispatch*, 21 February 1962. *Eastern Shore News* [Accomac, Va.], 9 September 1992, 19 September 1992.

Notes to Chapter 2: Indians and Europeans

1 The estimate is John Pory's in 1621; see John Smith, *The Generall Histories of Virginia, New England, and the Summer Isles* (London: Michael Sparkes, 1624; Readex Microprint reproduction, 1966), p. 143.

2 The transhumant lifestyle of the Indians of Virginia is described in Helen Rountree's *Young Pocahontas in the Indian World* (Yorktown, Va.: J & R Graphic Services Inc., 1995), pp. 18-19.

3 Helen F. Rountree, *Pocahontas's People: The Powhatan Indians of Virginia Through Four Centuries* (Norman: University of Oklahoma Press, 1990), p. 11.

4 Helen F. Rountree, *The Powhatan Indians, Their Traditional Culture* (Norman: University of Oklahoma Press, 1989), p. 11. John R. Swanton, *The Indian Tribes of North America* (Washington: Smithsonian Institution Press, 1952), p. 67.

5 Jennings C. Wise, *Ye Kingdome of Accawmacke, or the Eastern Shore of Virginia in the Seventeenth Century* (Richmond: Bell Book & Stationery Co., 1911), p. 59. See also Susie Mae Jones, "Eastern Shore Indians," *Eastern Shore News* [Cape Charles, Va.], 8 December 1922.

6 Whitelaw, pp. 281, 189-290.

7 Smith, p. 142.

8 Christian F. Feest, "Nanticoke and Neighboring Tribes," in William C. Sturtevant, ed., *Handbook of North American Indians, Vol. 15: Northeast* (Washington: Smithsonian Institution, 1978), p. 248.

9 Rountree, *Powhatan Indians*, p. 9.

10 Whitelaw, pp. 18-19.

11 Whitelaw, pp. 880, 885, 1044, 1065. Swanton, p. 69.

12 James E. Mears, *Hacks Neck and Its People, Past and Present* (Chicago: Published privately by the author, 1937), p. 1.

13 Whitelaw, p. 950. Swanton, p. 67. *Accomack Orders 1663-1666*, p. 2.

14 C. A. Weslager, *The Nanticoke Indians, Past and Present* (Newark: University of Delaware Press, 1983), p. 25.

15 Wise, p. 112. Whitelaw, p. 1351. Reginald V. Truitt and Millard G. LesCallette, *Worcester County, Maryland's Arcadia* (Snow Hill, Md.: Worcester County Historical Society, 1977), p. 17.

16 Whitelaw, p. 1299. C. A. Weslager, "Indians of the Eastern Shore of Maryland in Virginia," in Clark, vol. 1, p. 66n. Smith's map suggests, but not conclusively, that the Indian village of Wighcocomoco was located in what is now Virginia; see Smith, facing p. 40. Feest places the village in Maryland, not Virginia.

17 Whitelaw, pp. 19-20.

18 Wise, pp. 63-64.

19 Francis Jennings, *The Invasion of America: Indians, Colonialism, and the Cant of Conquest* (New York: W. W. Norton & Co., 1975), pp. 21-22, 30.

20 Jennings, p. 23.

21 Whitelaw, p. 22.

22 Smith, p. 56.

23 Jennings, p. 23. Philip L. Barbour, ed., *The Complete Works of Captain John Smith* (Chapel Hill: University of North Carolina Press, 1986), vol. 1, p. 225.

24 Clifford M. Lewis and Albert J. Loomie, *The Spanish-Jesuit Mission in Virginia, 1570-1572* (Chapel Hill: University of North Carolina Press, 1953), p. 192.
25 Lewis and Loomie, p. 188.
26 Lewis and Loomie, pp. 16-17, 56.
27 Wise, pp. 9-10. Nora Miller Turman, *The Eastern Shore of Virginia, 1603-1964* (Onancock: Eastern Shore News Inc., 1964), pp. 1-2.
28 J. Douglas Deal III, *Race and Class in Colonial Virginia: Indians, Englishmen, and Africanson the Eastern Shore During the 17th Century* (New York: Garland Publishing Col, 1993), pp. 10, 80n.
29 Only Wise considers this possibility, see p. 9.
30 Smith, p. 56, 143. Wise, p. 53ff.
31 Smith, pp. 55-56, 142. In fact, Smith does not refer to the chief of the Accomacks as "the Laughing King" in this 1608 expedition, though his description seems to fit "the Laughing King" that others mention later. Not until 1621 is there a specific mention of "the Laughing King," in the same work by John Smith.
32 Deal, p. 81n. This important work (while still unpublished) was the first to contend that the identification of Debedeavon as "the Laughing King" is incorrect and without documentary evidence. The first published contention was contained in the "Chronicles" column on 18 May 1985, from which this account is taken. More recent research has confirmed the fallacy of the traditional identification; see Rountree, *Pocahontas's People*, pp. 124-126.
33 Whitelaw, pp. 612-699. Deal, p. 81n.
34 Thomas T. Upshur, "Eastern Shore History," *Virginia Magazine of History and Biography* 9 (1901), pp. 88-99 and 10 (1902), pp. 65-71; see esp. 9, p. 91. Upshur also theorizes that "the Laughing King"/Debedeavon may also have been the same individual as Okiawampe (Wachiwampe), whose will of 1657 is on record in Eastville. While this identification is chronologically feasible, it is without documentary evidence, and illustrates this author's tendency to merge Indian names and assign them to one person (see 9, p. 91).
35 Wise and Whitelaw rely heavily on Upshur's Indian information. Although not challenging the "Laughing King"/Debedeavon identification, Ames implies that it is suspect when she asserts that "the Laughing King" died earlier than the 1660s; see Susie M. Ames, *Studies of the Virginia Eastern Shore in the Seventeenth Century* (Richmond: Dietz Press, 1940), pp. 5-6. Weslager is also reluctant to accept this identification, noting that Upshur "regrettably does not document his sources" and that Wise's book, which drew heavily on Upshur, is "rich with Eastern Shore lore;" see C. A. Weslager, *The Accomac and Accohannock Indians from Early Relations* (Onancock: Eastern Shore of Virginia Historical Society, 1961), pp. 4-5.
36 Weslager, *Accomac and Accohannock Indians*, p. 25.
37 Samuel Shepherd, *The Statutes at Large of Virginia* (New York: Ames Press, 1970), vol. I, p. 167.
38 Whitelaw, pp. 217, 219-220, 287.
39 Ames, pp. 5-6. Deal, pp. 28-29.
40 Whitelaw, p. 291. Deal, p. 81n.
41 *Northampton Deed Book #4*, p. 35. See also *Deed Book #7*, pp. 7-8 for the will of Wachiwampe (Okiawampe), where he signs with a non-figural signature.
42 Feest, p. 245.
43 Whitelaw, p. 947. *Accomack Orders 1663-1669*, fol. 39. A photograph of Ekeeks' signature appears in Anne B. Nock, *Child of the Bay, Present and Future* (Norfolk: Hampton Roads Publishing Col, 1992), p. 24.
44 *Accomack Orders 1663-1666*, fol. 64.
45 *Accomack Orders 1663-1666*, fol. 45.
46 *Accomack Orders 1663-1666*, p. 22.
47 *Accomack Orders 1663-1666*, pp. 38, fol. 40, p. 42, fol. 57. For identification of these "great men" as Occohannocks see Rountree, *Pocahontas's People*, p. 126.
48 *Accomack Orders 1664-1666*, p. 38, fol. 40, p. 41, p. 42, fol. 57, fol. 64. For these and other variant English spellings of Debedeavon's name see E. T. Crowson, *Life as Revealed Through Early American Court Records* (Easley, S.C.: Southern Historical Press, 1981), pp. 30, 37, 41, 69; Deal, pp. 18, 19; Whitelaw, p. 684.
49 Whitelaw, p. 947.
50 Rountree, *Powhatan Indians*, p. 114.

51 Rountree, *Pocahontas's People*, p. 126.
52 Wise, vii. L. Floyd Nock III, *Drummondtown, "A One Horse Town": Accomac Court House, Virginia* (Verona, Va.: McClure Press, 1976), p. 5.
53 Kirk Mariner, *Revival's Children: A Religious History of Virginia's Eastern Shore* (Salisbury, Md.: Peninsula Press, 1979), p. 539. James Murray, *History of Pocomoke City, Formerly Newtown, from Its Origins to the Present Time* (Baltimore: Curry Clay & Co., 1883), p. 50.
54 Mariner, *Revival's Children*, p. 506. Whitelaw, pp. 18-19.
55 Mary Frances Carey, *The Messongo Trader: A Family History* (Melbourne, Fla.: Edward L. Trader, 1980), pp. 24-25.
56 Whitelaw, pp. 1351, 1363. Wise, p. 112. Swanton, p. 67. Mariner, *Revival's Children*, p. 321. For a recent assertion of the local tradition that the Indians inhabited the island, see Lillian Mears Rew, *Assateague and Chincoteague As I Remember Them* ([n.p.], 1985), pp. 56-57. Kirk Mariner, *Once Upon an Island: The History of Chincoteague* (New Church, Va.: Miona Publications, 1996), pp. 4-5.
57 Deal, pp. 16-17, 24-25.
58 Helen C. Rountree, "The Indians of Virginia: A Third Race in a Biracial State," in Walter L. Williams, ed., *Southeastern Indians Since the Removal Era* (Athens: University of Georgia Press, 1979), pp. 30-31.
59 *Northampton Order Book #35*, pp. 416-417.
60 Rountree, "Indians of Virginia: A Third Race," pp. 31-32. Rountree, *Pocahontas's People*, p. 203. Frances Bibbins Latimer, *The Register of Free Negroes, Northampton County, Virginia, 1853 to 1861* (Bowie, Md.: Heritage Books Inc., 1992), pp. 7, 11, 13, 15-17, 21, 23, 32, 43.
61 Whitelaw, pp. 284-286.

Notes to Chapter 3: A Cast of Characters (Part I)

1 *Accomack Wills 1788-1794*, p. 16. Stratton Nottingham, *Wills and Administrations of Accomack County, Virginia, 1663-1800* (Onancock: Published by the author, 1931), p. 289. "Records of Accomack County, Virginia, Relating to The Rev. Francis Makemie," *Journal of Presbyterian History* 4 (December 1907), p. 194.
2 Mariner, *Revival's Children*, pp. 7-8.
3 Boyd S. Schlenther, *The Life and Writings of Francis Makemie* (Philadelphia: Presbyterian Historical Society, 1971), pp. 115-128. Whitelaw, pp. 1257, 1278, 1287, 1293, 1294.
4 H. P. Ford, "Francis Makemie's Picture," *The Westminster*, 16 May 1908, p. 10.
5 I. Marshall Page, *Old Buckingham by the Sea on the Eastern Shore of Maryland* (Philadelphia: Westminster Press, 1936), p. 79.
6 Ford, p. 10.
7 *Who Was Who in America* (Chicago: A. N. Marquis Co., 1942), vol. I, p. 912. See also brochure published by the Philatelic Service of Ireland to accompany the Makemie issue, 1982, in the author's collection.
8 *Who Was Who in America*, vol. 2, p. 97. Correspondence with Ms. Mary Plummer of the Presbyterian Historical Society, 12 February 1986. Calder's statue is depicted in the frontispiece of Schlenther's biography.
9 Whitelaw, p. 1284. See also special issue of *Journal of Presbyterian History* 4 (December 1908), an entire number on the Makemie Monument.
10 Telephone interview with Sarah B. Smith of Charlottesville and Rev. William Plonk of Onancock, 24 February 1986.
11 Littleton Purnell Bowen, *The Days of Makemie, or The Vine Planted* (Philadelphia: Presbyterian Board of Publication, 1885), pp. 79-80, 521.
12 Thomas T. Upshur, widely quoted by other writers, states that Blackbeard was from Accomack County, p. 95. For Franktown as the pirate's birthplace, see the files of the late Ernest C. Hallman, in the author's collection, where this unsubstantiated statement is recorded, probably dating from the 1930s. Dave Horner, "Blackbeard's Territory," *The Commonwealth* 37 (January 1970), pp. 27, 95. Reginald V. Truitt, *Assateague... The "Place Apart"* (College Park, Md.: Center for Environmental and Estuarine Studies, University of Maryland, 1971), p. 25. Robert E. Trevillian III and Francis Carter, *Treasure on the Chesapeake Bay* (Glen Burnie, Md.: Spyglass Enterprises, 1983), p. 6.
13 Shomette, p. 192. "Edward Teach," *Encyclopedia Brittanica*, p. 855.

14   Encyclopedia Brittanica, p. 855. I have deduced that he
"ended up in Jamaica" as the best way to account for the variant assert that he was born in Jamaica, found in Daniel
Defoe(?), A General History of the Robberies and Murders of the
Most Notorious Pyrates (reprint of the 1724 edition by Garland
Publishing Inc., New York, 1972), p. 86. Hugh F. Rankin, The
Golden Age of Piracy (New York: Holt, Rinehart & Winston Inc.,
1969), p. 106.
15   Shomette, pp. 193-194.
16   Defoe, pp. 99-100. Frank Sherry, Raiders and Rebels: The
Golden Age of Piracy (New York: Hearst Marine Books, 1986),
p. 235. Charles A. Mills, Treasure Legends of Virginia (Nokesville,
Va.: Apple Cheeks Press, 1984, p.8.
17   Shomette, p. 195.
18   Defoe, pp. 65-67, 87-97. Shomette, pp. 196, 208-216.
19   Whitelaw, p. 780. Information on maps is taken from
Morrison, pp. 18-77; "known" maps refer to maps in this
work.
20   Shomette, pp. 191, 194. For description of "careening,"
see Lloyd Haynes Williams, Pirates of Colonial Virginia
(Richmond: Dietz Press, 1937), p. 10.
21   "The Defence of Warner Mifflin," in Hilda Justis, Life and
Ancestry of Warner Mifflin (Philadelphia: Ferris & Leach, 1905),
p. 78.
22   Whitelaw, pp. 1373-1374. Kenneth Carroll, "Quakerism
on the Eastern Shore of Virginia," Virginia Magazine of History
and Biography 74 #2 (April 1966), p. 187. Mariner, Revival's
Children, pp. 6-7.
23   "Defence of Warner Mifflin," pp. 78-80, 81-82, 85, 87, 91.
Justis, pp. 56, 139-140.
24   Kenneth Carroll, Quakerism on the Eastern Shore
(Baltimore: Maryland Historical Society, 1970), pp. 131-133,
135, 137.
25   "Defence of Warner Mifflin," p. 84. Justis, p. 60.
26   Justis, pp. 70, 114.
27   Carroll, Quakerism on the Eastern Shore, p. 139. Justis, pp.
68, 117-127, 142.
28   Justis, pp. 39, 143-144, 145-146, 148, 150-153, 155.
29   Dictionary of American Biography (New York: Charles
Scribner's Sons, 1933), vol. 6, p. 609. "Defence of Warner
Mifflin," pp. 94-95.
30   Justis, pp. 39, 68, 95, 167ff, 170ff, 173ff.
31   David Brion Davis, The Problem of Slavery in the Age of
Revolution, 1770-1823 (Ithaca, N.Y.: Cornell University Press,
1975), pp. 28, 101.
32   Justis, pp. 185-189, 198ff. "Defence of Warner Mifflin," pp.
81, 100.
33   Justis, pp. 42, 45, 46-56, 63, 64-65, 74-75, 162-164.
34   Justis, pp. 16, 18-19, 40, 74-75, 76.
35   William H. Williams, The Garden of American Methodism:
The Delmarva Peninsula, 1769-1820 (Wilmington, Del.:
Scholarly Resources Inc., 1984), pp. 143-144, quoting from
Thomas Coke, Extracts from the Journals of the Rev. Dr. Coke's
Five Visits to America (London: G. Whitefield, 1793), p. 18.
36   Charles W. Ferguson, Organizing to Beat the Devil
(Garden City, N.Y.: Doubleday & Co. Inc., 1971), p. 107.
Williams, p. 143.
37   Henry Boehm, Reminiscences, Historical and Biographical
(New York: Carlton & Porter, 1865), p. 91.
38   "...Many would rather hear him than the bishops."
Boehm, p. 91.
39   Warren Thomas Smith, Harry Hosier, Circuit Rider
(Nashville, Tenn.: Upper Room, 1981), pp. 19, 21-22.
40   Francis Asbury, The Journal and Letters of Francis Asbury,
Elmer T. Clark, ed. (Nashville, Tenn.: Abingdon Press, 1958), vol.
I, pp. 362, 403, 413.
41   Thomas Coke, "The Journal of Thomas Coke, Bishop of
the Methodist Episcopal Church," Arminian Magazine I
(1789), p. 244.
42   Coke, p. 287.
43   Mariner, Revival's Children, pp. 22, 352-355, 386-389, 455,
515-517.
44   Coke, pp. 288-289.
45   Frederick Norwood, The Story of American Methodism
(Nashville, Tenn.: Abingdon Press, 1974), p. 168.
46   Warren Thomas Smith, p. 36.
47   Willis J. King, "The Negro Membership of the (Former)
Methodist Church in the (New) United Methodist Church,"
Methodist History 7 #3 (April 1969), p. 33. David H. Bradley,

"Francis Asbury and the Development of African Churches in
America," Methodist History 10 #1 (October 1971), p. 21.
48   Williams, p. 143.
49   Warren Thomas Smith, pp. 57-60.
50   Norwood, pp. 170-171.
51   Mariner, Revival's Children, pp. 96-98, 516.
52   John W. A. Elliott, Unwritten History of Eastern Shore
Methodism (unpublished manuscript, c. 1885), pp. 82-84. This is
the only source that specifically identifies the working-class
Gunter as a blacksmith.
53   Stratton Nottingham, Marriage License Bonds of
Northampton County, Virginia, 1706-1854 (Baltimore:
Genealogical Publishing Co., 1974), p. 41. Northampton Will
Book #34, pp. 385-391, sale of Michael Matthews' estate.
"Trumpery"—an old term for "odds and ends."
54   Journal of the Quarterly Conference of the Accomack Circuit,
1804-1867, 22 February 1817, 20 March 1818, 5 March 1819,
29 June 1822, 5 July 1823, et passim.
55   Hungars Parish Vestry Book, 1812-1936, pp. 16-18.
Northampton Order Book #31, p. 534. Tamar Gunter made her
mark as her signature to a conveyance to W. C. Pitts, 18
February 1842.
56   Northampton Will Book #5, fol. 56-p. 58. Susan Stitt, The
Importance of the Glebe to the History of Hungars Episcopal
Church (unpaginated pamphlet issued by the church, [n.d.]).
Mariner, Revival's Children, p. 436. Whitelaw, p. 431.
57   Northampton County, Va., 1850 Census, p. 310, family
561. Northampton Order Book #40, pp. 28, 70, 221. Nottingham,
Marriage License Bonds, pp. 21, 50.
58   Journal of the Quarterly Conference, 3 July 1824. Archives
of the Diocese of Virginia (from correspondence of Vernon
Perdue Davis of Richmond, 20 August 1985). Hungars Vestry
Book, pp. 18-19, 31, 34. Addison was Gunter's neighbor, and
may have been the original link between the preacher and the
Vestry; see Northampton Deed Book #27, p. 565 and
Northampton Order Book #39, p. 426.
59   Robert Emory, History of the Discipline of the Methodist
Episcopal Church (New York: Lane & Tippett, 1845), pp. 139-
140. Hungars Vestry Book, pp. 18-19, 21.
60   Northampton Order Book #40, pp. 28, 70, 221. Norfolk,
Va., 1850 Census (12 September), family 347, p. 224, line 13,
reel 328. Northampton Orphans Accounts #4 (1842-1850), pp.
1-5, 73-75. Hungars Parish Register (1836-1895), pp. 11, 13.
61   Interview with Mrs. Margaret Mears Vass of "Salt
Works," Jamesville, Virginia, a descendant of Gunter and
owner of the Bible which he used while serving at Hungars.
Inventories & Accounts, 1770-1870, Box G & H, Document #36.
62   Elliott, pp. 82-83.
63   Archives of the Diocese of Virginia. Francis L. Hawks, A
Narrative of Events Connected with the Rise and Progress of the
Protestant Episcopal Church in Virginia (New York: Harper Bros.,
1836), pp. 172, 188, 197-267, 327.
64   Hawks, pp. 267, 302, 327. Hungars Vestry Book, pp. 32, 36-
38.
65   Hungars Vestry Book, pp. 34, 38, 77. Inventories & Accounts,
Box G & H, Document #2, #36.
66   Whitelaw, p. 432. Stitt, loc. cit.
67   Nora Miller Turman, St. James Church and St. George
Parish, 1763-1990 (Onancock: Eastern Shore Printers, 1990),
pp. 26-27.
68   Nora Miller Turman, "Trompe l'oeil in Accomac: St. James
Episcopal Church," Virginia Cavalcade 23 #4 (Spring 1974), pp.
8-9.
69   National Recorder [Drummondtown, Va.], 2 November
1860. Nock, Drummondtown, p. 330.
70   R. Lewis Wright, Artists in Virginia before 1900: An
Annotated Checklist (Charlottesville: University of Virginia
Press, 1983), p. 130.
71   Potts' Address is reprinted in virtual entirety by James E.
Mears in "The Shoreline," Eastern Shore News, 26 April - 17
May 1946.
72   Letter from Potts to Major Sherman, 10 July 1867, in
Records of the Bureau of Refugees, Freedmen, and Abandoned
Lands, Drummondtown and Eastville, Virginia. Record Group
105. Letters Received.
73   Turman, "Trompe l'oeil in Accomac," p. 9. Barry W. Miles
and Moody K. Miles III, Marriage Records of Accomack County,
Virginia, 1854-1895 (Bowie, Md.: Heritage Books, 1997), pp. 74,
267.

Notes to Chapter 4: The Late Unpleasantness: Stories of the Civil War

1 Susie M. Ames, "Federal Policy Towards the Eastern Shore of Virginia in 1861," *Virginia Magazine of History and Biography* 69 (October 1961), p. 45. Leonard W. Johnson, *Ebb and Flow: The History of the Virginia Tip of the Delmarva Peninsula, 1561-1892* (Verona, Va.: McClure Printing Co., 1982), p. 160. See Lockwood's instructions from Dix in *The War of the Rebellion: A Compilation of the Official Records of the Union and Confederate Armies* (Washington: Government Printing Office, 1881), Series I, volume 5, pp. 424-425.

2 *Official Records of the Union and Confederate Armies*, Series I, volume 5, pp. 431-433.

3 *Official Records*, Series I, volume 5, pp. 433-434.

4 *Official Records*, Series I, volume 5, p. 434. James E. Mears, "The Virginia Eastern Shore During the War of Secession" in "The Shoreline," *Eastern Shore News*, 3 March 1950.

5 A. A. Hoehling, *Thunder at Hampton Roads* (New York: Da Capo Press, 1993), p. 126.

6 Lester J. Cappon, "The Yankee Press in Virginia, 1861-1865," *William and Mary Quarterly*, 2nd Series, 15 (1935), p. 82.

7 William R. Plum, *The Military Telegraph during the Civil War in the United States* (Chicago: Jansen, McClurg & Co., 1882), vol. 2, p. 359. *Regimental Flag* [Drummondtown, Va.], 6 February 1862, quoted in James E. Mears, *The Virginia Eastern Shore in the War of Secession and in the Reconstruction Period* (unpublished typescript, 1957), p. 143.

8 *Regimental Flag*, 13 February 1862, quoted in Mears, *War of Secession*, p. 143. *Official Records*, Series III, vol. 3, pp. 972-974. Hoehling, p. 71.

9 Richard N. Current et al., *American History: A Survey* (New York: Alfred A. Knopf, 1963), p. 287.

10 Plum, p. 359.

11 Scholars disagree on the date of the completion of the line. Ivan Musicant, *Divided Waters: The Naval History of the Civil War* (New York: HarperCollins Pubs., 1995), implies that the line was completed on Saturday, March 8, and that Wool's report of the battle to Washington was "the first message sent over the new 'submarine' cable" (p. 155). Hoehling (pp. 10, 147) states that the line became operational at 4:00 p.m. on Sunday, March 9—a crucial difference when considered against the backdrop of events concerning the *Monitor* and the *Merrimac* at Hampton Roads. This account is based on Hoehling; Wool's telegram of March 8 may well have come through Cherrystone, but perhaps not yet, as Musicant asserts, through the "submarine" cable.

12 Eric Mills, *Chesapeake Bay in the Civil War* (Centreville, Md.: Tidewater Publishers, 1996), p. 98ff.

13 Hoehling, p. 126. Musicant, pp. 154-156.

14 Hoehling, p. 10. *Official Records*, Series I, vol. 9, pp. 21-22.

15 *Official Records*, Series I, vol. 5, p. 764; vol. 11, part 3, pp. 379-380.

16 *Official Records*, Series I, vol. 11, part 1, pp. 87-88; part 3, pp. 379-380.

17 *Regimental Flag*, 13 February 1862, quoted in Mears, *War of Secession*, pp. 144-145.

18 Mears, *War of Secession*, p. 145. Whitelaw, p. 1014.

19 Kirk Mariner, "John Yates Beall, Rebel Raider of the Chesapeake," *Eastern Shore News*, 6 April 1985. *Official Records*, Series I, vol. 27, part 3, p. 665; vol. 29, part 2, p. 16.

20 *Official Records*, Series I, vol. 33, pp. 231-232; vol. 51, part 1, pp. 1150-1151.

21 *Official Records*, Series I, vol. 40, part 3, pp. 221, 248, 251, 274; vol. 46, part 2, p. 174. Plum, pp. 132, 140-141, 260.

22 Plum, pp. 321-322, 326, 340, 345, 346, 373.

23 Robert deGast, *Lighthouses of the Chesapeake* (Baltimore: Johns Hopkins University Press, 1973), p. 143.

24 Daniel Bedinger Lucas (ed.), *Memoir of John Yates Beall* (Montreal, Que.: John Lovell, 1865), pp. 24-25.

25 Lucas, pp. 1, 4, 15, 17-18.

26 Mears, "The Shoreline," *Eastern Shore News*, 9 February 1951. Lucas, pp. 24-25.

27 *Official Records*, Series I, vol. 29, part 2, p. 10. Mears, "The Shoreline," 9 February 1951, 2 March 1951.

28 Lucas, pp. 25-27.

29 *Official Records*, Series I, vol. 29, part 2, p. 23.

30 Lucas, p. 27.

31 Lucas, p. 28.

32 *Official Records*, Series I, vol. 29, part 1, pp. 639-640.

33 Lucas, pp. 28-29.

34 Lucas, p. 29. Mears, "The Shoreline," 2 March 1951.

35 Lucas, pp. 31, 33ff.

36 Lucas, pp. 74-75, 78-87.

37 *Official Records*, Series I, vol. 46, p. 716.

38 *Official Records*, Series I, vol. 46, p. 715. *Official Records of the Union and Confederate Navies*, Series I, vol. 5, p. 512.

39 *Official Records [Armies]*, Series I, vol. 46, p. 710. *Official Records [Navies]*, Series I, vol. 5, p. 512.

40 *Official Records [Armies]*, Series I, vol. 46, p. 710. *Official Records [Navies]*, Series I, vol. 5, p. 512.

41 *Official Records [Navies]*, Series I, vol. 5, pp. 512-513.

42 *Official Records [Armies]*, Series I, vol. 46, pp. 710-711, 715.

43 *Official Records [Navies]*, Series I, vol. 5, pp. 514-515.

44 *Official Records [Armies]*, Series I, vol. 46, p. 723.

45 *Official Records [Navies]*, Series I, vol. 5, pp. 514-515.

46 *Official Records [Navies]*, Series I, vol. 5, pp. 515-516.

47 *Peninsula Enterprise*, 21 July 1894, 23 April 1964. Jean M. Mihalyka (ed.), *Marriages: Northampton County, Virginia, 1660/1-1854* (Bowie, Md.: Heritage Books, 1991), p. 133. Nora Miller Turman, *Marriage Records of Accomack County, Virginia, 1776-1854* (Bowie, Md.: Heritage Books, 1994), p. 327. Whitelaw, p. 888. See also correspondence of the Winder/Kerr family in the collection of the Eastern Shore Historical Society, Kerr Place, Onancock. Much of the Winder family information in this article was supplied by the late Doris Adler, who researched this correspondence.

48 A. Parker Barnes, *Pungoteague to Petersburg: Eastern Shore Soldiers, Volume II: The Civil War, 1858-1865* (Onley, Va.: Lee Howard Co., 1988), pp. 20-21, 25. Mears, "The Shoreline," 8 April 1949, 15 May 1952, 19 June 1952. Nock, *Drummondtown*, p. 240. *Official Records [Armies]*, Series I, vol. 51, part 2, pp. 241-242; Series II, vol. 4, p. 911; vol. 7, p. 519; vol. 8, p. 730.

49 William Best Hesseltine, *Civil War Prisons: A Study in War Psychology* (New York: Frederick Ungar Pub. Co., 1964), pp. 133ff, p. 152.

50 *Official Records [Armies]*, Series II, vol. 6, pp. 962, 965-966, 972-973, 976-977, 985, 996, 1000, 1015, 1017-1018, 1028, 1054-1055, 1125; vol. 7, pp. 56, 89, 181-182, 402-403, 420, 451, 473, 519, 624-625; vol. 8, p. 731.

51 *Official Records [Armies]*, Series II, vol. 8, pp. 461, 534-535, 796-797.

52 *Official Records [Armies]*, Series II, vol. 8, pp. 736, 784-792, 797.

53 *Official Records [Armies]*, Series II, vol. 8, pp. 730-736.

54 *Official Records [Armies*, Series II, vol. 8, pp. 782-783, 799, 814-815, 819-820, 887-888.

55 Hesseltine, p. 246.

56 *Northampton Chancery Cases 1860-1867. Accomack Inventory Book 1865-1869*, pp. 610-611.

57 *Peninsula Enterprise*, 23 April 1964. Richard B. Winder to Sarah Caroline Winder Kerr, correspondence of 15 February 1868 at Kerr Place.

Notes to Chapter 5: A Cast of Characters (Part 2)

1 Letter of George Douglas Watson to Wessie Nock Eason, 10 April 1909, in unpublished papers of Eason in the possession of the author.

2 Eva M. Watson, *Glimpses of the Life and Work of George Douglas Watson* (Cincinnati: God's Bible School and Revivalist, 1929), pp. 21-28, 31.

3 Watson, pp. 18, 33-34, 58, 67-72, 74-77, 114.

4 Letter of Watson to Eason, 10 April 1909.

5 Watson, pp. 81-84, 87-88, 94-96, 98, 100, 102-103, 105, 109-113, 116, 121.

6 Evangelist J. H. Hames quoted in Watson, p. 125.

7 *Journal of the Baltimore Conference [The Methodist Church]*, 1941, p. 141.

8 W. B. Judefind (ed.), *On Wings of Love* (Baltimore: Judefind Bros., 1902), *passim*.

9 W. B. Judefind et al. (eds.), *Exultant Praises* (Baltimore: Judefind Bros., 1910), *passim*.

10 Interview with Miss Nell Scott of Parksley, 21 February 1985.

11 *Journal of the Baltimore Conference (The Methodist Church)*, 1941, p. 142.

12 R. Pitcher Woodward, *On a Donkey's Hurricane Deck, A Tempestuous Voyage of Four Thousand and Ninety-Six Miles Across the American Continent on a Burro in 340 Days and 2 Hours*

(New York: I. H. Blanchard Co., 1902), p. 39.
13   Woodward, pp. 1-2, 8-10.
14   Woodward, pp. 27-28, 59-60, 102, 108, 123-124, 126, 129-130, 137, 154, 174, 179, 189, 193, 196, 220-221, 225, 232-233, 236, 239, 288, 304, 325, 328-329, 339, 350, 371ff, 408.
15   Woodward, pp. 44, 81, 209, 213, 313ff, 412-414.
16   Northampton Marriage Register #3, p. 39. Information supplied by Woodward's daughter, Mrs. Maybelle Kniffin, East Chester, New York.
17   Woodward, pp. viii, 416.
18   John Kobler, Ardent Spirits: The Rise and Fall of Prohibition (London: Michael Joseph, 1974), p. 150. Robert Lewis Taylor, Vessel of Wrath: The Life and Times of Carry Nation (New York: New American Library, 1966), pp. 94, 113-120.
19   Kobler, p. 147.
20   Kobler, pp. 151-152. Taylor, pp. 10, 131-132, 195ff, 210ff, 227-228, 230, 241-245, 256, 299-300, 311ff, 339-340, 360.
21   Accomack News [Onancock, Va.], 22 October 1910, 29 October 1910.
22   Accomack News, 29 October 1910. Peninsula Enterprise, 29 October 1910.
23   Accomack News, 5 November 1910. Peninsula Enterprise, 29 October 1910. Mariner, Once Upon an Island, p. 85.
24   Taylor, pp. 332-336, 358-361.
25   James E. Mears et al., The Temperance Movement on Virginia's Eastern Shore (Onancock: Eastern Shore News, 1966), pp. 77-78. Kobler, p. 146. Taylor, p. 122.
26   Mariner, Revival's Children, p. 183.
27   Taylor, p. 361.
28   Eastern Shore News, 3 April 1925, 10 April 1925. Peninsula Enterprise, 11 April 1925. The News estimated Sunday's crowd at over 6,000, the Enterprise at 2,500 with about 1,000-1,500 standing.
29   Kirk Mariner, Historical Origins of Contemporary American Evangelicalism (Washington, D.C.: unpublished doctoral thesis, Wesley Theological Seminary, 1979), pp. 31-33.
30   Eastern Shore News, 27 March 1925. Peninsula Enterprise, 11 April 1925.
31   Eastern Shore News, 3 April 1925, 10 April 1925.
32   Mariner, Historical Origins, p. 32-33. 35.
33   Eastern Shore News, 5 June 1926. Mariner, Revival's Children, p. 206.
34   Methodist Protestant Recorder [Baltimore, Md.] 3 #50 (22 July 1932), p. 3.
35   Mariner, Historical Origins, p.32.
36   Interview with Nora Miller Turman, whose reminiscences are used throughout this sketch on Johnson. Eastern Shore News, 20 July 1934.
37   Pete Daniel and Raymond Smock, A Talent for Detail: The Photographs of Miss Frances Benjamin Johnston, 1889-1910 (New York: Harmony Books, 1974), pp. 5-6, 11-13, 87, 95 et passim. Lincoln Kirstein, The Hampton Album (New York: Doubleday & Co. Inc., 1974), p. 55.
38   Daniel and Smock, p. 32. Henry Brock, Colonial Churches in Virginia (Richmond: Dale Press, 1930), pp. 26-29.
39   Daniel and Smock, pp. 27, 32. Kirstein, p. 50.
40   Kirstein, p. 54.
41   Some of Johnston's Eastern Shore photographs appear in H. Chandlee Forman's The Virginia Eastern Shore and Its British Origins (Easton, Md.: Eastern Shore Publishers Association, 1975) and in Nock, Drummondtown. Daniel and Smock, p. 34.
42   Howard Koch, The Panic Broadcast (Boston: Little Brown & Co., 1970), pp. 13-15.
43   Interview with U. Kerr Henderson of Accomack, 1988.
44   Eastern Shore News, 4 November 1938.
45   Eastern Shore News, 4 November 1938. Peninsula Enterprise, 4 November 1938.
46   Barbara Leaming, Orson Welles (New York: Viking Penguin Inc., 1983), pp. 159, 161.
47   Eastern Shore News, 4 November 1938.

Notes to Chapter 6: Presidential Visitations
1   Peninsula Enterpise, 15 November 1884, 29 November 1884.
2   Peninsula Enterprise, 29 November 1884.
3   Peninsula Enterprise, 11 April 1885, 18 April 1885. Justus D. Doenecke, The Presidencies of James A. Garfield and Chester A. Arthur (Lawrence: The Regents Press of Kansas, 1981), p. 80.

4   Peninsula Enterprise, an unidentified notice of May 1886 quoted in Mears, "The Shoreline," 26 September 1968.
5   Peninsula Enterprise, 20 October 1888, and 27 October 1888.
6   Peninsula Enterprise, 12 November 1892, 19 November 1892, 19 October 1988.
7   James Wharton, "Virginia's Drowned Village," Virginia Cavalcade 7 (Winter 1957), p. 9. Henry A. Fleckenstein, Jr., Southern Decoys of Virginia and the Carolinas (Exton, Pa.: Schiffer Pub. Ltd., 1983), pp. 143-144. John S. Wise, Recollections of Thirteen Presidents (New York: Doubleday &Page, 1906), pp. 172, 186.
8   Dennis Tilden Lynch, Grover Cleveland: A Man Four-Square (New York: Horace Liveright Inc., 1932), p. 420.
9   Peninsula Enterprise 26 November 1892, 10 December 1892.
10   Brooks Miles Barnes and Barry R. Truitt, Seashore Chronicles: Three Centuries of the Virginia Barrier Islands (Charlottesville: University Press of Virginia, 1997), p. 240 (n. 166).
11   Correspondence with Ethel Downing Mullaly, granddaughter of Johnston, 28 July 1987.
12   Eastern Shore News, 9 June 1960. Correspondence (1992) with C. E. "Duke" Doughty, citing reminiscences of Lloyd Thomas Doughty; see The Doughty Tree 1 #2 (June 1977), p. 13; 2 #4 (1978), p. 76.
13   Peninsula Enterprise, 3 June 1954, 19 July 1956.
14   Mears, "The Shoreline," 26 September 1968. Peninsula Enterprise, 9 November 1901. John S. Wise, p. 186.
15   Wharton, p. 9. Fleckenstein, p. 144. Mears, "The Shoreline," 7 July 1931.
16   Montcalm Oldham, Jr., later Clerk of Court for Accomack County, attended Cleveland's inauguration in 1885 and shook hands with the new President; see Eastern Shore news, 4 March 1987.
17   There were four Brittingham children unmarried in April 1892: John W., age 18; Mary Elizabeth, age 14; Grover Cleveland, and Edna, not yet 2 years old. The oldest of the Brittingham children, Edward J., was also unmarried at that time, but almost 30 years old and apparently not living with the family. Genealogical information furnished by Carolyn Jones of Pocomoke City, Md.
18   This paragraph based largely on an item in Peninsula Enterprise, 16 April 1892, which authenticates the Brittingham family tradition of the President's visit in several details.
19   The story of the meeting between President Benjamin Harrison and Grover Cleveland Brittingham is based largely on an address made at the Brittingham family reunion at Melbourne's Landing, Worcester County, Md., by Jim Bishop, Summer of 1982 and again in 1983. Taped version supplied by Carolyn Jones.
20   Genealogical information on the Brittingham family supplied by Carolyn Jones.
21   John S. Wise, p. 198.
22   Accomack News, 7 April 1916.
23   Edith Bolling Wilson, My Memoir (Indianapolis, Ind.: Bobbs-Merrill Co., 1938), pp. 96-98. Kirk Mariner, God's Island: The History of Tangier (New Church, Va.: Miona Publications, 1999), pp. 93-95.
24   Peninsula Enterprise, 9 November 1928, 20 August·1932. Washington Post, 17 August 1932. Mariner, God's Island, p. 110.
25   Peninsula Enterprise, 22 July 1933.
26   Northampton Times [Cape Charles, Va.], 25 April 1946. Eastern Shore News, 26 April 1946.
27   Northampton Times, 21 May 1953. Eastern Shore News, 21 May 1953. Peninsula Enterprise, 21 May 1953.
28   "George and Barbara Bush: When Virginia Went to War," The Virginian 11 #3 (May-June 1989), pp. 12-13. Walter Scott, "Personality Parade," Parade, 23 April 1989, p. 2. Mariner, Once Upon an Island, p. 130.

Notes to Chapter 7: A Little Murder, A Little Mayhem, and a Ghost or Two
1   Carolyn C. Jones, "The Dix Family of Bulbegger, Virginia" (unpublished typescript, [n.d.]), p. 1. Whitelaw, p. 1296.
2   Carolyn Jones, pp. 1-2.
3   Accomack Will Book 1846-1882, pp. 326-327.
4   Correspondence from Carolyn C. Jones and Mary Frances Carey 1 September 1988.
5   Carolyn Jones, p. 3. This account of the Dix murder is

drawn entirely from family traditions collected by Jones.

6 For "Buzzard's Roost," see Robert S. Burton, "Eastville's Historical Commercial Buildings" (unpublished typescript, 1975). Testimony at the inquest makes it clear that witnesses of the shooting were on the opposite side of the street from the old drugstore; see Norfolk Landmark, 30 March 1878.

7 Norfolk [Va.] Landmark, 30 March 1878.

8 Duelling was already illegal in Virginia in 1878. For a discussion on the end of the code duello, in which some Eastern Shoremen figured frequently and prominently, see Curtis Carroll Davis, "The Small Bang at Bangs," Virginia Cavalcade 11 #2 (Autumn 1961), pp. 4-9, and James T. Moore, "The Death of the Duel: The Code Duello in Readjuster Virginia, 1879-1883," Virginia Magazine of History and Biography 83 #3 (July 1975), pp. 250-276.

9 Norfolk Landmark, 18 May 1875.

10 Paul Brandon Barringer et al., University of Virginia: Its History, Influence, Equipment, and Characteristics (New York: Lewis Publishing Co., 1904), pp. 142-143. Peninsula Enterprise, 20 May 1899.

11 Norfolk Landmark, 30 March 1878, 25 April 1878.

12 Barringer, p. 143.

13 Peninsula Enterprise, 22 February 1935.

14 Whitelaw, p. 1078.

15 Eastern Shore News, 22 July 1982.

16 Mariner, Once Upon an Island, pp. 90-92. This account of the Hill-Freeman murders is drawn largely from the unpublished papers of Victoria Pruitt, in the collection of the Eastern Shore Public Library in Accomac. The Pruitt Papers include undated articles from Peninsula Enterprise. See also the souvenir history of Christ United Methodist Church distributed at the 155th anniversary celebration on 30 June 1984.

17 Mariner, Once Upon an Island, p. 92.

18 Peninsula Enterprise, 17 April 1920, 22 May 1920, 26 June 1920, 9 October 1920, 16 May 1931, 2 September 1949. Mariner, God's Island, pp. 103-103. The reminiscences of Ruth Wallace Clarke were invaluable in reconstructing this event.

19 Whitelaw, p. 1511.

20 Northampton Times, 13 September 1934.

21 Eastern Shore News, 24 July 1936. Mount Airy [N.C.] News, 23 July 1936, 12 November 1936. Northampton Times, 18 June 1936, 7 October 1936.

22 Eastern Shore News, 9 October 1936.

23 Eastern Shore Herald [Eastville, Va.], 25 July 1936. Eastern Shore News, 24 July 1936. Northampton Times, 23 July 1936. Mount Airy News, 7 October 1936.

24 Eastern Shore News, 24 July 1936. Northampton Times, 23 July 1936.

25 Mount Airy News, 30 July 1936, 22 May 1980. Northampton Times, 30 July 1936.

26 Northampton Times, 23 July 1936, 30 July 1936. Eastern Shore News, 24 July 1936, 31 July 1936. Mount Airy News, 30 July 1936, 20 August 1936.

27 Mount Airy News, 6 August 1936, 20 August 1936.

28 Northampton Times, 17 September 1936.

29 Mount Airy News, 7 October 1936, 12 November 1936.

30 Northampton Times, 15 October 1936.

31 Mount Airy News, 7 October 1936. Northampton Times, 8 October 1936.

32 Northampton Times, 15 October 1936.

33 Mount Airy News, 20 August 1936, 15 October 1936, 22 October 1936, 12 November 1936, 22 May 1980. Northampton Times, 15 October 1936. Eastern Shore News, 31 July 1936.

34 Richmond Times-Dispatch, 23 July 1936, 24 July 1936, 25 July 1936, 29 July 1936, 6 October 1936, 8 October 1936, 12 October 1936, 13 October 1936, 23 October 1936. Washington Post, 23 July 1936, 7 October 1936. Evening Herald & Express [Los Angeles, Ca.], 23 July 1936, 12 October 1936.

35 Richard Hirsch, "Postmarked for Prison: Behind the Scenes with the U.S. Postal Inspectors," True Detective 35 #5 (February 1941), pp. 56-59, 107-111.

36 Correspondence with Jim Lewis, Salisbury, Md., 8 March 1992.

37 Mount Airy News, 3 January 1992.

Notes to Chapter 8: Almost Forgotten: Little Places That Are No More

1 Nora Miller Turman and Gladys Lee Hamilton, "The Daughter of Francis Makemie," The Colonial Genealogist 12 #25-26 (1984), pp. 13, 17.

2 Whitelaw, pp. 1305-1306. 1310.

3 Katherine Scarborough, Homes of the Cavaliers (New York: Macmillan Co. 1930), p. 387. Truitt and LesCallette, p. 178.

4 Biographical Dictionary of the American Congress, 1774-1971 (Washington: Government Printing Office, 1971), pp. 848-849.

5 Accomack Wills 1807-1830, p. 170. Whitelaw, p. 1306.

6 Alan Palmer, An Encyclopaedia of Napoleon's Europe (New York: St. Martin's Press, 1984), p. 285.

7 Truitt & LesCallette, p. 306.

8 This and all other information in this sketch concerning the Wagram post office is from Claude A. Tull, "Wagram," Eastern Shore News, 7 February 1947.

9 Genealogical information supplied by Mary Frances Carey.

10 Accomack News, 28 February 1891.

11 Callahan's photographs have been reprinted in Julie V. Nordstrom, The Eastern Shore of Virginia in Days Past (Sarasota, Fla.: Serbin Printing Co., 1981), pp. 75-76.

12 Much of the information concerning the final days of Wagram is based upon the reminiscences of Algea C. Tull (1891-1987) of New Church.

13 See advertisement for Atlantic Female College in National Recorder, 2 November 1860. S. T. Ross, "Recollections of Onancock, 1850," Eastern Shore News, 3 July 1980.

14 Whitelaw, pp. 932-933.

15 Blanche Sydnor White, History of the Baptists on the Eastern Shore of Virginia, 1776-1959 (Baltimore: J. H. Furst Co., 1959), p. 32. Whitelaw, p. 932. Robert Williamson, A Brief History of the Origin and Progress of the Baptists on the Eastern Shore of Virginia (Baltimore: J. F. Weishampel, 1878), pp. 39, 61, 103. National Recorder, 2 November 1860.

16 "Old Atlantic Female College Book Found," Eastern Shore News, 4 February 1987.

17 Eastern Shore News, 1 February 1962, reprints the names and addresses of some of the students.

18 National Recorder, 2 November 1860.

19 National Recorder, 2 November 1860. Eastern Shore News, 1 February 1962.

20 Whitelaw, p. 725. Lucy Ames Edwards, Ames, Mears, and Allied Lines ([n.p.], 1967), p. 206. James E. Mears, "The Eastern Shore of Virginia in the Nineteenth and Twentieth Centuries," in Clark, vol. 2, p. 626n. Jean Merritt Mihalyka and Faye Downing Wilson, Graven Stones of Lower Accomack County, Virginia (Bowie, Md.: Heritage Books, 1986), p. 16.

21 Letter of George C. Tyler of Onancock to Gen. Benjamin F. Butler, 25 March 1864, in Mears, "The Shoreline," 5 July 1951.

22 Turman, Eastern Shore of Virginia, pp. 197-198. Lynn Ballard, "Education in Onancock," Eastern Shore News, 28 June 1973.

23 Whitelaw, p. 932. Ballard, loc. cit.

24 Whitelaw, pp. 179-180. Much of the information concerning the final days of the Boykin's school is based on the reminiscences of Elizabeth A. Waters of Cape Charles, supplied by Jean M. Mihalyka.

25 Northampton Deed Book #48, pp. 182, 183, 424, 440; #49, pp. 439, 483; #50, p. 39; #51, p. 237; #52, p. 289; #54, p. 110; #58, p. 237; #59, p. 155. Whitelaw, p. 180.

26 Constance P. Fox, "A History of Tidewater Institute," Eastern Shore News, 13 September 1986. See also Eastern Shore News, 17 September 1986.

27 Accomack Marriage Register #1-2, p. 4. This and other genealogical information supplied by Mary Frances Carey.

28 John Neely Mears, Miscellaneous Papers (unpublished folios and scrapbooks in the collection of the Eastern Shore Historical Society, Kerr Place, Onancock).

29 Accomack Marriage Register #3, p. 125. Eastern Shore News, 31 August 1934.

30 Eastern Shore News, 31 August 1934.

31 This story supplied by L. Floyd Nock III (1932-1997).

32 Mariner, Revival's Children, p. 574.

33 Accomack News, 9 June 1906.

34 Peninsula Enterprise, 7 July 1906, 4 August 1906. Accomack News, 4 August 1906.

35 Accomack News, 7 July 1906, 11 August 1906, 18 August

1906, 25 August 1906, 8 September 1906, 15 September 1906, 29 September 1906, 27 October 1906. *Peninsula Enterprise*, 11 August 1906, 8 September 1906, 22 September 1906.
36   *Accomack News*, 27 April 1907, 29 June 1907, 31 August 1907, 27 October 1907, 4 July 1908. *Peninsula Enterprise*, 15 August 1908.
37   *Peninsula Enterprise*, 13 May 1905. Mariner, *Once Upon an Island*, pp. 16, 85-86.
38   *Peninsula Enterprise*, 14 July 1906; 21 July 1906; 4 August 1906. *Accomack News*, 16 March 1907; 27 June 1908; 24 October 1908.
39   Rew, p. 47. *Accomack News*, 10 April 1909; 15 May 1909; 29 May 1909; 26 June 1909.
40   Mariner, *Once Upon an Island*, pp. 86-87. *Accomack News*, 8 August 1908. Kirk Mariner, "Sinnickson and Red Hills," *Eastern Shore News*, 22 January 1997.
41   *Accomack News*, 12 March 1910; 9 April 1910; 3 September 1910; 13 May 1911; 18 April 1914. *Accomack Deed Book #97*, p. 377.
42   *Accomack News*, 26 June 1909.
43   Whitelaw, p. 877.
44   Helen Henry, "Old Houses Moved to Live Again," *Baltimore Sun Magazine*, 9 February 1975, pp. 27-29.
45   James C. Wilfong, Jr., "Lower Marlboro Faces Major Changes," *The News Leader* [Laurel, Md.], 2 September 1971. The identification of the location of the house that Van Vleck called "Gargaphia Savannah" was supplied by William Samuel Phillips. Despite this use of that name, this house is not to be confused with the older "Gargaphia Savannah" described in Whitelaw, p. 1160.
46   Lee Flor, "Restoring Houses," *The Evening Star* [Washington, D.C.], 24 March 1972. Betty Briscoe, "Shabby Hall," *The Independent* [Prince Frederick, Md.], 3 October 1973. Wilfong, *loc cit.*
47   Paula Mask, "A Gallery of Historic Districts," *The Calvert Historian* 5 #1 (Spring 1990), p. 29. Correspondence of Ethel Downing Mullaly, Onancock, 21 August 1987.
48   *Calvert Independent*, 5 October 1971. *Calvert Independent* [Prince Frederick, Md.], 14 October 1971. Henry, p. 26.
49   Henry, p. 26. Mask, p. 33. Whitelaw, p. 597. Van Vleck dated the Edmond's Place at c. 1740, older than the 1797 date assigned by Whitelaw. Pierce Eichelberger remembers that interior paneling had been removed from the house prior to Van Vleck's purchase, even though Van Vleck (Henry, p. 26) reported that it still had its original paneling.
50   Whitelaw, pp. 1089-1090. Information about Van Vleck's purchased of the Northam Place supplied by L. Floyd Nock III, of the Edmond's Place by Pierce Eichelberger. Henry, p. 29. James C. Wilfong, Jr., "Edmonds Place," *Calvert Independent*, 18 October 1971 See advertisements of Anchor Properties Inc. in June 1986 issue of *Washingtonian Magazine*.

Notes to Chapter 9: As the World Watches: Brief Moments in the Limelight
1   *Baltimore Sun*, 12 October 1891, quoted in Joan Charles, *Mid-Atlantic Shipwreck Accounts to 1899* (Hampton, Va.: Published privately by the author, 1997), p. 96. *Peninsula Enterprise*, 14 November 1891. Strictly speaking, the *Despatch* was a yacht for the use of the Secretary of the Navy, yet it was also frequently put at the disposal of the President. Chester Alan Arthur "used the vessel as his private yacht during his Administration," see *New York Times*, 12 October 1891.
2   *New York Times*, 12 October 1891. George and Suzanne Hurley, *Shipwrecks and Rescues Along the Barrier Islands of Delaware, Maryland, and Virginia* (Norfolk, Va.: Donning Co. Publishers, 1984), p. 83. *Richmond* [Va.] *Dispatch*, 15 October 1891.
3   *Peninsula Enterprise*, 17 November 1891. *New York Herald*, 12 October 1891. *New York Times*, 12 October 1891. *Baltimore Sun*, 12 October 1891. Sources disagree about the size of the crew of the *Despatch*: 74 according to *Peninsula Enterprise*, 75 according to *New York Herald*, 79 according to Hurley, p. 81.
4   *New York Herald*, 12 October 1891. *Richmond Dispatch*, 15 October 191. For location of the Assateague Beach Life Saving Station, see Mariner, *Once Upon an Island*, p. 104.
5   *New York Times*, 11 October 1891. *New York Herald*, 12 October 1891; 13 October 1891. For "wrecking," see Barnes and Truitt, *Seashore Chronicles*, pp. 8, 10.

6   The *Sun's* report of Monday, 12 October, was undoubtedly written on Sunday, 11 October, since it states that the wreck occurred "yesterday," *i.e.*, Saturday, 10 October. *New York Herald*, 12 October 1891; 13 October 1891; 14 October 1891; 15 October 1891. Hurley, p. 81. Chincoteague Island had no telegraph until 1896, see Mariner, *Once Upon an Island*, p. 83. It can be deduced from some of these newspaper accounts that reporters sent their articles from Pocomoke City, Maryland, and from Georgetown and Lewes, Delaware. The *Herald* reporter states that he returned to Assateague over twenty miles of "miry road and tempestuous bay [from] the nearest telegraph station," probably at Pocomoke City; *New York Herald*, 13 October 1891.
7   *New York Herald*, 12 October 1891; 15 October 1891. Mariner, *Once Upon an Island*, pp. 65, 79, 90.
8   *Peninsula Enterprise*, 17 October 1891.
9   *New York Herald*, 18 October 1891.
10   *New York Herald*, 15 October 1891. *Peninsula Enterprise*, 24 October 1891.
11   Hurley, p. 82.
12   Mary Frances Carey, *Tombstone Inscriptions of Upper Accomack County, Virginia* (Bowie, Md.: Heritage Books Inc., 1995), p. 275. *Accomack News*, 20 May 1911. Mariner, *Once Upon an Island*, p. 104. Hurley, p. 74.
13   *National Cyclopaedia of American Biography* (New York: James T. White Co., 1933), vol. 23, pp. 116-117. *Who Was Who in America*, vol. 1, p. 267.
14   *New York Times*, 11 October 1891. *Peninsula Enterprise*, 14 November 1891. *Accomack Times*, 29 July 1905.
15   Burke Davis, *The Billy Mitchell Affair* (New York: Random House, 1967), p. 73.
16   Robert H. Burgess, *This Was Chesapeake Bay* (Cambridge, Md.: Cornell Maritime Press, Inc., 1963), pp. 26-27. Maurice Dukes, "The San Marcos Wreck," *Chesapeake Bay Magazine* 13 #7 (November 1983), p. 31.
17   Davis, *Billy Mitchell Affair*, p. 68.
18   Davis, pp. 80-81, 94, 97-101, 107-108, 111.
19   Davis, pp. 95, 124-125. *Accomack News*, 8 July 1921.
20   *Accomack News*, 30 September 1921.
21   E. Frank Dize, *Something Fishy from Tangier* ([n.p.], [n.d.]), p. 10.
22   Burgess, pp. 27-29. Duke, p. 31. A. Hughlett Mason, *History of Steam Navigation to the Eastern Shore of Virginia* (Richmond: Dietz Press, 1973), pp. 2, 40. Robert H. Burgess and H. Graham Wood, *Steamboats Out of Baltimore* (Cambridge, Md.: Tidewater Publishers, 1968), p. 146. Gary Gentile, *Shipwrecks of Virginia* (Philadelphia: Gary Gentile Productions, 1992), pp. 143ff. *Eastern Shore News*, 3 September 1959.
23   Christopher Chant, *The Zeppelin: The History of German Airships from 1900 to 1937* (New York: Barnes & Noble Books Inc., 2000), pp. 8, 91, 94.
24   *Richmond Times-Dispatch*, 14 October 1928; 15 October 1928. *Virginian-Pilot* [Norfolk, Va.], 15 October 1928; 16 October 1928.
25   Chant, pp. 94, 96, 100. *Virginian-Pilot*, 15 October 1928. *Richmond Times-Dispatch*, 14 October 1928; 15 October 1928.
26   *Virginian-Pilot*, 15 October 1928. *Richmond Times-Dispatch*, 15 October 1928.
27   *Virginian-Pilot*, 16 October 1928.
28   Correspondence to the author from Edwin S. Jacob, Southampton, N.Y.; Bernice F. Sigreon, Takoma Park, Md.; and E. Thomas Crowson, Rock Hill, S.C., May-June 2001. *Eastern Shore News*, 19 October 1928. *Virginian-Pilot*, 15 October 1928; 16 October 1928. *Richmond Times-Dispatch*, 16 October 1928.
29   *Eastern Shore News*, 19 October 1928. *Virginian-Pilot*, 15 October 1928; 16 October 1928. *Richmond Times-Dispatch*, 16 October 1928. Chant, p. 94.
30   *Virginian-Pilot*, 16 October 1928. Chant, pp. 90, 101-106.
31   Chant, p. 106.
32   This account was gathered from contemporary newspaper sources: *Eastern Shore News*, 7 July 1977; 21 July 1977. *Daily Press* [Newport News, Va.], 17 July 1977. *Richmond Times-Dispatch*, 16 July 1977. *Virginian-Pilot*, 17 July 1977. Also from interviews with Rev. Stan Mulford of Williamsburg, Capt. Freddie Pruitt of Onancock, and John Pruitt of Suffolk, Va.

Bibliography

Books

I. The Eastern Shore

Ames, Susie M. *Studies of the Virginia Eastern Shore in the Seventeenth Century.* Richmond: Dietz Press, 1940.

Barnes, A. Parker. *Pungoteague to Petersburg, Vol. II: Eastern Shore Soldiers, The Civil War, 1858-1865.* Onley, Va.: Lee Howard Co., 1988.

Barnes, Brooks Miles and Barry R. Truitt. *Seashore Chronicles: Three Centuries of the Virginia Barrier Islands.* Charlottesville: University Press of Virginia, 1997.

Bowen, Littleton Purnell. *The Days of Makemie, or The Vine Planted.* Philadelphia: Presbyterian Board of Education, 1885.

Burgess, Robert H. *This Was Chesapeake Bay.* Cambridge, Md.: Cornell Maritime Press Inc., 1963.

Burgess, Robert H. and H. Graham Wood. *Steamboats Out of Baltimore.* Cambridge, Md.: Tidewater Publishers, 1968.

Carroll, Kenneth. *Quakerism on the Eastern Shore.* Baltimore: Maryland Historical Society, 1970.

Clark, Charles B. *The Eastern Shore of Maryland and Virginia.* New York: Lewis Historical Publishing Co., 1950.

Crowson, E. T. *Life as Revealed Through Early American Court Records.* Easley, S.C.: Southern Historical Press, 1981.

Deal, J. Douglas III. *Race and Class in Colonial Virginia: Indians, Englishmen, and Africans on the Eastern Shore During the 17th Century.* New York: Garland Publishing Co., 1993.

DeGast, Robert. *The Lighthouses of the Chesapeake.* Baltimore: Johns Hopkins University Press, 1973.

Dize, E. Frank. *Something Fishy from Tangier.* [n.p], [n.d.].

Footner, Hulbert. *Rivers of the Eastern Shore.* New York: Farrar & Rhinehart Inc., 1944.

Forman, H. Chandlee. *The Virginia Eastern Shore and Its British Origins.* Easton, Md.: Eastern Shore Publishers Association, 1975.

Hurley, George and Suzanne Hurley. *Shipwrecks and Rescues Along the Barrier Islands of Delaware, Maryland, and Virginia.* Norfolk, Va.: Donning Co. Publishers, 1984.

Johnson, Leonard W. *Ebb and Flow: The History of the Virginia Tip of the Delmarva Peninsula, 1561-1892.* Verona, Va.: McClure Printing Co. Inc., 1982.

Mariner, Kirk. *God's Island: The History of Tangier.* New Church, Va.: Miona Publications, 1999.

Mariner, Kirk. *Once Upon an Island: The History of Chincoteague.* New Church, Va.: Miona Publications, 1996.

Mariner, Kirk. *Revival's Children: A Religious History of Virginia's Eastern Shore.* Salisbury, Md.: Peninsula Press, 1979.

Mason, A. Hughlett. *History of Steam Navigation to the Eastern Shore of Virginia.* Richmond: Dietz Press, 1973.

Mears, James E. *Hacks Neck and Its People, Past and Present.* Published privately by the author, 1937.

Mears, James E. *The Temperance Movement on the Eastern Shore of Virginia.* Onancock: Eastern Shore News, 1966.

Mills, Eric. *Chesapeake Bay in the Civil War.* Centreville, Md.: Tidewater Publishers, 1996.

Murray, James. *History of Pocomoke City, Formerly Newtown, from Its Origins to the Present Time.* Baltimore: Curry Clay & Co., 1883.

Nock, Anne B. *Child of the Bay: Past, Present, and Future.* Norfolk: Hampton Roads Publishing Co., 1992.

Nock, L Floyd III. *Drummondtown: 'A One Horse Town:' Accomac Court House, Virginia.* Verona, Va.: McClure Press, 1976.

Nordstrom, Julie V. *The Eastern Shore of Virginia in Days Past.* Sarasota, Fla.: Serbin Printing Co., 1981.

Page, I. Marshall. *Old Buckingham by the Sea on the Eastern Shore of Maryland.* Philadelphia: Westminster Press, 1936.

Perry, James R. *The Formation of a Society on Virginia's Eastern Shore, 1615-1655.* Chapel Hill: University of North Carolina Press, 1990.

Rew, Lillian Mears. *Assateague and Chincoteague As I Remember Them.* [n.p.], 1985.

Shomette, Donald G. *Pirates on the Chesapeake.* Centreville, Md.: Tidewater Publishers, 1985.

Trevillian, Robert E. III and Francis Carter, *Treasure on the Chesapeake Bay.* Glen Burnie, Md.: Spyglass Enterprises, 1983.

Truitt, Reginald V. *Assateague...the "Place Apart."* College Park: University of Maryland, 1971.

Truitt, Reginald V. and Millard G. LesCallette, *Worcester County, Maryland's Arcadia.* Snow Hill, Md., Worcester County Historical Society, 1977.

Turman, Nora M. *The Eastern Shore of Virginia, 1603-1964.* Onancock, Va.: Eastern

Shore News Inc., 1964.

Turman, Nora M. *St. James Church and St. George Parish, 1763-1990.* Onancock, Va.: Eastern Shore Printers, 1990.

Vanlandigham, Edward Noble. *Delaware and the Eastern Shore.* Philadelphia: J. B. Lippincott, 1922.

Weslager, C. A. *The Accomac and Accohannock Indians from Early Relations.* Onancock, Va.: Eastern Shore of Virginia Historical Society, 1961.

Weslager, C. A. *The Nanticoke Indians, Past and Present.* Newark: University of Delaware Press, 1983.

Whealton, Louis N. *The Maryland and Virginia Boundary Controversy, 1668-1894.* New York: Albert J. Leon, 1897.

White, Blanche Sydnor. *History of the Baptists on the Eastern Shore of Virginia, 1776-1959.* Baltimore: J. H. Furst Co., 1959.

Whitelaw, Ralph T. *Virginia's Eastern Shore.* Richmond: Virginia Historical Society, 1951.

Williams, William H. *The Garden of American Methodism: The Delmarva Peninsula, 1769-1820.* Wilmington, Del.: Scholarly Resources Inc., 1984.

Williamson, Robert. *A Brief History of the Origin and Progress of the Baptists on the Eastern Shore of Virginia.* Baltimore: J. F. Weishampel, 1878.

Wise, Jennings C. *Ye Kingdome of Accawmacke, or the Eastern Shore of Virginia in the Seventeenth Century.* Richmond: Bell Book & Stationery Co, 1911.

II. Genealogical Works

Carey, Mary Frances. *The Messongo Traders: A Family History.* Melbourne, Fl.: Edward L. Trader, 1980.

Carey, Mary Frances. *Tombstone Inscriptions of Upper Accomack County, Virginia.* Bowie, Md.: Heritage Books Inc., 1995.

Edward, Lucy Ames and Nannie Ames Mears. *Ames, Mears, and Allied Lines.* Onancock: Eastern Shore of Virginia Historical Society, 1967.

Latimer, Frances Bibbins. *The Register of Free Negroes, Northampton County, Virginia, 1853 to 1861.* Bowie, Md.: Heritage Books Inc., 1992.

Mihalyka, Jean M. and Faye Downing Wilson, *Graven Stones of Lower Accomack County, Virginia.* Bowie, Md.: Heritage Books Inc., 1986.

Mihalyka, Jean M. (ed.), *Marriages: Northampton County, Virginia, 1660/1-1854.* Bowie, Md.: Heritage Books, 1991.

Miles, Barry W. and Moody K. Miles III. *Marriage Records of Accomack County, Virginia, 1854-1895.* Bowie, Md.: Heritage Books, 1997.

Nottingham, Stratton. *Marriage License Bonds of Northampton County, Virginia, 1706-1854.*

Baltimore: Genealogical Publishing Co., 1974.

Nottingham, Stratton. *Wills and Administrations of Accomack County, Virginia, 1663-1800.* Onancock: Published privately by the author, 1931.

Turman, Nora M. *Marriage Records of Accomack County, Virginia, 1776-1854.* Bowie, Md.: Heritage Books, 1994.

III. Virginia

Barringer, Paul Brandon et al., *University of Virginia: Its History, Influence, Equipment, and Characteristics.* New York: Lewis Publishing Co., 1904.

Brock, Henry. *Colonial Churches in Virginia.* Richmond: Dale Press, 1930.

Charles, Joan. *Mid-Atlantic Shipwreck Accounts to 1899.* Hampton, Va.: Published privately by the author, 1997.

Gentile, Gary. *Shipwrecks of Virginia.* Philadelphia: Gary Gentile Productions, 1992.

Hoehling, A. A. *Thunder at Hampton Roads.* New York: Da Capo Press, 1993.

Lewis, Clifford M. and Albert J. Loomie. *The Spanish-Jesuit Mission in Virginia, 1570-1572.* Chapel Hill: University of North Carolina Press, 1953.

Mills, Charles A. *Treasure Legends of Virginia.* Nokesville, Va.: Apple Cheeks Press, 1984.

Rountree, Helen F. *Pocahontas's People: The Powhatan Indians of Virginia Through Four Centuries.* Norman: University of Oklahoma Press, 1990.

Rountree, Helen F. *The Powhatan Indians, Their Traditional Culture..* Norman: University of Oklahoma Press, 1989.

Sanchez-Saavedra, E. M. *A Description of the Country: Virginia's Cartographers and Their Maps, 1607-1881.* Richmond: Virginia State Library, 1975.

Shepherd, Samuel. *The Statutes at Large of Virginia.* New York: Ames Press, 1970.

Wright, R. Lewis. *Artists in Virginia Before 1900: An Annotated Checklist.* Charlottesville: University of Virginia Press, 1983.

IV. General

Chant, Christopher. *The Zeppelin: The History of German Airships from 1900 to 1937.* New York: Barnes & Noble Books Inc., 2000.

Current, Richard N. et al. *American History: A Survey.* New York: Alfred A. Knopf, 1963.

Davis, David Brion. *The Problem of Slavery in the Age of Revolution, 1770-1823.* Ithaca, N.Y.: Cornell University Press, 1975.

Defoe, Daniel. *A General History of the Robberies and Murders of the Most Notorious Pyrates.* New York: Garland Publishing Co., 1972 (reprint of 1724 edition).

Emory, Robert. *History of the Discipline of the*

Methodist Episcopal Church. New York: Lane & Tippett, 1845.

Ferguson, Charles H. *Organizing to Beat the Devil.* Garden City, N.Y.: Doubleday & Co. Inc., 1971.

Fleckenstein, Henry J. Jr. *Southern Decoys of Virginia and the Carolinas.* Exton, Pa.: Schiffer Pub. Ltd., 1983.

Hawkes, Francis L. *A Narrative of Events Connected with the Rise and Progress of the Protestant Episcopal Church in Virginia.* New York: Harper Bros., 1836.

Jennings, Francis. *The Invasion of America: Indians, Colonization, and the Cant of Conquest.* New York: W.W. Norton & Co., 1975.

Judefind, William B. (ed.). *Exultant Praises.* Baltimore, Md.: Judefind Bros., 1910.

Judefind, William B. (ed.). *On Wings of Love.* Baltimore, Md: Judefind Bros., 1902.

Kirstein, Lincoln. *The Hampton Album.* New York: Doubleday & Co., 1966.

Kobler, John. *Ardent Spirits: The Rise and Fall of Prohibition.* London: Michael Joseph, 1974.

Koch, Howard. *The Panic Broadcast.* Boston: Little Brown & Co., 1970.

Marvel, William. *Andersonville: The Last Depot.* Chapel Hill: University of North Carolina Press, 1994.

Morrison, Russell et al. *On the Map: Maryland and the Chesapeake Bay.* Chestertown, Md.: Washington College, 1983.

Musicant, Ivan. *Divided Waters: The Naval History of the Civil War.* New York: HarperCollins Pubs., 1995.

Norwood, Frederick. *The Story of American Methodism.* Nashville, Tenn.: Abingdon Press, 1974.

Palmer, Alan. *An Encyclopaedia of Napoleon's Europe.* New York: St. Martin's Press, 1984.

Plum, William R. *The Military Telegraph During the Civil War in the United States.* Chicago: Jansen, McClurg & Co., 1882.

Rankin, Hugh F. *The Golden Age of Piracy.* New York: Holt, Rhinehart & Winston Inc., 1969.

Scarborough, Katherine, *Homes of the Cavaliers.* New York: Macmillan Co., 1930.

Sherry, Frank. *Raiders and Rebels: The Golden Age of Piracy.* New York: Hearst Marine Books, 1986.

Sturdevant, William C. (ed.). *Handbook of North American Indians, Vol. 15: Northeast.* Washington, D.C.: Smithsonian Institution, 1978.

Swanton, John R. *The Indian Tribes of North America.* Washington, D.C.: Smithsonian Institution Press, 1952.

Williams, Lloyd Haynes. *Pirates of Colonial Virginia.* Richmond: Dietz Press, 1937.

Williams, Walter L. (ed.). *Southeastern Indians Since the Removal Era.* Athens, Ga.: University of Georgia Press, 1979.

V. Biography

Asbury, Francis. *The Journal and Letters of Francis Asbury,* Elmer T. Clark, ed. Nashville: Abingdon Press, 1958.

Barbour, Philip L. (ed.). *The Complete Works of Captain John Smith.* Chapel Hill: University of North Carolina Press, 1986.

Biographical Dictionary of the American Congress, 1774-1971. Washington, D.C.: Government Printing Office, 1971.

Boehm, Henry. *Reminiscences, Historical and Biographical.* New York: Carlton & Porter, 1865.

Daniel, Pete and Raymond Smock. *A Talent for Detail: The Photographs of Miss Frances Benjamin Johnston, 1889-1910.* New York: Harmony Books, 1974.

Davis, Burke. *The Billy Mitchell Affair.* New York: Random House, 1967.

Dictionary of American Biography. New York: Charles Scribner's Sons, 1933.

Doenecke, Justus D. *The Presidencies of James A. Garfield and Chester A. Arthur.* Lawrence: The Regents Press of Kansas, 1981.

Hale, Nathaniel C. *Virginia Venturer: A Historical Biography of William Claiborne, 1600-1677.* Richmond: Dietz Press, 1951.

Justis, Hilda. *Life and Ancestry of Warner Mifflin.* Philadelphia: Ferris & Leach, 1905.

Leaming, Barbara. *Orson Welles.* New York: Viking Penguin Inc., 1983.

Daniel Bedinger Lucas, *Memoir of John Yates Beall.* Montreal, Que.: John Lovell, 1865.

Lynch, Denis Tilden. *Grover Cleveland: A Man Four-Square.* New York: Horace Liveright Inc., 1932.

National Cyclopaedia of American Biography. New York: James T. White Co., 1933.

Schlenther, Boyd S. *The Life and Writings of Francis Makemie.* Philadelphia: Presbyterian Historical Society, 1971.

Smith, John, *The Generall Historie of Virginia, New England, and the Summer Isles.* London: Michael Sparkes, 1624; Readex Microprint Reproduction, 1966.

Smith, Warren Thomas. *Harry Hosier, Circuit Rider.* Nashville: Upper Room, 1981.

Taylor, Robert Lewis. *Vessel of Wrath: The Life and Times of Carry Nation.* New York: New American Library, 1966.

Watson, Eva M. *Glimpses of the Life and Work of George Douglas Watson.* Cincinnati, Ohio: God's Bible School and Revivalist, 1929.

Who Was Who in America (Vol. 1: 1897-1942)). Chicago: A. N. Marquis Co., 1942.

Wilson, Edith Bolling. *My Memoir.* Indianapolis: Boobs Merrill Co., 1938.

Wise, John S. *Recollections of Thirteen*

Presidents. New York: Doubleday & Page, 1906.

Woodward, Robert P. *On a Donkey's Hurricane Deck, A Tempestuous Voyage of Four Thousand and Ninety-Six Miles Across the American Continent on a Burro in 340 Days and 2 Hours.* New York: I. H. Blanchard Co., 1902.

Periodicals

Ames, Susie M., "Federal Policy Towards the Eastern Shore of Virginia in 1861," *Virginia Magazine of History and Biography* 69 (October 1961).

Bradley, David H., "Francis Asbury and the Development of African Churches in America," *Methodist History* 10 #1 (October 1971).

Cappon, Lester J., "The Yankee Press in Virginia, 1861-1865," *William and Mary College Quarterly* 15 [2nd series] (1935).

Carroll, Kenneth, "Quakerism on the Eastern Shore of Virginia," *Virginia Magazine of History and Biography* 74 #2 (April 1966).

Coke, Thomas, "The Journal of Thomas Coke, Bishop of the Methodist Episcopal Church," *Arminian Magazine* 1 (1789).

Davis, Curtis Carroll, "The Small Bang at Bangs," *Virginia Cavalcade* 11 #2 (Autumn 1961).

Duke, Maurice, "The San Marcos Wreck," *Chesapeake Bay Magazine* 13 #7 (November 1983).

Ford, H. P., "Francis Makemie's Picture," *The Westminster,* 16 May 1908.

Henry, Helen, "Old Houses Moved to Live Again," *Baltimore Sun Magazine,* 9 February 1975.

Hirsch, Richard, "Postmarked for Prison: Behind the Scenes with the U.S. Postal Inspectors," *True Detective* 35 #5 (1941).

Horner, Dave, "Blackbeard's Territory," *The Commonwealth* 37 (January 1970).

King, Willis J., "The Negro Membership of the (Former) Methodist Church in the (New) United Methodist Church," *Methodist History* 7 #3 (April 1969).

Mask, Paula, "A Gallery of Historic Districts," *The Calvert Historian* 5 #1 (Spring 1990).

Moore, James T., "The Death of the Duel: The *Code Duello* in Readjuster Virginia, 1879-1883," *Virginia Magazine of History and Biography* 83 #3 (1975).

Schaun, George, "Isle of Kent," *Chesapeake Bay Magazine* 11 #3 (July 1981).

Scott, Walter, "Personality Parade," *Parade,* 23 April 1989.

Turman, Nora M., "*Trompe d'oeil* in Accomac: St. James Episcopal Church," *Virginia Cavalcade* 23 #4 (Spring 1974).

Turman, Nora M. and Gladys Lee Hamilton, "The Daughter of Francis Makemie," *The Colonial Genealogist* 12 #25-26 (1984).

Upshur, Thomas T., "Eastern Shore History," *Virginia Magazine of History and Biography* 9 (1901), 10 (1902).

Wharton, James, "Virginia's Drowned Village," *Virginia Cavalcade* 7 (Winter 1957).

_____, "George and Barbara Bush: When Virginia Went to War," *The Virginian* 11 #3 (May-June 1989).

_____, "Records of Accomack County, Virginia, Relating to The Rev. Francis Makemie," *Journal of Presbyterian History* 4 (December 1907).

Unpublished Manuscripts and Articles

Burton, Robert S. *Eastville's Historical Commercial Buildings.* Unpublished typescript, 1975.

Eason, Wessie Nock. *Unpublished Papers,* in possession of the author.

Elliott, John W. A. *Unwritten History of Eastern Shore Methodism,* ca. 1885.

Jones, Carolyn C. *The Dix Family of Bulbegger, Virginia.* Unpublished typescript, [n.d.].

Mariner, Kirk. *Historical Origins of Contemporary American Evangelicalism.* Unpublished doctoral thesis, Wesley Theological Seminary, 1979.

Mears, James Egbert. *The Virginia Eastern Shore in the War of Secession and in the Reconstruction Period.* Unpublished typescript, 1957.

Mears, John Neely. *Miscellaneous Papers.* Unpublished folios and scrapbooks in the Eastern Shore of Virginia Historical Society, Kerr Place, Onancock, Va.

Pruitt, Victoria. *The Pruitt Papers.* Unpublished typescript in Eastern Shore Public Library, [n.d.], edited by Robert L. Krieger, 1979.

Stitt, Susan. *The Importance of the Glebe to the History of Hungars Episcopal Church.* Unpaginated pamphlet issued by the church, [n.d.].

Newspaper Articles

Ballard, Lynn, "Education in Onancock," *Eastern Shore News,* 28 June 1973.

Briscoe, Betty, "Shabby Hall," *The Independent* [Prince Frederick, Md.], 3 October 1973.

Flor, Lee, "Restoring Houses," *The Evening Star* [Washington, D.C.], 24 March 1972.

Fox, Constance P., "A History of Tidewater Institute," *Eastern Shore News,* 13 September 1986.

Jones, Susie Mae, "Eastern Shore Indians," *Eastern Shore News* [Cape Charles], 8 December

1922.

Mariner, Kirk, "The Eastern Shore of Virginia in 1608: Examining John Smith's Map," *Eastern Shore News*, 6 March 1991.

Mariner, Kirk, "John Yates Beall, Rebel Raider of the Chesapeake," *Eastern Shore News*, 6-20 April 1985.

Mariner, Kirk, "Sinnickson and Red Hills," *Eastern Shore News*, 15-29 January 1997.

Mears, James Egbert, "The Virginia Eastern Shore During the War of Secession," *Eastern Shore News*, 1949-1952.

Mears, James Egbert, "The Shoreline," *Eastern Shore News*, 1931, 1946, 1951, 1968.

Ross, S.T., "Recollections of Onancock, 1850," *Eastern Shore News*, 3 July 1980.

Tull, Claude A., "Wagram," *Eastern Shore News*, 7 February 1947.

Wilfong, James C., "Edmonds Place," *Calvert Independent* [Prince Frederick, Md.], 18 October 1976.

Wilfong, James C., "Lower Marlboro Faces Major Changes," *The News Leader* [Laurel, Md.], 2 September 1971.

_____, "Old Atlantic Female College Book Found," *Eastern Shore News*, 4 February 1987.

Newspapers

Accomack News [Onancock, Va.], 1905, 1906, 1907, 1908, 1910, 1911, 1916, 1921.

Baltimore [Md.] *Sun*, 1891.

Calvert Independent [Prince Frederick, Md.], 1971.

Daily Press [Newport News, Va.], 1977.

Eastern Shore Herald [Eastville, Va.], 1928, 1936.

Eastern Shore News [Accomac, Va.], 1925, 1926, 1928, 1934, 1936, 1938, 1946, 1953, 1959, 1960, 1962, 1971, 1977, 1980, 1982, 1986, 1987, 1992.

Eastern Shore News [Cape Charles, Va.], 1922.

Evening Herald & Express [Los Angeles, Ca.], 1936.

Methodist Protestant Recorder [Baltimore, Md.], 1932.

Mount Airy [N.C.] *News*, 1936, 1980, 1992.

National Recorder [Drummondtown, Va.], 1860.

New York [N.Y.] *Herald*, 1891.

New York [N.Y.] *Times*, 1891.

News Leader [Laurel, Md.], 1971.

Norfolk [Va.] *Landmark*, 1875, 1878.

Norfolk [Va.] *Virginian-Pilot*, 1928.

Northampton Times [Cape Charles, Va.], 1934, 1936, 1946, 1953.

Peninsula Enterprise [Accomac, Va.], 1884, 1885, 1886, 1888, 1891, 1892, 1899, 1901, 1906,

1908, 1910, 1925, 1928, 1932, 1933, 1935, 1938, 1954, 1956.

Richmond [Va.] *Dispatch*, 1891.

Richmond [Va.] *Times-Dispatch*, 1928, 1936, 1962, 1977.

Washington [D.C.] *Post*, 1932, 1936.

Church Records

Archives of the Diocese of Virginia.
Hungars Parish Register, 1836-1895.
Hungars Parish Vestry Book, 1812-1836.
Journal of the Baltimore Conference, The Methodist Church, 1941.
Journal of the Quarterly Conference of the Accomack Circuit, 1804-1867.

Public Records and Documents

Accomack County, Virginia
Deed Book #47, #97.
Marriage Register, #1-2, #3.
Orders, 1663-1666.
Wills, 1788-1794, 1807-1830, 1846-1882.

Northampton County, Virginia
Deed Book #4, #7, #27, #48, #49, #50, #51, #52, #54, #58, #59.
Inventories and Accounts, 1700-1870.
Marriage Register #3.
Order Book #31, #35, #39, #40.
Orphans Accounts #4.
Will Book #5, #34.

Commonwealth of Virginia:
Communication from the Governor of Virginia Transmitting Report of the Commissioners to Arbitrate the Boundary Line Between Virginia and Maryland. Richmond: Senate Document XII, 1877.
Virginia House of Delegates, 1859-60, Document #40.

United States of America
Census Records, 1850.
Official Records of the Union and Confederate Armies, Series I, Vol. #5, #11, #29, #33, #40, #46, #51. Series III, Vol. 3.
Official Records of the Union and Confederate Navies, Series I, Vol. #5.
Records of the Bureau of Refugees, Freedmen, and Abandoned Lands, Drummondtown and Eastville, Virginia. Record Group 105. Letters Received.

Interviews and Correspondence

*Adler, Doris, Silver Beach, Va.
Barnes, B. Miles, Onancock, Va.
Carey, Mary Francis, New Church, Va.

Clarke, Ruth Wallace, Tangier, Va.
Crowson, E. Thomas, Rock Hill, S.C.
Davis, Vernon Perdue, Richmond, Va.
*Dennis, John V., Princess Anne, Md.
Doughty, C. E. "Duke," Mays Landing, N.J.
Eichelberger, Pierce, Quinby, Va.
Enright, Maury, Wattsville, Va.
Fisher, Arthur K., Parksley, Va.
*Henderson, U. Kerr, Accomac, Va.
Jacob, Edwin S., Southampton, N.Y.
Jones, Carolyn C., Pocomoke City, Md.
Kniffin, Maybelle Woodward, E. Chester, N.Y.
Latimer, Frances B., Eastville, Va.
Lewis, Jim, Salisbury, Md.
*Lusk, Adelaide, Cherrystone, Virginia
Mihalyka, Jean M. Cheriton, Va.
Mulford, Stanley, Williamsburg, Va.
Mullaly, Ethel Downing, Onancock, Va.
Nock, Anne B., Onancock, Va.
*Nock, L. Floyd III, Onancock, Va.
Phillips, William Samuel, Mutton Hunk, Va.
Plonk, Rev. William, Onancock, Va.
Plummer, Mary, Philadelphia, Pa.
Pruitt, Freddie, Suffolk, Va.
Pruitt, John, Suffolk, Va.
*Scott, Nell, Parksley, Va.
Sigreon, Bernice F., Takoma Park, Md.
Smith, Sarah B., Charlottesville, Va.
*Tull, Algea C., New Church, Va.
*Turman, Nora Miller, Parksley, Va.
Vass, Margaret Mears, Jamesville, Va.
*Waters, Elizabeth A., Cape Charles, Va.
*Whitehead, Marguerite, Nassawadox, Va.
(* = deceased)

Picture Credits

Baltimore Sun Magazine, 9 February 1975: 150 (top).

Barringer, Paul Brandon, *University of Virginia: Its History*: p. 119.

Chant, Christopher, *The Zeppelin: The History of German Airships*: pp. 163, 165.

Claiborne, John Herbert, *William Claiborne of Virginia* (New York: G. P. Putnam's Sons, 1917): p. 2.

Davis, Burke, *The Billy Mitchell Affair*: pp. 159, 161.

Doughty, C. D. "Duke," Mays Landing, N.J.: p. 103.

Eastern Shore of Virginia Historical Society, Onancock, Va.: pp. 102, 122, 123.

Eastern Shore Public Library, Accomac, Va.: pp. 62, 132, 133, 137.

Ellis, William T., *"Billy" Sunday: The Man and His Message* ([n.p.]: L. T. Myers, 1917): pp. 89, 90.

Ferm, Vergilius, *Pictorial History of Protestantism* (New York: Philosophial Library,

1957): p. 29.

Fisher, Arthur King, Parksley, Va.: p. 140.

Hale, Nathaniel C., *Virginia Venturer: A Historical Biography of William Claiborne*: p. 3.

Harper's New Monthly Magazine, May 1879: p. 117.

Harper's Weekly, 17 October 1891: p. 155.

Hoehling, A. A., *Thunder at Hampton Roads*: p. 58.

Jones, Carolyn C., Pocomoke City, Md.: p. 106.

Justis, Hilda, *Life and Ancestry of Warner Mifflin*: pp. 35, 38.

Leaming, Barbara, *Orson Welles*: p. 96.

Library of Congress, Prints and Photographs Division: pp. 92, 94.

Lucas, Daniel Bedinger, *Memoir of John Yates Beall*: p. 64.

Mariner, Anne Marie, Onancock, Va.: p. 135.

Marvel, William, *Andersonville: The Last Depot*: pp. 71, 73.

Morrison, Russell, *On the Map: Maryland and the Chesapeake Bay*: p. 32.

Mulford, Stan, Williamsburg, Va.: p. 167.

Nation, Carry A., *The Use and Need of the Life of Carry A. Nation* (Topeka, Kan.: F. M. Steves & Sons, 1909): p. 87.

New York Herald, 14 October 1891: pp. 154, 156, 157.

Nock, Anne B., Onancock, Virginia: p. 54.

Once a Week, 3 December 1892: p. 102.

Pruitt, Freddie, Onancock, Va.: p. 168.

Sherry, Frank, *Raiders and Rebels: The Golden Age of Piracy*: p. 31.

Smith, Warren Thomas, *Harry Hosier, Circuit Rider*: p. 42.

Taylor, Robert Lewis, *Vessel of Wrath: The Life and Times of Carry Nation*: pp. 86, 87.

True Detective, February 1941: p. 126.

Washington Star, 16 July 1977: pp. 169, 170.

Watson, Eva M., *Glimpses of the Life and Work of George Douglas Watson*: p. 75.

Whitelaw, Ralph T., *Virginia's Eastern Shore*: pp. 120, 148 (top), 151 (top).

Woodward, Robert P., *On a Donkey's Hurricane Back*: pp. 82, 83.

Worcester Democrat [Pocomoke City, Md.]: June 1955 (Special Anniversary Edition): p. 111.

_____, "Painting the Peninsula: The War in Watercolors," *Civil War Times Illustrated* 18 #8 (December 1979): p. 55.

Index

Accomac, 19, 22, 30, 49, 57, 59, 60, 66, 67, 69, 71, 74, 91, 93, 95, 99
Accomack Indians, 11, 13, 14, 22, 23
Addison, Thomas, 45
African Methodist Episcopal Church (A.M.E.), 43
Agnew, Eleanor "Judy," 81
Allen, Richard, 43
Andersonville Prison, 71 74
Arthur, Chester Alan, 100
Asbury, Francis, 41, 43
Assateague Island, 31
Assawoman, 22
Awosseconsul (Indian), 20
Assateague Island, 7, 153 158
Atlantic, 99, 101
Atlantic Female College, 134-136

Baptists, 23, 134-139
Battaile, Henry, 136
Battle of the Pocomoke, 1-3
Beall, John Yates, 60, 61-67
Belinda, 139-141
Belle Haven, 96
Benezet, Anthony, 36
"Beverley," 10, 104, 110, 131
Blackbeard, 31-34
Blackbeard's Cove, 33-34
Bloodworth Cottage, 93
Bodley, Avalon D., 140-141
Bowen, Littleton P., 30
Boykin, Arthur L., 137-139

Bradford, Frank, 123
Bridgetown, 44
Brittingham, Elijah, 118; Grover C., 104-106; John A., 53-56, 104-105; John E., 104-106
"Brownsville," 13, 93, 104
Bullbegger, 113-116
Burton, Thomas, 42
Bush, George H. W., 112

Calder, Alexander Sterling, 28-30
Caldwell, W. D., 143-145
Callahan, Griffin, 132-134
Calvert, Philip, 5-7
Calvert-Scarburgh Boundary, 5-7
Cape Charles, 11, 22, 85, 88, 91, 100, 111; 125-128, 159, 164
Captain's Cove, 34
Cathell, Levi, 10
Cedar Straits, 6
Charlton, Stephen, 44-45
Cheriton, 11, 139
Cherrystone, 18, 57-61, 68, 69, 70, 137-139
Cherrystone Creek, 15, 137
Chesapeake Bay, exploration by Spanish, 15-16; US military exercises, 158-162
Chesapeake Bay Bridge, 3, 10
Chesconessex, 20, 21
Chesconessex Indians, 13, 20
Chincoteague, 6, 7, 23, 87, 96, 99, 101, 121-123, 145-148, 155, 157
Chincoteague Indians, 13, 23
Chincoteague Naval Air Station, 112
Civil War, 50-51, 52-74, 75, 77, 115, 136
Claiborne, William, 1-3
Clarke, Ruth W., 108
Cleveland, Grover, 99-106, 158
Coke, Thomas, 41-43
Colbert, William, 43

Colonna, W. E., 118
Connorton, Charles "Bud," 124-125
Corbin Hall, 23
Craddockville, 93, 96
Crisfield (MD), 6, 7, 77, 110, 112, 164, 167-168, 170
Crockett, Henry, 142, 145; Hobson 166; John, 110; Vienna, 166, 168
Crowson, E. Thomas, 164

Debedeavon, 16-18, 20, 21
de Bry, Theodore, 18
Delmarva, 1, 8-10
Deep Creek, 4
Deep Hole, 121-123
Dennis, Littleton P., 10, 131; S. Burton, 125-148
Despatch [yacht], 153-158
Dix, Julia, 113-116; Thorogood, 113, 115
Dize, E. Frank, 160
Doughty, Henry Warren, 103; Mary Anna, 103; Thomas Major, 103
Dover (DE), 8
Dover (MD), 8
Downing, William, 42
Drummond, Belinda, 139-141; Herbert A., 140
Drummond's Mill, 94-95
Drummondtown, see Accomac

Easton (MD), 8-10
Eastville, 17, 19, 24-25, 47, 48, 57, 59, 69, 71, 85, 116, 119, 164
"Edmond's Place," 151-151
Eisenhower, Dwight D., 111-112
Ekeeks (Indian), 20, 21
Episcopalians, 44-48, 49
Exmore, 101, 164

Fitchett, Edward P., 51
Fitzhugh, Thaddeus, 60
Flag Pond Landing, 3
Franktown, 22, 31, 35
Freeman, Thomas W., 121 123

"Gargaphia Savannah," 149, 151
Garrettson, Freeborn, 43
Garrison, Jonathan, 34
ghosts, 119-121
Gilbert, Bartholemew, 16
Gingaskin, 13, 23-25
Gonzales, Vicente, 15
Graf Zeppelin, 162-166
Grant, Ulysses S., 73
Greenbackville, 6, 7, 34
Grotons, 23
Guilford, 35
Gunter, Benjamin T., 50-51; Stephen, 44-48

Harborton, 101
Harrison, Benjamin, 100, 158
Hege, Harvey, 126-128
"Hermitage" [Cape Charles], 125-128; [Craddockville], 93
Herrmann, Augustine, 6, 7
Hill, Jennie, 121-123; Timothy, 121; Zipporah, 121-123
Hills Farm, 93
Hitchens, David, 51
Hog Island, 31, 63-64, 65, 70, 101-104, 164
Holden, Ann Makemie, 27 28, 129
Holden's Creek, 28, 30
Hoover, Herbert, 109-110
Horntown, 6, 7, 55, 105
Hosier, "Black Harry", 41-43
Hungars Episcopal Church, 44-48, 93
Hungars Glebe, 44-46, 48
Hungars Parish, 24-25, 44-48
Hungars Wharf, 118
"Huntington," 137-139

Indiantown, 23-25
Indians, 1, 11-25

Jamestown, 1
Janes Island (MD), 6-7
Jenifer, Daniel, 6
Jenkins Bridge, 129

Johnson, Henry Clay, 101, 149; Lucie, 103
Johnston, Frances Benjamin, 91-95
Jolley's Neck, 3, 113
Judefind, William B., 79-81
Justisville, 164

Kent Island (MD), 1-3
Kickotan Indians, 13
King's Creek, 22
Kiptopeake (house), 104
Kiptopeake (Indian), 13
Kokewiss (Indian), 20, 21

Lankford, C. M., 127
"Laughing King," 11, 13, 16-19
Lewis, Levin D., 121
Lighthouses: Assateague Island, 65; Cape Charles, 51, 61-63; Hog Island, 63 64, 70
Lincoln, Abraham, 58, 67
Little Hell, 141-142
Locustville, 93, 99, 148-149
Luna Park, 142-145

Machipongo, 22
Machipongo Indians, 13
Machipongo River, 22
Magotha Indians, 13
Makemie, Francis, 27-30, 129; Naomi, 27
Makemie Monument, 29-30
Makemie Presbyterian Church, 30
Mappsville, 99
Margaret Academy, 136
"Marino," 119-121
Marionville, 164
Maryland, founding of 1-3; boundary with Virginia 4-7; Eastern Shore separatism, 8-10
Matahoquic (Indian), 20
Matom (Indian), 20
Matomkin Indians, 13, 20
Mattawoman Creek, 13, 23
McClellan, George B., 59
McIlwaine, William, 55
Mears, A. F., 99
Mearsville, 99,101

Melson, Annie Willett, 121
Mencken, H. L., 8,10
Merrimack (warship), 57-59
Messongo, 22-23, 139
Messongo Creek, 6, 22
Methodists, 22, 41-43, 44-48, 75, 81, 141-142
Michler, Nathaniel, 6
Mifflin, Daniel, 34-35, 37; Warner, 34-41
Mihalyka, Jean M., 44
Mitchell, William, 159-162
Modest Town, 99
Monitor (warship), 57-59
Mosquito Creek, 13
Mount Hope, 93
Mulford, Stan, 166-170

Nandua Indians, 13, 17
Nassawadox, 22
Nation, Carry A., 85-88
New Church, 6, 53-56, 77, 104-105, 134
New Kent County (VA), 3
Newtown, see Pocomoke City
Norris (Indian), 19-20
Nottingham, L. J., 118
Nowthothrawen (Indian), 20

Oak Hall, 42, 50
"Oatlands," 13
Occohannock Indians, 13, 14, 19, 20
Ogden, Henry A., 28-30
Okiawampe (Indian), 19-20
Oldtown Neck, 18, 23
Onancock, 27-28, 69, 77, 86-87, 96, 99, 134-136, 142-145, 164
Onancock Creek, 4
Onancock Indians, 13, 20
Onley, 86-87
Oyster, 164

Painter, 75, 150
Parks, Annie K., 108; George P., 119-121; Roland, 124-125
Parksley, 79-81
Parramore, Thomas, 34
Parramore Island, 31

"Pharsalia," 34-35, 37
Phillips, J. H., 134
Pitts Creek, 129
Pitts, Major S., 117-119
Pitts Wharf, 13
Pocomoke City (MD), 22, 60, 77, 110-111
Pocomoke Indians, 13
Pocomoke River, 2, 3-7, 10, 22, 129
Potts, Jean G., 49-51
Press, Edmund, 25
Pruitt, Freddie, 167-168
Pungoteague, 59, 69, 142
"Pythagoras Pod," 82-85

Quakers, 4, 22, 34-41

Raleigh, Walter, 16
Red Hills, 147
Rehobeth (MD), 28
Revels Island, 31
Rittenhouse, Bob, 111
Roberts Bros. Circus, 166 170
Robins, Obedience, 18
Rogue Island, 31
Roosevelt, Franklin D., 110-111

St. James Episcopal Church, 49-50
St. Mary's City (MD), 1-2
Sandy Island, 15
Sanford, 3, 22, 23, 139
Savage, Hanna, 19; Thomas, 18
Savage Neck, 19
Saxis, 6, 7, 23
Scarburgh, Edmund, 4-7, 19
Sentman, J. B., 127
"Shabby Hall," 148-149
Smith, Capt. John, 14-16; Sarah B., 29; Nathaniel S., 145-148; Capt. Thomas, 3
Smith Island (MD), 68, 70
Smith Island (VA), 33-34, 51, 61-63
Snow Hill (MD), 28, 77, 85, 110
Somerset County (MD), 4-7, 10, 28
Stone, William, 23

Sunday, Billy, 88-91
Swan's Gut Creek, 5, 34
Tangier, 106-110, 123-125, 144, 159-162, 166-170
Tangier Sound, 70
Tasley, 164
Taylor, Frank H., 102-103; Philip, 24
Teach, Edward, 31-34
Teach's Island, 32-33
telegraph, 56-61
temperance movement, 85 87
Temperanceville, 6, 7, 59, 99
Thom, Alfred P., 117-119
Thomas, Curry S., 125-128
Thorne, Robert, 167
Tidewater Institute, 139
Tracy, James, 154, 157, 158
Travis, Bryan, 111
Tull, Levi C., 133; William T., 133
Truman, Harry S, 111
Turlington, S. Bayly, 93
Turman, Nora Miller, 92
Turner, George T., 127; Nat, 25

Upshur, Abel P., 45; Thomas T., 17, 104

van Vleck, Perry, 148-151
Vaucluse, 93

Wachapreague, 101, 164
Wachapreague Inlet, 64-65
Wagram, 129-134
"War of the Worlds," 95-97
Washington, George, 39, 40
Watchesagon (Indian), 20, 21
Watkins' Point, 4-6
Watson, George D., 75-79
Watts Island, 77
Webb, B. B., 127
Welles, Orson, 95-97
Wells, H. G., 95
White, Frank J., 69-70
Whitehead, Marguerite, 121

"Wighco River," 4
Williams, William F. D., 103
Willis Wharf, 71, 101, 149 151
Wilson, Samuel, 28; Woodrow, 106-109
Winder, John H., 73; Richard B., 71-74
Wirz, Henry, 71-73
Wise, Henry A., 50, 77, 101; John, 20; John J., 51; John S., 101, 103, 106
Womble, John R., 127
"Woodlands," 13
Woodward, Robert P., 82-85
Woolman, John, 36
Worcester County (MD), 5, 104-106, 129-134

Yeardley, George, 18